Aimé Césaire:
Cahier d'un retour au pays natal

AIMÉ CÉSAIRE

CAHIER D'UN RETOUR
AU PAYS NATAL

Edited, with Introduction, Commentary
and Notes by

Abiola Irele

NEW HORN PRESS LIMITED, IBADAN

First published 1994 by
New Horn Press Limited
P.O. Box 4138
University Post Office,
Ibadan (Oyo State),
Nigeria.

ISBN 978–2266–25–6

Typeset by Harlan Graphics

Printed and bound in Great Britain by
Antony Rowe Ltd., Chippenham, Wiltshire

Printed on acid-free paper

CONTENTS

GUADELOUPE

GRAND-TERRE

Point-à-Pitre

BASSE-TERRE

Marie Galante

MARTINIQUE

Grande Rivière   Basse-Pointe

Δ
*Montagne
Pelée*

POINT DU
DIABLE

Saint-Pierre   la Trinité

Fort-de-France

Rivière
Salée

Sainte-Anne

THE FRENCH WEST INDIES

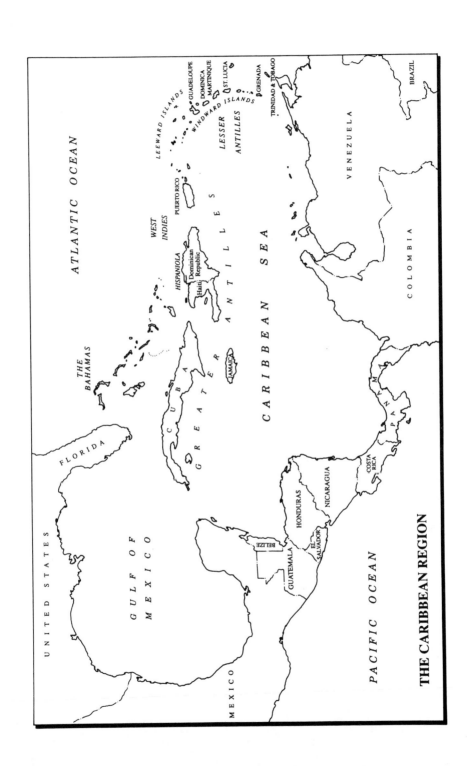

THE CARIBBEAN REGION

PREFACE

Aimé Césaire's long poem, *Cahier d'un retour au pays natal*, is noted as much for its formidable difficulty as for its rare power of poetic expression. In preparing this edition of the poem, I have had in mind primarily the needs of English-speaking university students of French whose program of study includes the work and for whom this difficulty may constitute a barrier to a proper appreciation of its singular qualities. My approach has been governed by a basic principle: to provide a guide for a *meaningful* reading of the poem, in every sense of the word. I have therefore endeavored in the notes to elucidate as many points as possible, so as to make the poem comprehensible, both in relation to its objective historical reference and within the framework of its individual poetic idiom. For this reason, I have had occasional recourse to paraphrase in order to clear up obscurities in certain passages, believing as I do that the poem can only gain in its impact from the very words that constitute it as imaginative structure and textual event being understood, to the extent that the poem's idiom permits. My aim has been, on the whole, to make clear the inner workings of the poem which contribute to its essential tension.

Because of the extent of the editorial matter and in order to facilitate its use, this edition reproduces the complete text of the poem twice. In the first section, the text stands on its own, with each stanza numbered consecutively for easy reference. Users of the book are advised to first read the poem through in this section, in order to obtain an initial feel of its tone and movement, without the distraction of the editorial matter. In the second section, the text, now in bold print, is broken up into its constituent stanzas, with each stanza or group of stanzas accompanied by a commentary and followed by a series of notes on references, allusions and points of stylistic interest arising from the text.

For the text itself, I have generally followed the 1956 edition published by Présence Africaine, to whom grateful acknowledgment is made for permission for its reprint in this edition. However, I have taken cognizance of other editions of the work, especially with regard to stanza division, which differs from one edition to another. This is particularly so with the French text, printed opposite the German translation by Janheinz Jahn, in the bilingual edition published in Frankfurt in 1962. Césaire is known to have worked closely with Jahn in the preparation of this edition, so that its deviations from the 1956 Paris edition can be considered to have met with his approval. I have departed here and there from the latter edition in order to adopt the stanza division in the German edition where this seemed to me more in keeping with the logic of the poem's development.

I am aware that the present annotated edition raises a pedagogical question, that of the utility of presenting a work in French through an editorial apparatus in English. But if ever there was a work that justified the time-honored convention, now apparently falling into disfavor, by which editorial matter in English has been provided to help students with literary texts in foreign languages, Cahier is that work. For apart from its difficulty, the poem contains so many points of unfamiliar French usage that students require explanations in a language with which they are already familiar in order to cope with its complexities. It seems to me, therefore, quite simply an illusion to imagine that the English-speaking student can achieve a full experience of Césaire's poem from an edition in which the editorial apparatus is also in French, a language with which the student is still grappling. Moreover, the argument against the use of English in annotated editions of foreign language texts is undermined by the fact that, in the English-speaking world, the overwhelming majority of critical and secondary literature on foreign literature to which students are often referred continues to be published in English. There is thus good reason in this case for reverting to what has long been considered a practical method—and indeed a respectable tradition—of foreign language teaching. At all events, I dare hope that the editorial matter I have supplied will be found helpful not only by students but by the many English-speaking admirers of Césaire's masterpiece who have sufficient knowledge of French to tackle the poem and who desire a closer acquaintance with the work in its original language of composition.

It remains for me to add that, in preparing this edition, I have benefited immensely from the consideration of a great number of people, beginning with Aimé Césaire himself, who in the mid-sixties, when I was preparing my doctoral dissertation on his work, was kind enough to spend many hours with me explaining some of the references and intricacies of his poetry. Without the initial light thrown upon Cahier by the poet himself during these sessions, I would never have advanced very far in its comprehension. I would like here to express my appreciation for his help. I would also like to extend this appreciation to his son, Jean-Paul, whose hospitality on the occasion of two visits I made to Martinique has had a direct effect upon my work on this edition: driving me in his car round the island, he made me even more aware than I'd been previously of the way in which the distinctive character of the landscape of Martinique has, as it were, formed the very sinews of Césaire's poetic language.

I also owe a great debt of gratitude to Michael Black for his input into this work right from its inception. He not only initiated this project before he retired as Publisher of Cambridge University Press, but he continued to take an interest in it long afterwards. He read and commented on several drafts of the work at every stage of its preparation and his suggestions have proved invaluable, especially for the notes. Gregson Davis of Cornell University and Joan Dayan of the University of Arizona both read early drafts of the work; they not only provided me with insight into key passages of the poem, but also saved me from some serious errors of interpretation. Albert Gérard sent me from Belgium a copy of the only extant number of *L'Etudiant Noir*, a collegial gesture which enabled me to consult this publication directly. Josaphat Kubayanda and Richard Bjornson, my friends and colleagues here at The Ohio State University, gave constant encouragement up to the time of their untimely deaths; my satisfaction in completing this edition and offering it to the public is overcast by profound regret that neither of them has lived to see the work in print.

Beyond these named individuals who have, in one way or the other, helped to advance my work on this edition, my indebtedness to the authors of the now impressive secondary literature on Aimé Césaire will be evident from the selected bibliography at the end of the volume. It has not been possible, however, to list all the critical and secondary literature I have consulted; I have had, in particular, for reasons of space, to leave out the many excellent articles which have illuminated for me important aspects of Césaire's poetry in general, and of *Cahier* in particular.

I cannot fail to mention the contribution of generations of students at the University of Ibadan, whose questions over the years, while I struggled to make meaning of *Cahier* to them, prompted me to undertake this edition in the first place. I have also benefited from the questions and responses to the poem by students at the Université Nationale du Bénin (Cotonou) and, more recently, at The Ohio State University. I am grateful to The Ohio State University College of Humanities and in particular to Dean Riley, for making available the support and facilities that enabled me to make progress with the edition at a critical stage in its preparation. I want to say a special word of thanks to Diana Philips Nelson, who provided able assistance with the word processor, and to Yvonne Holsinger, who prepared the maps. Finally, my thanks go to Ruthmarie Mitsch for her competent editing of the typescript and handling of the entire production process.

Columbus, Ohio
September, 1993

INTRODUCTION

Le front d'or dompte les nuages, où tournoient des aigles glacés,
O pensée qui lui ceint le front! La tête du serpent est son oeil cardinal.

Léopold Sédar Senghor, *Ethiopiques*

Aimé Césaire's *Cahier d'un retour au pays natal* has acquired the status of a classic of black literature, that is, of that area of imaginative discourse which has been concerned with giving symbolic form to the distinctive experience of black people in the modern world. It is without question the most impassioned statement of the racial sentiment of Africans and people of African descent, a sentiment deriving from their problematic historical relationship with the Western world. The very fact that the term *Négritude* which designates this sentiment in its comprehensive scope comes out of the poem is sufficient testimony to its unique significance in this respect. *Cahier* has also been acknowledged as a masterpiece of modern French literature, as a work that fully exploits the modes of a recognizably modern aesthetic and in its own peculiar way gives it a triumphant vindication.

It has sometimes been suggested that these two terms of reference of the poem—as indeed of Césaire's entire imaginative work—are in some way at odds with each other, and that, moreover, there exists an incompatibility between its explicit ideological content and purpose, on one hand, and its fine exemplification of form in resolutely modernist terms, on the other. Césaire's poem raises in an acute way two sets of problems: that of the relationship between literature and reality, and that of so-called minority literatures to the dominant, "mainstream" corpus which constitutes the "canon" against which they are measured. To both of these questions, a consideration of the place of Césaire's poem within the French literary tradition to which it is bound by language affords a first line of approach.

It is true that in its theme, as in the attitudes it proclaims, the poem is a violent rejection by a colonial subject of French political and cultural domination. Moreover, its procedures dramatize this essential gesture by working against the very grain of the language by which it is bound to the French literary inheritance and which determines the poem's structure of expression. The poet's avowed purpose is to sever the bonds that attach him to that language as represented by its conventional forms, a language that is, moreover, symbolic of a condition that he experiences as a form of alienation. In its subversion of the protocols that regulate the use of that language, the poem enacts the movement of resurgence of a repressed consciousness.

Yet it is these procedures that account for its poetic effects. The degree of lyrical intensity with which the poet explores his condition and at the same time articulates the feelings and dispositions of the racial and historical community to whose cause his expression is committed accounts in large part for his vigorous manipulation of the resources of the French language and endows the poem with its particular force. There is thus a sense in which the poem is animated by a tension between its public theme, with the complex of associations it carries, and its formal means of discourse, as determined by the language of its expression.

But if the relation between Césaire's poem and the French literary tradition is particularized in this way, *Cahier* has a significance beyond its grounding in a specific national speech and what may be considered its contribution to and extension of an established literary tradition. It remains a work whose energy of poetic statement ultimately reflects the pressure upon human speech of strong emotions and of an intensely held apprehension of the world—the pressure from which all great literature springs. The particular circumstances of Césaire's situation ensured that the only language available to him was French. Because the poem itself draws directly upon those circumstances for its statement and plays upon the paradoxes they involve for its internal effects, their consideration becomes essential for an appreciation of the poem's range of reference and significance.

LIFE AND BACKGROUND

The island of Martinique, "le pays natal" which is the focus of Césaire's poem, has been associated with France for over 350 years. It owes its present name to Christopher Columbus, who landed there in 1502 and thus opened the way to its occupation at various times by Europeans of several nationalities, including the English, the Dutch, the Danish, and the Spanish. With its annexation in 1635 to the French crown, it became part of the group of French possessions in the Caribbean, along with Saint-Domingue (later renamed Haïti), Guadeloupe, and other island outposts, all of which were collectively referred to as "Les Indes Occidentales." Despite constant challenges from other European nations, especially England, which lasted right up to the early years of the nineteenth century, the French have maintained an effective presence in Martinique ever since, with hardly any interruption .

The introduction of the black population into the island began in the seventeenth century. It is estimated that in the last quarter of that century alone, over one hundred thousand slaves were imported to work on the extensive sugar plantations established by European settlers and colonists. Sugar became the foundation of the island's economy and its export brought great prosperity to the settlers.

With the steady importation of more slaves and natural increase, the black population had become the largest single element in the racial composition of the island's inhabitants by the middle of the eighteenth century. By this time too, a substantial mulatto element, the offspring of white colonists and black slaves, had also developed, gradually coming to form an intermediary racial and social category between a dominant class of white settlers and the black slave majority. This socioeconomic distribution of the island's inhabitants along the color line came to mark the pattern of human relations in the context of slavery and was to prevail long after the abolition of slavery.

As in other parts of the New World, slavery has been central to the political and social fortunes as well as the collective awareness of the black population in the French West Indies. There, the French Revolution of 1789 gave a historic turn to the issue. The upheavals that the revolution provoked in France itself were immediately followed by severe repercussions in the colonies, in the form of divisions within the ranks of the white settlers between adherents of the revolution and defenders of the old order, and of widespread unrest among the slaves. It was as much the danger to the new republic inherent in this confused situation in the colonies as the liberal ideas to which the new revolutionary government in Paris suscribed that persuaded the members of the Convention to decree the abolition of slavery in 1794. However, when Napoleon Bonaparte came to power a few years later, he was determined to impose total control over the colonies, which had begun to assume autonomy with regard to Paris. He considered the institution of slavery indispensable to the government of the colonies and therefore revoked the abolition decree in 1802.

Napoleon's action sparked off a wave of violent slave revolts throughout the French West Indies. The most serious of these took place in Guadeloupe, where Louis Delgrès organized armed resistance to the reimposition of the hated institution, and in Saint Domingue, where Toussaint L'Ouverture, a former slave who had risen, thanks to abolition, to administrator of the colony, decided upon a course of defiance to Napoleon. The French were able to subdue the revolt in Guadeloupe,[1] but although

---

[1] Louis Delgrès and his followers blew themselves up at the town of Matouba, which they were holding, rather than give themselves up to General Richepanse, the French commander.

Toussaint L'Ouverture was captured by a ruse and deported to France where he later died in captivity, the slaves in Saint Domingue defeated the French expeditionary force sent out against them and declared the independence of the colony under its original Carib name of *Haïti*.[2]

Meanwhile, slavery had been restored in Martinique and Guadeloupe, and it was to take almost another fifty years before, in the wake of another revolution in France and a further wave of disturbances, it was finally abolished in 1848. The new freedom did not, however, bring about a significant change in the condition of the black population, which was simply transformed into a mass of rural poor, now obliged to work for meager wages on the white man's sugar plantations. The racial divide continued to determine individual destiny, with the difference that education, which was open to all, at least in principle, provided an avenue of escape for a few from the depressed condition of the black population.[3]

Education was not simply a means of social promotion; it was also an instrument of French colonial policy, consciously geared toward an unconditional adherence to French culture, presented as the very model of an achieved human existence. It served as a psychological mode of cooptation into the system of colonial domination of the local middle class of mulattoes and isolated blacks who had obtained positions at various levels in the civil service and the professions. The superiority of French culture was an article of faith for this class, whose members demonstrated a total subservience to French norms in social manners. This collective state of mind was reflected in the literature that was produced by the intelligentsia which had evolved from within its ranks.

From about the late nineteenth century until well beyond the first quarter of this century, the French West Indies, including Haïti, witnessed an appreciable flourishing of letters due to the efforts of its educated élite. It is perhaps in the area of poetry that this effort is most notable, as much for its indication of the effectiveness of French colonial policy in education and culture as for its character and orientation, against which later writers in the region were to react. It was a poetry that drew upon the exotic appeal of metropolitan writers such as José-Maria Hérédia and Leconte de Lisle—an appeal that, it ought to be noted, Charles Baudelaire also exploited in some of his poems—and aspired to the polish of a high classical style, or its neo-

---

[2]C. L. R. James's classic work *The Black Jacobins*, first published in 1943, provides the most comprehensive account of the Haitian revolution; Aimé Césaire's 1960 biography of Toussaint L'Ouverture has an even more immediate relevance to *Cahier*.

[3]This is the background to Joseph Zobel's autobiographical novel, *La rue Cases-nègres*, which has been made into a very successful film by Euzhan Palcy; the film has become well known in the English-speaking world under the title *Sugarcane Alley*.

classical variant as exemplified by the Parnassians. It needs to be said that the motivation behind this effort was legitimate, to the extent that the Caribbean region offered much of the primary material that fed the imagination of the poets in the metropolis; it was thus simply a matter of authenticating the theme of exoticism by relating it more directly to a local inspiration. But the almost total fixation upon landscape in its purely decorative aspect, deprived of the resonance of a full human relation to the natural environment, presented in this poetry as an object of superficial contemplation, condemned it to the status of a derived and ineffectual mode. Moreover, the assiduous cultivation of an idiom that had been rendered obsolete by the poetic revolution of the latter part of the nineteenth century in France could not but create the impression of an inherent feebleness which no level of proficient versification in the conventional manner could disguise. Not the least importance of Césaire's *Cahier* was the decisive way it put an end to French West Indian poetry of exotic orientation.

The exclusion of a human reference in this earlier poetry was not only a sign of its superficiality, it was also symptomatic of the social attitude and psychological disposition of the educated élite, its anxiety to put a distance between itself and the common people whose vibrant presence it refused to acknowledge. Implicit in this refusal was a gesture of self-refusal, dictated by a complex so deeply implanted as to be unsettling. The élite's mental conditioning not only prescribed conformity to French standards as a positive mode of upliftment but also discouraged any form of identification with folkways represented as a vestigial African barbarism. Assimilation to French culture compelled a flight of the élite from its own moral and cultural anchor in the common people, which was thus left disinherited and demoralized. This was the situation into which Aimé Césaire was born, in which he grew up and formed his earliest impressions, and with which his mature consciousness was confronted, calling forth the response of which *Cahier* is a powerful testimony.

The second son in a family of modest condition which came to include four other children, Césaire was born on June 26, 1913, at Basse-Pointe, in the north of Martinique. It was here that he spent his childhood and received his early education. While the evocations of his childhood in *Cahier* cannot be read as strictly biographical, they offer a composite image of the realities he was accustomed to in a household such as that of his family, amidst the general poverty of the black population within which his origins placed him. There is good reason to suppose, too, that the natural milieu of his birthplace, with its rugged landscape and tropical exuberance and its backdrop of the sea with its breaking waves, became imprinted upon his mind, later to emerge as a primordial register of his imagination.

When, in 1924, Césaire moved to Fort-de-France, the colony's capital, to begin his secondary education as a scholarship student at the Lycée Schoelcher, he came face to face with the attitudes displayed by children of the middle class toward race and with the social and cultural implications which it had assumed as a factor of history in the order of life in the colony. Césaire was later to remark upon his uneasiness in their company at the lycée, and while this does not suggest any feeling of insecurity, it points to a sensitivity that must have set him apart. It was here, too, that he first met Léon Damas, from the French colony of Guyane on the South American mainland, who was also a student at the lycée. This was the first of many encounters that were to shape his future course in life and letters.

The education Césaire received at the lycée was oriented toward the humanities and was based on the standard curriculum in the French system. This consisted mainly of courses in Latin and Greek, classical French literature, and French history, to which was added philosophy in the terminal year. Césaire obtained his *baccalauréat* in 1932 with such distinction that he was awarded another scholarship to continue his education in France. He arrived in Paris in September of that year and was admitted to the Lycée Louis-le-Grand, where he enrolled in the preparatory class for the entrance examination to the prestigious Ecole Normale Supérieure. It was shortly after his arrival that he made the acquaintance of Léopold Sédar Senghor, who was also a student at the lycée preparing for the same examination. Despite the difference in age—Senghor was seven years his senior—in background and in temperament, they struck up a friendship that was to endure and to be one of the most remarkable in literary history, comparable in its nature and consequences to that between Wordsworth and Coleridge in English letters.

Césaire has summed up the effect upon him of his encounter with Senghor in these words: "Quand j'ai connu Senghor, je me suis dit africain." By this he meant that Senghor brought him the revelation of an Africa that was far removed from the primitive image to which he was accustomed and which he was taught to reject as being in any way related to him. That revelation initiated a reconversion of consciousness that enabled him to identify with the ancestral continent and thus to arrive at self-acceptance as a black man in a world where his racial origins had been devalued. The importance of his discovery of Africa through meeting Senghor cannot therefore be overemphasized for Césaire's eventual development both as a political leader and as a poet.[4] It brought him, as a West Indian cut off by history and the

---

[4]Césaire was to recall in moving terms the details of this meeting and its significance for him in his speech of welcome on the occasion of President Senghor's visit to Martinique in February 1976. See "Discours prononcé en l'honneur de la visite de L.S. Senghor," *Oeuvres Complètes*, Vol. 3, pp. 539-45.

cultural interposition of the colonial order from his African antecedents, the realization of a wider belonging than was afforded by his immediate Caribbean background and the exclusively French frame of reference of his education and upbringing. And, if it can be surmised from Césaire's remark that the very relation between his French attachments and Caribbean belonging had already proved problematic for him, it becomes clear that his discovery of Africa restored to his sense of identity a dimension that it lacked. There can be no doubt that this discovery became a factor in defining for him the mission he has sought to fulfil in all his writing.

Césaire's meeting with Senghor cannot be said to have been altogether fortuitous, for it was implied by the very logic of the colonial situation that made Paris, capital of one of the great colonial empires of modern times, the meeting place of expatriate intellectuals from all over the world. French colonialism was in its heyday, and its apparent triumph had been celebrated with the spectacle of the Exposition Coloniale of 1931. Yet that event drew attention to the colonial question, which was already being raised as part of what was then termed "the national question" in Europe itself, in the aftermath of the First World War. The resolve of the European powers to limit the application of the Wilsonian principle of self-determination, which had been implemented after that war in the creation of new states in Central and Eastern Europe out of the ruins of the Austro-Hungarian Empire, was emphasized by the decision to strip Germany of its overseas colonies and redistribute them to the victorious powers. The inequity involved in the lack of consideration of subject races in the non-Western world became a rallying point for anti-colonial movements within which black intellectuals were both active and prominent. This was especially the case with the American W. E. B. Du Bois, whose Pan-African movement took shape in the immediate postwar period,[5] and with Lamine Senghor, whose radical politics and trade union activities placed him in the forefront of African nationalism in the interwar years.

The atmosphere of political and social turmoil that characterized the European scene in the 1930s contributed an element of disenchantment that undermined the notion of white racial superiority on which, as an intellectual proposition, the whole idea of colonialism had come to be predicated. The impact of the Bolshevik revolution in Russia as well as the enormous influence it gave to Marxism in promoting socialist ideas fostered hopes of an imminent social revolution that would sweep the world. Such hopes were sharpened by the widespread economic and human distress caused by the Great Depression, which was interpreted by all radicals as the

---

[5] As a result of Du Bois's attempt to place the colonial question on the agenda at the Versailles Peace Conference.

sign of a profound crisis in the capitalist system that would lead inevitably to its demise. But socialist movements had, at the same time, to reckon with the countervailing pressure of conservative forces and especially with the stark emergence of Fascism as a threat not only to the realization of their hoped-for new social order but to the peace of Europe and of the world. These internal contradictions, graphically reflected in the disorder of social agitation and violent political clashes, could not but compromise the claim of Europe to world mastery.

Such was the troubled state of Europe throughout Césaire's years as a student in Paris. Like other black intellectuals attentive to events around them, he was quickly attracted to Marxism and its development by Lenin and Stalin, who extended its radical critique of capitalism and bourgeois society to embrace the colonial question, and thus identified Communism with a resolutely anti-imperialist and anti-colonial position. But if Marxism largely addressed what might be considered the objective aspects of human life and its social organization, other currents of thought went to the heart of what was widely felt as a crisis of Western civilization, brought on by the horror of the unprecedented carnage and destruction of the First World War. The mood of disillusionment that ensued produced a deep anxiety about the future direction of the Western world, as is well reflected in Paul Valéry's anguished cry, "Nous autres civilisations, nous savons maintenant que nous sommes mortelles," and by the dispiriting landscape of T. S. Eliot's *The Waste Land*.

In this atmosphere, marked by a general loss of faith in the values of traditional humanism, the quest for new intellectual and moral horizons became a preoccupation of Western thought. Henri Bergson undertook to demonstrate the inadequacy of discursive processes to encompass the full reality of experience and insisted upon the value of an inner surge of life (*élan vital*) as a complementary resource for an awareness of being. His philosophy came into its own at this time, along with the message of Oswald Spengler, whose vitalism derived from Nietzsche's earlier call for a revitalization of civilization in what he termed a "transvaluation of values." At the same time, Sigmund Freud was expounding his ideas on the compulsions exerted upon human behavior by the obscure forces of the unconscious. A certain attraction to the irrational began to creep into the European mind. Nor were the new findings in the natural sciences peripheral to the unsettling effects of these currents: If the universe itself could no longer be seen as perfectly adjusted to the operations of human intelligence, the very basis of faith in those operations could no longer be said to hold. Rationalism, previously held as the governing principle of the European mind, seemed at the time to be in a state of retreat. The primacy of the senses over the intellect was becoming for many indeed an article of faith.

The anxieties and preoccupations of the age were fully registered in the arts, especially in the domain of literature where Césaire encountered them in their most expressive form. Of particular significance was the Surrealist movement, which was at its height in the interwar years. It offered a theory of literature, based on Freudian psychoanalysis, that combined an artistic revolt against social conventions and established categories of thought with a new outlook on life, a new mode of organization of the powers of the imagination.

The high valuation of the creative process by the Surrealists, in particular of the poetic medium—"*le diamant audible*," for André Breton—was in reality the culmination of a steady development in the second half of the nineteenth century of a renewal of the language of French poetry, which took it away from a rhetorical preoccupation with explicit ideas and sentiments, often involving didacticism, toward an evocation of deep spiritual states. Surrealism's roots within the French literary tradition lay in the late romanticism of the Victor Hugo of *Les Feuilles d'automne* and *Les Contemplations*, which contained poems that hinted at an order of reality beyond ordinary human perception, beyond even the possibility of articulation in language. Baudelaire's theory of correspondence, advanced by the annunciatory poem of that title in the volume *Les Fleurs du Mal*, sought to expand upon and give coherence to intimations, of the kind expressed by Hugo, of the world as endowed with a sacred character—"la Nature est un temple," Baudelaire declared. His own practice opened up perspectives of feeling and vision that later poets were to explore. The highly sensuous and introspective expression of Verlaine and the assertive visionary mode of Rimbaud with its daring use of language and violent imagery carried Baudelaire's insights further, preparing the way for the hieratic conception of poetry that animated Mallarmé's work. Mallarmé's incessant effort to refine language—even to the point of preciosity—was bent towards making poetry an analogue in language of an elusive reality and involved a mystical devotion to a cult whose aim was no less than to arrive at a form of revelation of the mystery of the universe—as he himself put it, "l'explication orphique de la terre." No less significant in these developments were the hallucinatory evocations of Gérard de Nerval and of Lautréamont (Isidore Ducasse), in the former case as a reponse to a somber apprehension of the world, in the latter as a mode of aggressive confrontation with an oppressive reality.

This was the heritage the nineteenth-century French poets passed on to the twentieth, and which was taken up by poets as dissimilar as Paul Valéry, who continued largely in the vein of Mallarmé; by Paul Claudel, who converted the devotional tenor of Rimbaud's poetry to the service of religious orthodoxy; and by Apollinaire, who related poetry to a pagan vision and coined the term *Surrealism* by which the movement of that name came to be known. It was this heritage that Breton was to build upon for his project of psychological and metaphysical liberation.

Césaire absorbed these developments in his student days and all his work bears their imprint, beginning with *Cahier*. It needs to be recalled in this respect that the poem started out as a youthful effort; Césaire had not yet fully integrated the various influences that converged to mold his expression, although his individual idiom had already emerged in the poem. For *Cahier* is not by any means a patchwork of influences but a fully developed work in its own right. The impact of Surrealism upon Césaire's work is pervasive, but it is fair to observe that if *Cahier* derives much of its impulse and texture from Breton's aesthetic of total experience, it is the robust muscularity of Rimbaud that prevails in its general tone, while its mystical orientation draws upon Mallarmé's conception of the poetic function, which is given a new meaning by Césaire's conscious effort to recover an original sense of myth and ritual suggested by his Caribbean environment and his distant African background. For if the developments summarized above provided Césaire with an idiom he could adopt as both up-to-date and in consonance with his expressive needs, while also offering a philosophy of the imagination that bore a relation to his vision, the substance of his expression was imposed in an imperious fashion by the collective agony of his race, its feeling grounded in the historical passion of its drama in which he was implicated. This thematic ground of Césaire's expression was prepared by important literary developments in the black world itself.

In June 1932, on the eve of Césaire's arrival, a group of young Martinican students and intellectuals launched a new journal in Paris. *Légitime Défense*, the name they gave to the journal, was a deliberate echo of the title of a previous publication by André Breton; the name announced their literary objectives and affiliations, which they made clear in the joint editorial that served as a manifesto for the group:

> Nous nous dressons ici contre tous ceux qui ne sont pas suffoqués par ce monde capitaliste, chrétien, bourgeois dont à notre corps defendant nous faisons partie.

Declaring their adherence to both Marxism and Surrealism as the twin channels of their attack upon Western civilization, they wrote:

> Et c'est en grinçant horriblement les dents que nous supportons l'abominable système de contraintes et de restrictions, d'exterminations de l'amour et la limitation du rêve généralement désigné sous le nom de civilisation occidentale.

In one article after another, they presented an uncompromising analysis of the economic and social conditions of their native island and a ruthless exposure of the fetters placed upon the mind of the local middle class, factors which they readily attributed to the global system of oppression represented by the colonial situation. The article entitled "Généralités sur 'l'écrivain' de couleur antillais" by René Ménil begins with this general statement:

> En même temps que les gendarmes, les administrateurs, les outils de travail et de police arrivent, dans les pays colonisés, les idées qu'il convient de faire penser aux indigènes pour l'exploitation heureuse du sol conquis.

Ménil goes on to describe the alienated character of the literature produced by the middle class in the French West Indian colonies. But it is especially in the essay entitled "Misère d'une poésie," written by Etienne Léro, that the connection is drawn in the most forthright way between what he saw as the exceptional mediocrity of this literature and the social situation in the colony:

> L'étranger chercherait vainement dans cette littérature un accent original ou profond, l'imagination sensuelle et colorée du noir, l'écho des haines et des aspirations d'un peuple opprimé.

This original accent he discerned in the literature of the new generation of black writers in the United States and Haiti, whose obvious affinities of experience were enough to set them up as appropriate models for the colonized West Indian writer. The terms in which he drew attention to their work are indicative of the revolution in consciousness that was beginning to take place among the younger elements of the French West Indian intellectual élite:

> Le vent qui monte de l'Amérique noire aura vite fait, espérons-le, de nettoyer nos Antilles des fruits avortés d'une culture caduque. Langston Hughes et Claude McKay, les deux poètes noirs révolutionnaires, nous ont apporté, marinés dans l'alcool rouge, l'amour africain de la vie, la joie africaine de l'amour, le rêve africain de la mort. Et déjà, de jeunes poètes Haïtiens nous livrent des vers gonflés d'un futur dynamisme.

The enthusiastic reception to which these words attest of the literature of what has come to be known as the Harlem Renaissance can be ascribed primarily to the militant character of the literature, centered on the unhappy situation of the black population in the United States. But the terms of Léro's tribute point as well to the innovative significance of the literature in its break with "mainstream" models, its refusal of a patronizing use of "dialect" (as in the work of Paul Lawrence Dunbar), and its cultivation of forms that were derived from or suggestive of an authentic black cultural expression as represented by the blues tradition and jazz. This feature, notable in the work of Langston Hughes, was intended not only to create a distinctive tone of address but also to promote the sense of a communal fund of culture and of social and moral values to which black people in America

could lay an original claim. This was a literature that sought to bring into
the open the suppressed feelings as well as the repressed energies of an
oppressed minority. There is no better statement of this purpose than this
passage from the essay "The Negro Poet and the Racial Mountain" written
by Langston Hughes and published in 1926:

> We younger Negro artists who create now intend to express our indi-
> vidual dark-skinned selves without fear or shame. If white people are
> pleased we are glad. If they are not, it doesn't matter. We know we are
> beautiful. And ugly, too. The tom-tom cries and the tom-tom laughs.
> If colored people are pleased we are glad. If they are not, their displea-
> sure doesn't matter either. We build our temples for tomorrow, strong
> as we know how, and we stand on top of the mountain, free within our-
> selves.

A significant component of this process of revaluation of the black self
in the literature of the Harlem Renaissance was the exploration of the
African theme. In this connection, Du Bois's book *The Souls of Black Folk*,
published as early as 1903, exerted a major influence in determining a new
attitude on the part of black intellectuals toward the way of life—the culture, in other words—of the black folk which had its roots in an African
past. This past was itself endowed with a poetic halo that gave it at once a
mysterious and spiritual dimension. "The shadow of a mighty Negro past,"
DuBois wrote, " flits through the tale of Ethiopia the Shadowy and of Egypt
the Sphinx." Such prose established Africa as a reference for the African-
American imagination, so that in such poems as Countee Cullen's
"Heritage," Claude McKay's "Outcast," and Langston Hughes's "Afro-
American Fragment," despite a lingering undertone of ambivalence, a clear
note of romantic longing for the ancestral homeland is struck, a note that is
given an elemental resonance in one of the best-known poems by Langston
Hughes, "The Negro Speaks of Rivers":

> I've known rivers:
> I've known rivers ancient as the world and older than the flow
>   of human blood in human veins
>
> My soul has grown deep like the rivers.

It was in accents such as these that the Harlem poets made their deep
impression on the minds of the group around *Légitime Défense*. They were
all the more ready to identify with this literature since Paris itself had
become the center of a vogue centered on blackness. Jazz had made its
impact not only as a form of popular music but also as an idiom that offered
resources to serious composers like Igor Stravinsky and Darius Milhaud.
With the active encouragement of the poet Guillaume Apollinaire and
prominent art critics, African sculpture became a source for the revitalization of Western art in the work of leading artists of the day, its influence

having become determinant in the development of Cubism. Besides, Claude McKay and Langston Hughes had been acclaimed in French literary circles, their work held up by its left-wing members as pointers to the advent of a world revolution. Such recognition in the colonial metropolis could not be a matter of indifference to the group; at the same time, it could not but induce in them, and all the more keenly, a feeling of disappointment at the marginality of their own homeland to these developments.

In one respect, however, the *Légitime Défense* group had cause for a certain optimism, of which Léro's brief reference to the work of the younger Haïtian poets is an indication. The Harlem Renaissance served as the immediate precedent for this work, which grew out of the reaction of the Haïtian intellectual élite to the occupation of their country by the United States from 1915 to 1934, an action that reduced Haiti once more to the status of a colony. A strong element of racial prejudice marked the administration and the general attitude of Americans, a factor of the occupation that disposed the Haitians to a large response to the themes of black writers in the United States. Moreover, they had in Jean Price-Mars an intellectual guide whose work *Ainsi parla l'Oncle* fulfilled for them an inspirational function similar to that of *The Souls of Black Folk*, awakening them to the need for an acceptance of their African ancestry and its inheritance, made manifest in an even more obvious way than in North America in the folkways and belief systems of the Haitian people. Thus, the themes of the Harlem Renaissance passed into the French language in the new literature of the Haitians, in the work of such writers as Jean Brière, Camille Rousseau, René Bélance, Jacques Roumain, and, later, René Depestre.

But although Léro drew the attention of his countrymen to this work, his own poetry and that of his collaborators were strikingly different, affecting a deliberate avant-garde manner that—with the possible exception of two poems in the journal contributed by Jules Monnerot—bore no visible relationship to any form of social inspiration.[6] It might be conjectured that this discrepancy between the declared objective of the group and its actual

---

[6]In his introduction to the 1979 reprint of the single number of the journal, René Ménil concedes as much when he writes, "D'une part, nous prenions en compte la société coloniale antillaise et nous en faisions une critique et une description réaliste. Mais, d'autre part, nous produisions des poèmes sans enracinement dans cette société, des poèmes de nulle part, des poèmes de personne." Ménil adds, moreover, that it took the publication of Césaire's *Cahier* to correct this anomaly. It must be said, however, that Jules-Marcel Monnerot does anticipate Césaire in some of his pieces published in the journal; the social reference of the following extract from an untitled poem is clear from the imagery and can be said to prepare Césaire's style and approach: *D'invisibles fusils qui tirent dans nos rêves / Font éclore de beaux marais automobiles / Il ne reste plus que des visages de buvard / Et l'usine s'arrête de battre / Dans l'attente du crime sauveur.*

realization in poetry would have been corrected with time, but only one issue of the journal ever appeared, for it was immediately suppressed by the French authorities for what was considered its seditious character, and Etienne Léro, the moving spirit of the group, died shortly afterwards. But the journal had struck a note whose reverberations could not be stilled and which Césaire was to amplify. It can be said that in writing *Cahier*, he set out to fulfil the program outlined by *Légitime Défense* and in a sense to take up the mantle of Etienne Léro.

All the indications are that Césaire had already acquired a certain reputation within the Caribbean community in Paris and had become a prominent member of its intellectual wing when, in March 1935, at his suggestion, a new journal, entitled more discretely *L'Etudiant Noir*, was launched to replace *Légitime Défense*. Judging from the single number that has survived, the tone was more moderate, but it went a significant step further than the earlier journal, for although it was concerned specifically with Martinique—its subtitle was "Journal de l'Association des Etudiants Martiniquais en France"—its horizons were decidedly Pan-African, as indicated by the section of the journal devoted to "Les Idées et les Lettres." Here could be found an article by Senghor on the African novels of the Martinican writer René Maran, that stressed his African sensibility and expatiated on the idea of a black personality as a factor of the interaction of races and cultures—an early pointer to Senghor's later elaboration of the concept of négritude. Another revelatory contribution was the short article on "Langage et musique chez les Nègres du Congo," by Henri Eboué, the son of the Guyanese-born Governor-General of French Equatorial Africa, in which an allusion is made to the similarities between the musical instruments of the population of the region and those that had become symbolic of black Caribbean history. The most trenchant contribution came from Césaire himself, in an article entitled "Négrerie: Jeunesse noire et assimilation" in which he denounced assimilation as contradictory and stultifying and in his own way restated the literary program of the group associated with *Légitime Défense*:

> La jeunesse noire veut agir et créer. Elle veut avoir ses poètes, ses romanciers, qui lui diront à elle ses malheurs à elle; elle veut contribuer à la vie universelle, à l'humanisation de l'humanité; et pour cela...il faut se conserver ou se retrouver: c'est le primat du soi.

The statement represents a summary of the theme and dialectic of *Cahier*. Césaire was giving notice of a mission toward which he was advancing on the broad front of a racial solidarity based as much on a shared condition as on a sense of a common identity. The presiding idea here is already that of négritude.

Césaire gained admission to the Ecole Normale Supérieure that same year, and it is more than likely that he had already begun to try his hand at poetry. Nothing has survived of his efforts prior to *Cahier* and he is reported to have said that once the idea of the poem had taken shape in his mind, he destroyed all his earlier work. He began to compose *Cahier* in the autumn of 1936, after his return from a trip to Yugoslavia in the company of his friend Petar Guberina.[7] An anecdote associated with this trip has it that Guberina took him to the island of Martinska in the Aegean Sea; the name of the island and its general aspect is said to have recalled to Césaire his island homeland so vividly that it stirred in him powerful emotions that he felt he had to record. He began to consign these emotions, reworked as images, in a student notebook, which explains the first word of the title. It is possible that the other elements of the title were suggested to Césaire by "Retour au pays maudit," a poem by the Surrealist poet René Daumal, which Césaire had almost certainly encountered in the course of his reading, and whose grim and nightmarish evocation of a landscape of the mind could well have evoked for him the dejected state of his native Martinique. At all events, it is this vivid reality that he expands upon in his poem as the dominant key of its thematic development.

Césaire was still working on the poem when, in 1937, Léon Damas published the collection *Pigments*, with a preface by Robert Desnos, one of the leading French poets of the day. The collection was well received and the impression it made was enforced as much by the subject matter as by the range of moods it encompassed, its striking use of imagery within a forth-right poetic diction leaning toward a colloquial style and its free deployment of French versification pointing up its message. These characteristics of the volume are well illustrated by the poem "La complainte du nègre" which contains this passage:

Ils me l'ont rendue
la vie
plus lourde et lasse

Mes aujourd'huis ont chacun sur mon jadis
de gros yeux qui roulent de rancoeur
et de honte.

In another poem, "Obsession," Damas gives an unusual turn to the Symbolist manner through an image that dramatizes his inner tension:

un goût de sang me vient
âcrement vertical
pareil
à l'obsession païenne

---

[7]Guberina was later to write the preface to the definitive edition of the poem pub-lished by Présence Africaine in 1956.

des encensoirs.

In its development of a sequence of poems centered upon a strongly articulated theme, *Pigments* is comparable in its structure and its effects to *Cahier*, and although Damas was later to be somewhat overshadowed by Césaire, its publication represented an important landmark in the evolution of French-speaking black poetry. Indeed, the volume has always enjoyed a consideration almost equal to that bestowed on Césaire's poem.

It seems that Césaire himself was going through a period of stress at this time. He had married in the meantime, and a child was expected—an allusion to this fact in *Cahier*[8] indicates that the poem was in active gestation, and the two events came to be associated in his mind, in Mallarméan fashion, with the slow maturation of the creative process itself. The material problems of starting out on family life may have had something to do with his not presenting himself for the *Agrégation*, the final examination that normally concluded studies at the Ecole Normale Supérieure. However, he obtained a *Diplôme d'Etudes Supérieures* with a thesis on the theme of the South in African-American Literature—indicative of the interests which the influence of the Harlem Renaissance and his activities had determined for him—and completed the first version of *Cahier*. In the meantime one of his professors at the Ecole Nornale, M. Petitbon, became aware of its existence after being struck by the original turns of phrase and general vigor of style in Césaire's essays; he inquired from his student if he did any creative writing, whereupon Césaire showed him the poem. It was thus with his assistance that *Cahier* was published in the little-known journal *Volontés* in its number for August 1939.

There can be no doubt that *Cahier* was born out of a compelling inner necessity and that its writing and publication represented an immense deliverance for Césaire. In it, he exteriorized all the inner drama of the collective history and personal experience that ravaged his mind. In the Postface to *Ethiopiques*, Senghor, who was a witness to the circumstances under which the poem was composed, provides a revealing testimony of the therapeutic function that the writing of the poem performed for Césaire as sentient individual:

> Le *Cahier d'un retour au pays natal* d'Aimé Césaire fut une parturition dans la souffrance. Il s'en fallut de peu que la mère y laissât sa vie, je veux dire: la raison.

Césaire left Paris for Martinique shortly after the publication of the poem, which went unnoticed in the tense situation that prevailed in Paris on the eve of the Second World War, which duly broke out just at the time

---

[8]See stanza 112.

Césaire arrived in Martinique. He immediately took up a position as *professeur de lettres* at his old lycée, which counted among its students at the time Frantz Fanon, Edouard Glissant, and Georges Desportes, all of whom were later to distinguish themselves as writers.

The Martinique to which Césaire returned had long-standing problems as a colonial outpost that were now exacerbated by the difficulties of the war. After the early defeat of France by Germany in 1940, the island came under the control of the Vichy regime, whose willingness to collaborate with the Nazi victors was facilitated, among other factors, by its commitment to a narrow conception of the French nation and a strong aversion to the liberal, egalitarian, and secular principles on which, at least nominally, the institutions of the Third Republic had been based. Vichy imposed on the colony a conservative, authoritarian administration, whose ideological options, coupled with the influx of intolerant whites from metropolitan France, favored an intensification of the racism that had always been a pervasive element of human relations on the island. The situation was further complicated by its isolation, material privations, and the general atmosphere of apprehension caused by the naval blockade of the island by Allied forces.

As an immediate consequence of this situation, despite his meager resources, Césaire decided to found a publication that would address the complex problems of Martinique and thus bring home, as it were, the spirit of *Légitime Défense* and *L'Etudiant Noir* to its population. With the collaboration of his wife Suzanne, of René Ménil, who had also returned to Martinique and taught philosophy at the lycée, as well as other like-minded compatriots, he began to bring out *Tropiques*, as the publication was called, in April 1941. Despite the vicissitudes associated with initiatives of this kind, the difficulties arising from the war situation, and, above all, the hostility of the political and ecclesiastical authorities, with whom his team kept up a running battle, they were able to take the journal through twelve issues until the end of the war in 1945, when it ceased publication.

The function that Césaire envisaged for *Tropiques* was essentially an educative one, but the urgent import of the events taking place on the world stage and their implications for his homeland claimed his attention in the "Présentation" he wrote to introduce the first number of the journal:

> Où que nous regardions, l'ombre gagne. L'un après l'autre les foyers s'éteignent. Le cercle d'ombre se resserre, parmis les cris d'hommes et des hurlements de fauves. Pourtant, nous sommes de ceux qui disent *non* à l'ombre. Nous savons que le salut du monde dépend de nous aussi. Que la terre a besoin de n'importe lesquels d'entre ses fils. Les plus humbles.

But while a pronounced political and social concern runs through the

journal, either as the explicit subject of articles and features or as the implicit motivation of the entire enterprise, the fundamental interests of the group
found expression in the remarkable series of cultural and intellectual essays
that dominated each issue of the journal. They fall into two broad categories: essays on literature, the arts, and general ideas, whose theme was the
significance of creative and intellectual endeavors as a general proposition,
on one hand, and on the other, those devoted specifically to the
Martinican/Caribbean environment, with the declared objective of promoting an awareness of its unique mode of collective insertion into the world.
The postulate from which the theme of these articles derived was the existence of an autonomous culture and personality of the Caribbean population, composed of elements in its triple inheritance: the Caribbean, the
French/Western, and the African.

In the circumstances, they felt an obligation to insist upon the African
element, as a means of bringing the Caribbean to a reconciliation with this
element that was unavowed but which, they maintained, remained a living
presence in the profound recesses of the collective being. The African
theme was carried on a stream of racial and cultural notions that had their
source in anthropological literature, especially in the work of Leo Frobenius,
who exercised what can only be called a fascination on the mind of the
Césaires. Indeed, on this point, Suzanne can be considered to have been the
theoretician of a Caribbean version of négritude that is as vigorously formulated as that of Senghor. The conviction that she put into her various essays
on this question can be judged from this passage from her essay entitled
"Malaise d'une civilisation," published in the fifth issue of *Tropiques*, dated
April 1942:

> Qu'est-ce que le Martiniquais?
> — L'homme plante
> Comme elle, abandon au rythme universel. Point d'effort pour dominer
> la nature. Médiocre agriculteur. Peut-être. Je ne dis pas qu'il fait
> pousser la plante; je dis qu'il pousse, qu'il vit en plante . . . Abandon à
> soi, aux saisons, à la lune, au jour plus ou moins long. Cueillette. Et
> toujours et partout, dans les moindres représentations, primat de la
> plante, la plante piétinée mais vivante, morte, mais renaissante, la
> plante libre, silencieuse et fière...
> Ouvrez les oreilles. Un des contes populaires du folklore martiniquais:
> l'herbe qui pousse sur la tombe est la vivante chevelure de la morte, qui
> proteste contre la mort. Toujours le même symbole: la plante.
> Sentiment vif d'une communauté vie-mort. Bref, *sentiment éthiopien de
> la vie*.
> Donc, le Martiniquais est typiquement éthiopien. Dans les profondeurs
> de sa conscience, il est l'homme-plante et s'identifiant à la plante, son
> désir est de s'abandonner au rythme de la vie.

The correspondence between this extract and some of the key passages in *Cahier*[9] hardly needs to be stressed. But apart from the indication it provides of the close collaboration that existed between Césaire and his wife, and beyond the romanticism with which the image of Africa is charged in their vision at this point of their development, it points to the redemptive value that Africa assumed for them as a symbol of inner liberation, which they urged upon their community. As the rest of Suzanne Césaire's essay makes clear, the open avowal of an African presence in Caribbean forms of life and expression had a precise psychological function in the context of French colonialism, as an unburdening of the self. The massive introjection of the ideological and moral premises of assimilation had become unsettling and dysfunctional for the West Indian mind. Africa thus offered the prospect of a healthy integration of the personality, even in its quotidian manifestations, the mode of a normal adherence to a framework of self-awareness and expression constituted by the immediate, native background of collective life.

Césaire has more recently put the matter in its proper perspective :

> Quand je me revendique de l'Afrique, cela signifie que je me revendique *des valeurs culturelles africaines*. Nous sommes le produit de la biologie, mais nous sommes, en très grande partie, le produit de la *culture*. Et la biologie ne devient intéressante que quand on la transcende en élément culturel. (Italics in the original)

What this further implies is that Africa served as a reference for what must be acknowledged as an incipient nationalist consciousness, as a maximal symbol in a process of self-differentiation in reaction to the cultural imperialism that sustained the political, as a claim to cultural legitimacy of a distinctive Martinican feeling for life and relation to the world. It is the aspiration toward a sense of a national community grounded in a creative relationship to its environment, to the sense of a homeland in the most intense and meaningful sense of the word, that all Césaire's work seeks to promote through the suggestive power of poetry. This aspiration comes through admirably, albeit in negative terms, in the peremptory but urgent tone of the statement with which Césaire introduced the journal to his people:

> Terre muette et stérile. C'est de la nôtre que je parle... Point de ville. Point d'art. Point de poésie. Point de civilisation, je veux dire cette projection de l'homme sur le monde, ce modelage du monde par l'homme, cette frappe de l'univers à l'effigie de l'homme.

The nationalist impulse behind this statement and its relation to the inspiration of Césaire's poetry become clarified in another statement on the function of poetry and its specific modality in the Martinican context that

---

[9]See in particular stanzas 114-18.

opens his essay "Maintenir la poésie":

> Se défendre du social par la création d'une zone d'incandescence, en
> deçà de laquelle, à l'intérieur de laquelle fleurit dans une sécurité terri-
> ble la fleur inouïe du "Je"; dépouiller toute l'existence matérielle dans le
> silence et les hauts feux glacés de l'humour; que ce soit par la création
> d'une zone de feux; que ce soit par la création d'une zone de silence
> gelé, conquérir par la révolte la part franche où se susciter soi-même,
> intégral, telles sont quelques-unes des exigences qui depuis un siècle
> bientôt tendent à s'imposer au poète.

In this declaration, it is the heritage of Rimbaud and the Surrealists
that Césaire assumes in order to apply it to his historical and existential situation. As against the reassurance dispensed by an earlier generation of
French West Indian poets, which gave no hint of the brutal reality of life in
the island colonies and even served to enforce a numbing attitude of acceptance, Césaire envisages a poetry of insurrection for the remaking of his people. This is the precise sense of Suzanne Césaire's provocative conclusion to
"Misère d'une poésie" (in a reprise of the title of Léro's essay in *Légitime
Défense*), her 1942 review of a volume of poems by a member of this earlier
generation of poets: "La poésie martiniquaise sera cannibale, ou ne sera pas,"
a deliberate echo of a line from *Cahier*,[10] whose aesthetic implications and
symbolic connotations form an integral part of Césaire's poetic revolt.

Apart from offering Césaire and his group a channel for reflection and
expression, *Tropiques* brought an element of sustained urgency and high-
mindedness to the discussion of the problems of the French West Indies
which the colonies had not known before, and was more immediate in its
impact because it was published locally. It was perhaps this element, as well
as the obviously informed level of discourse of its contributions, that struck
André Breton, *chef de file* of the Surrealist movement when, during a
stopover in Fort-de-France in April 1941, on his way to voluntary exile in
the United States, he came by chance across the first number of the review,
which had just then appeared. He was so taken by its content that he
expressed an interest in making the acquaintance of those responsible for its
publication. In the essay "Un Grand Poète noir," written as a preface for
the bilingual edition of *Cahier* which he later arranged to have published in
New York, Breton has given an account of the meeting that ensued between
him and Césaire and his wife, René Menil, and others of the group, the cor-
diality that marked his relations with them, and, above all, the profound
impression made upon him by *Cahier*, which he was later to describe as "le
plus grand monument lyrique de ce temps."

Breton's enthusiasm can be explained in part by the circumstances of
his encounter with the poem and its author and by the moral significance it

---

[10]See stanza 48.

assumed in those dark times beyond its immediate reference to the social situation in Martinique, a significance that was highlighted by Césaire's coura-
geous stand in his introduction to the first number of *Tropiques*. Moreover,
the anecdotal aspects of the encounter as recounted by Breton could not but
strike him as a marvelous confirmation in real life of his idea of "le hasard
objectif," which he championed as a principle of artistic creation. There
can be no doubt, however, that the intrinsic qualities of the poem were
responsible in the main for his whole-hearted response to Césaire's *Cahier*,
its exemplary illustration of the canons of thought and vision that he had
been defending for some twenty years. Indeed, Breton was the perfect reader
for *Cahier*, and as he put it in the essay, "L'enjeu, tout compte tenu du génie
propre de Césaire, était notre conception commune de la vie." In other
words, from what may have seemed to Breton the most unlikely of sources,
Cahier brought a vindication of Surrealism through what the French critic
Alain Bosquet has termed "la preuve par les tropiques."[11]

It is not likely that *Cahier* would ever under any circumstances have
sunk into oblivion, but Breton's intervention, leading to its publication in
volume form, with the warm endorsement of a magnificent preface, has been
crucial in the esteem it has enjoyed ever since. Moreover, Breton's active
promotion of Césaire's work through publication of his early poems in various Surrealist journals contributed to the growth of his reputation as a poet.
This had soon become considerable enough to justify his being invited to
deliver a keynote address at an international conference on philosophy in
Port-au-Prince, the capital of Haiti, in September 1944.

Césaire's address, entitled "Poésie et Connaissance," which has
remained perhaps his best-known essay—certainly his most significant—
amounts to a resounding declaration of faith in the cognitive potential of
poetry, which, it is essential to stress, he views not so much as a relation of
opposition, but as one of complementarity to science, as is clear from the
sixth of the seven propositions with which, in the manner of Karl Marx's
Gotha Program, he concludes his communication: "La vérité scientifique a
pour signe la cohérence et l'éfficacité. La vérité poétique a pour signe la
beauté." But while he acknowledges the practical function of science as a
means of orientation in what he calls "la forêt des phénomènes," with its
legitimacy at its own level of operations, he insists upon the impoverishment
of the human mind that these entail, and upon the transcendent power of

---

[11]In *Verbe et vertige: situations de la poésie contemporaine*, Paris, Hachette, 1961, p. 74.
Breton himself has expounded on this point in "Le Dialogue créole," written in collaboration with André Masson and included in *Martinique, charmeuse de serpents*; the
volume also contains "Un Grand Poète noir" and other essays on his impressions of
Martinique, in particular "Eaux troubles," which offers a testimony of the tense
atmosphere on the island and a report on its social situation under the Vichy regime.

the poetic mode of knowledge. The thrust of his argument is that poetry, when not restricted in its scope to a merely rhetorical figuration of the world, is capable of extending human experience into the obscure realm of consciousness and imagination through the evocative force of image and symbol, and hence of grasping the profound reality of the universe they signify. Thus Césaire declares:

> Autrement dit, poésie est épanouissement.
> Epanouissement de l'homme à la mesure du monde; dilatation verti-
> gineuse. Et on peut dire que toute grande poésie, sans jamais renoncer à
> être humaine, à un très mystérieux moment, cesse d'être strictement
> humaine pour commencer à être cosmique.

It is significant to note the conjunction in this declaration of Césaire's preoccupation with the immediate human relevance of poetry—in other words, with its social and existential significance—and his conception of its visionary import. It is a conjunction that is characteristic and informs the definition with which he concludes the address:

> Le poète est cet être très vieux et très neuf, très complexe et très simple
> qui aux confins vécus du rêve et du réel, du jour et de la nuit, entre
> absence et présence, cherche et reçoit dans le déclenchement soudain
> des cataclysmes intérieurs le mot de passe de la connivence et de la
> puissance.

Accompanied by his wife, Césaire spent a total of seven months in Haiti, from mid-May to mid-December 1944; the visit afforded them an opportunity to make intimate contact with a country and a people with whom they could feel the closest of affinities through the local forms of speech and immediate sympathy for an evolved authenticity of life,[12] and with the writers associated with the Haitian Renaissance with whom they kept up a busy program of lectures and discussions.

At the end of the war the following year, Césaire was elected mayor of Fort-de-France and, as a member of the French Communist Party, one of the deputies for Martinique to the Constituent Assembly. His activities were henceforth to proceed on the two fronts of the political and the literary, which, he had become convinced, had to be closely associated in his espousal of the cause of his people. It was at this point that he took the momentous initiative of introducing, in February 1946, a bill in the French parliament for the transformation of the "creole" colonies—Martinique and Guadeloupe in the Caribbean, Guyane on the South American mainland,

---

[12]Although Haitian créole is different from the Martinican, they are mutually intelligible. On the question of cultural and religious practices, Césaire has remarked that the Haitian *hougan* (officiating priest of the Vodun cult) is really the equivalent of the *quimboiseur* in the equally African-derived religion of the Martinican folk.

and Réunion in the Indian Ocean—into constituent departments of France, with full rights of citizenship for all their inhabitants. Despite the reticence of his metropolitan colleagues, he pushed the bill through the French National Assembly until it became law.

Césaire has been bitterly reproached for this initiative by the younger radical elements in the French Caribbean who are calling for independence, which the granting of departmental status seems to them to have compromised, if not foreclosed. Césaire's action requires, however, to be understood in the context of the time. This was the era of the Liberation, which seemed to signal a new beginning for France. The defeat of Fascism had rekindled socialist hopes everywhere and the optimistic mood of the French people was reflected in the strong representation of the Communist party in the French parliament and in the government.[13] Moreover, the colonies had played a notable role in the Resistance, highlighted by the rallying of Equatorial Africa under its Guyanese-born Governor-General Félix Eboué to General de Gaulle's cause.[14] Affected no doubt by the general euphoria that reigned at the time, it seemed to Césaire that integration into a reformed France promised redress of old grievances and a reversal of the terms and conditions of the existing colonial form of association. Césaire's action was thus a response to the hopeful signs of the day; in the general perspective of this outlook, far from being a contradiction in his position, it was indeed in full conformity with the universalism consistently proclaimed in his poetry. However, Césaire was soon to be disillusioned. The steady drift to the right of the Fourth Republic—in part as a consequence of the politics of the cold war—and its reaffirmation of the old concept of empire made for a situation in which no practical distinction was made between the overseas departments and the colonies.

The publication in 1946 of *Les Armes miraculeuses* established Césaire as a major poet, firmly associated with the Surrealist movement, of which he was considered a new and leading light. The following year, he took part in the founding of the review *Présence Africaine* for which the primary initiative was due to Alioune Diop, who also secured the collaboration of Césaire's old friends Senghor and Damas, both of whom had returned to Paris as deputies, and of prominent French writers and intellectuals such as

---

[13]Maurice Thorez, General Secretary of the Party, was *Vice-Président du Conseil* (Deputy Prime Minister) at the time.

[14]It must be recalled that at the Brazzaville Conference in 1944, De Gaulle himself outlined comprehensive reforms of French colonial policy to be implemented after the war. This raised immense hopes in the colonies, and although the promise of Brazzaville was never fulfilled, a move was made toward granting French citizenship to selected Africans under the law named after the Senegalese deputy, Lamine Guèye.

André Gide, Albert Camus, and Emmanuel Mounier. The review, which also started a book publishing section, has proved to be the most durable of all African or black publications and has played and continues to play an invaluable role in the intellectual life of the black world.

The growing importance of the new black literature in French was demonstrated that same year by the appearance of *Poètes d'expression française*, edited by Damas, who wrote an introduction tracing the development in the pre-war years of the poetic and intellectual movement that culminated in the selection he was offering. The real consecration of this literature came, however, with the publication in 1948 of Senghor's *Anthologie de la nouvelle poésie nègre et malgache*, where in his introduction, he advanced the term *négritude* coined by Césaire, as a common reference for the work of the poets of the anthology. This provided Jean-Paul Sartre with a cue for his now celebrated prefatory essay "Orphée noir," in which he gave an extended formulation to the concept, defining it, in terms of his existentialist philosophy, as "l'être-dans-le-monde du noir."

Sartre's essay is too well-known to require discussion here. It is sufficient to note that it launched négritude as a movement whose fortune has been various and given rise to an ongoing debate concerning its meaning and implications. It is also important to observe that for Sartre, Césaire was clearly the most impressive of the poets of the anthology, the writer whose work offered the most meaningful signposts to the collective state of mind represented by the term *négritude* and illustrated its most far-reaching significance. And in view of Sartre's limited interest in poetry, the effect of Césaire's work on him can be said to have been salutary, for if his characterization of certain passages of *Cahier* is open to question, there can be no doubt that the poem elicited from him a response that was full and deep.

The year 1948 also saw the publication of *Soleil cou coupé*, a volume that confirmed Césaire's Surrealist affiliations, as much by its title (taken from Apollinaire's "Zone") as by the general cast of the poems it contained. The year was also the centenary of the abolition of slavery by France, and Césaire contributed a warmly eulogistic introduction to the collection of essays by Victor Schoelcher that had been brought out to mark the occasion. Another volume, *Corps perdu*, appeared the following year, in a limited edition illustrated by Picasso. Although the poems in this volume were more terse in tone and spare in texture than those of the preceding volume, they continued his previous vein of intransigent defiance as to theme, and of hermeticism as to form. Césaire later revised the poems in the two volumes, shearing them somewhat of their luxuriance, and brought them together in *Cadastre*, whose title was intended to mark more pointedly their plotting of an outer world of events and of solicitations as registered upon an inner landscape of experience.

In 1950, Césaire turned to discursive prose for his *Discours sur le colo-*

nialisme, an indictment that has become in its own way a classic of the polemical genre. He singled out for attack a book that had received considerable attention, *Psychologie de la colonisation,* which happens to have been written by one of his former teachers at the lycée, Octave Mannoni, for what he considered its invidious attempt to lend the authority of science to the colonial enterprise.[15] Rejecting the notion of "mission civilisatrice" that had been employed to justify the colonisation of non-Western races, he described in detail the atrocities committed in the course of French colonial conquest and, pointing out their dehumanizing effects, summed up his view in a formulaic sentence: "De la colonisation à la civilisation, la distance est infinie."

He returned to this theme in the address "Culture et Colonisation," which he delivered at the Premier Congrès des Ecrivains Noirs, organized by Présence Africaine in September 1956. Observing that what brought together the participants at the Congress, writers and intellectuals from Africa and of African descent in the New World, was the common experience of the colonial situation, he went on to point out the cultural implications of this situation:

> Limitation de la civilisation colonisée.
> Suppression ou abâtardissement de tout ce qui la structure, comment dans ces conditions s'étonner de la suppression de ce qui est une des caractéristiques de toute civilisation vivante: la faculté de renouvellement.

Césaire thus gave an unambiguous political meaning to the declared cultural objectives of the Congress, a meaning that Frantz Fanon was to expand upon in the communication that he sent to the Second Congress held in Rome three years later. Césaire did not, however, lose sight of the cultural perspectives within which the process of African renewal, which remained at the center of his preoccupations, would take place:

> Je crois que la civilisation qui a donné au monde l'art de la sculpture nègre; que la civilisation qui a donné au monde politique et social des institutions communautaires originales, comme par exemple la démocratie villageoise ou la fraternité d'âge et tant d'institutions marquées au coin de l'esprit de la solidarité; que cette civilisation, la même qui sur un autre plan a donné au monde moral une philosophie originale

---

[15]Mannoni's book, published in an English translation under the title *Prospero and Caliban,* was written as an attempt to explain, in psychoanalytic terms, the deep causes of the 1947 uprising in Madagascar against the French. Mannoni put forward the theory of a "dependency syndrome" within Malagasy culture which had gone unfulfilled by the French, leading to frustration and armed revolt. The uprising was put down with exceptional brutality by the French, hence Césaire's bitter denunciation of Mannoni's book.

fondée sur le respect de la vie et l'intégration dans le cosmos, je refuse
de croire que cette civilisation-là, pour insuffisante qu'elle soit, son
anéantissement et son reniement soient une condition de la renaissance
des peuples noirs.

A connection exists between Césaire's advocacy of cultural independence as a condition for African and black re-emergence into history and his
break with the Communist Party that occurred a few weeks after the
Congress of black writers. As he makes clear in his *Lettre à Maurice Thorez*,
the immediate reason for his decision to leave the party was Nikita
Krushchev's exposure of the sinister character of the Stalinist regime in the
Soviet Union. Césaire's commitment to freedom and justice could not be
reconciled with the reality of the crimes confirmed so spectacularly as having been committed in the name of Communism. But his disaffection had
been prepared by his uneasy relations with the hierarchy of the party whose
dogmatism he had found intolerable. The readiness of the Communist Party
to subordinate the interests of black people to an ideological orthodoxy nar-
rowly defined and pursued appeared to Césaire as a form of imperialism and
a reflection of its monolithic intolerance of a necessary pluralism. This led
Césaire to insist upon the specificity of the black cause:

Singularité de notre "situation dans le monde" qui ne se confond avec
nulle autre. Singularité de nos problèmes qui ne se ramènent à nul autre
problème. Singularité de notre histoire, coupée de terribles avatars qui
n'appartiennent qu'à elle. Singularité de notre culture que nous
voulons vivre de manière de plus en plus réelle.

He proceeded thereafter to found his own party, le Parti Progressiste
Martiniquais, as a new platform for his political activities which, as its name
implies, retained the socialist orientation of his earlier commitments, and
through which he has maintained a devoted following on his native island
ever since.

The next few years witnessed an acceleration of events in France that,
under the stress of the Algerian War, led to the collapse of the Fourth
Republic and the return to power of Charles de Gaulle, who put in train a
series of measures which, starting with the breakaway of Sekou Touré's
Guinea in 1958, was to culminate in a cascade of independence in 1960 for
the French colonies in Africa. With similar developments elsewhere on the
continent, the year seemed the *annus mirabilis* presaging a general reawaken-
ing of Africa. The volume *Ferrements*, which was published that year,
reflected a dual response on the part of Césaire to these events: on the one
hand, a mood of exhilaration at the pace with which his hopes were being
realized on the mother continent, expressed in such poems as "Salut à la
Guinée," "Pour Saluer le Tiers Monde," and especially "Afrique"; on the
other hand, a despondency about the situation in his own homeland, quali-

fied as "une île bien en peine," a mood that predominates in such poems as the liminary which gives the volume its title and the oft-quoted "Hors des jours étrangers," which begins:

> mon peuple
>
> quand
> hors des jours étrangers
> germeras-tu une tête bien tienne sur tes épaules renouées
> et ta parole

The volume is also distinguished by a remarkable coherence of imagery and a greater deliberation in its expression, by a nobility of diction attaining a rhetorical quality, in the series of commemorative poems represented by "Statue de Lafcadio Hearn," "Mémorial de Louis Delgrès," and, in particular, "Tombeau de Paul Eluard." In this last poem, arguably the finest single composition by Césaire up to that point in his poetic career, a steady flow of opulent images functions as dense background and symbolic counterpoint to the solemnity of the poet's elegiac tone of address.

There is good reason to consider *Ferrements* as having brought Césaire's writing to a new level of maturity. In it, he found a new voice with which to sustain his habitual constellation of images and, at the same time, draw his audience more directly into the structure of thought and vision they embodied. The need to put across this vision in a more accessible form led him further in this direction with his writing of the historical play *La Tragédie du Roi Christophe*, which was serialized in *Présence Africaine* from 1961 to 1963 and published as a volume shortly after. The connection between this play and Césaire's biography of Toussaint L'Ouverture which had appeared in 1960 is not only historical and thematic but more profoundly moral. Both works, each in its own way, represent a meditation upon the Haitian experience as representative of the vicissitudes of black history, the exalted moments as well as the troughs in its uncertain course toward some form of accomplishment.

In its bearing upon the contemporary scene in Africa, through the parallel it strikes with the post-independence situation in Haiti and the ominous unfolding of events in postcolonial Africa—of which the Congolese crisis in the early sixties was a premonition—*La Tragédie du Roi Christophe* presented itself as a demonstration of the perils and responsibilities that lay ahead. It assumes in that light a didactic significance that the poet-playwright's audience was invited to consider and to ponder. The didactic intent of the play is pursued and made more pointed in *Une Saison au Congo*, which followed in 1965 and in which Césaire dramatized the meaning of the Congo crisis itself. For while the historical personality of Lumumba is celebrated in this play, the emphasis of the dramatic action is placed upon the

external as well as the internal forces against which he had to contend, and
which contributed to his fall and martyrdom. Both plays present a political
message with a clear pedagogical underpinning: the need for lucidity as a
necessary complement to a heroic disposition and passion. In this light, the
two plays combine to project a new direction of Césaire's historical intelligence and racial sentiment in what might be called a postcolonial négritude.

All the while, Césaire maintained an intense activity on the political
front, which had become complicated by the development in the French
West Indies of a movement for autonomy, a movement that translated the
frustration of the local population, especially the younger elements, with the
reality of departmental status[16] and manifested itself in unrest and occasional
violence. Given his personal disillusionment with a measure attached to his
name, Césaire had come to identify with this movement, although he could
not give his assent to its radical wing which had indicated it would settle for
nothing less than total independence from France. In Césaire's view, while
autonomy had become a political and administrative imperative, independence could only be meaningful in the context of a West Indian federation;
the conditions did not appear to him for the moment encouraging, especially in the light of the failure registered in this matter in the English-speaking
parts of the region.[17] At all events, his conviction on the question of autonomy was made clear in his address of welcome as mayor of Fort-de-France on
the occasion of De Gaulle's visit to Martinique in March 1964. However,
despite the extreme courtesy of the exchange between the two men, there
seemed little possibility of understanding between Césaire and De Gaulle
who in his reply described the islands of the Caribbean as "ces grains de

---

[16]As a member of the autonomy movement put it, instead of making them "des
Français à part entière," departmental status meant in reality that the French West
Indians had become "des Français entièrement à part."

[17]Césaire's reservations in this regard have earned him the strictures of the radicals,
notably Daniel Boukman, whose play Chants pour hâter la mort d'Orphée is a direct
attack on Césaire, though ironically, its whole style reflects the strong influence of
Césaire himself. A more direct questioning of Césaire's position is contained in an
open letter addressed to him by one of the radicals, Guy Cabort-Masson—see his
"Lettre ouverte à Aimé Césaire," published in Peuples Noirs/Peuples Africains, No. 22,
July-Aug. 1981. It cannot, however, be said that attacks like these have had any
effect on Césaire's political and intellectual standing, for his continuing force and
appeal for a large section of the younger generation of the French West Indian intelligentsia were demonstrated at a conference held in Paris in October 1985 as a form
of homage to him; the conference was organized by Editions Caribbéennes, founded
and run by a substantial element of this group. (The proceedings of this conference
have been published in the volume Aimé Césaire ou l'athanor d'un alchimiste.)

poussière dans l'océan."[18] It was not until 1981, with the return of the
Socialists to power and the regional policy of François Mitterand's presiden-
cy, that a move was made to give satisfaction to local particularities. The
regional assembly created for Martinique and Guadeloupe under this policy,
of which Césaire became president in 1982, has gone some way to respond-
ing to the nationalist sentiment reflected in the autonomy movement.

Césaire's preoccupations in the above circumstances impart an espe-
cial vigor to his refocussing of the island theme in the play *Une Tempête*,
which appeared in 1969. This was followed in 1981 by the collection *moi,*
laminaire, containing most of the poems published earlier under the title
Noria as an appendix to *Oeuvres Complètes*, which had appeared in 1976.
The archetypal form that Shakespeare's imagination had given to the colonial conflict in terms of dramatic setting, action, and meaning provided an
ideal model, in the real sense of the term, for a reworking by Césaire, himself
an historical embodiment of Caliban. Césaire redirected the powerful flow
of the English master's language, with its immense pressure on his own consciousness, toward his project of revolt and liberation. Rather than an
updating of Shakespeare, Césaire's adaptation is a way of giving intertextual
resonance to the Prospero-Caliban dialectic, of moving its reference into an
area of sensibility and of vision that the original text could not anticipate.
That area is defined by the scope of Césaire's négritude, in which the poet's
African sentiment lays the ground for an attachment to his island homeland
and conditions his hope for the regeneration of its people. It is to this hope
that Césaire gives voice in the final lines of the poem "J'ai guidé du troupeau
la transhumance," from the volume *moi, laminaire*, a poem in which the
imagery endows the subject with a clear personal reference:

> il s'est arrêté un moment
> le temps pour un nuage d'installer une belle parade de trochilidés
> l'éventail à n'en pas douter à éventer d'or jeune
> la partie la plus plutonique d'une pépite qui n'est pas autre chose que le
> ventre flammé d'un beau temps
> récessif.

It is in *Cahier* that we first encounter the determined confrontation
with history these lines bespeak. We now turn to the poem to examine how
this is realized at both the thematic and symbolic level of its articulation.

---

[18]André Malraux has provided an account of the meeting between Césaire and De
Gaulle in his *Antimémoires*.

THE POEM

Cahier d'un retour au pays natal has had a remarkable textual history. The text of the poem as we have it today is the result of a process of composition and revision stretching over a period of more than twenty years. It should be recalled that Césaire began the poem late in 1935 and worked on it for the next four years, completing the first version in time for its publication in *Volontés* just before the outbreak of the Second World War and his return to Martinique in 1939. This first version he almost certainly considered tentative, for although the poem did not attract attention at the time, he attached enough importance to it to continue to revise it, in the obvious hope of bringing it out as a volume in a more finished form some day. What is more, Césaire wrote a number of new poems during the war that were published in *Tropiques* and which he must have conceived in some kind of organic relation to the first completed version of *Cahier*. This is the case in particular with the poem "En guise de manifeste littéraire," which appeared in the review's issue for April 1942 and was dedicated to André Breton, whom he had met the year before. This poem was later incorporated with revisions into the volume edition, now considerably augmented with new material, which Breton arranged to have published in New York in 1947, with the French text accompanied by an English translation, and for which he wrote the preface. It is this edition, without the English translation, that was reissued, with minor modifications, by Bordas in Paris later the same year.

Césaire continued to work on the poem, adding or deleting material, rearranging the sequence of stanzas or individual passages, and revising the text as a whole, for a new edition which was published in 1956 by Présence Africaine, with a preface by his old friend Petar Guberina, to whom, as we have seen, he owed the occasion that triggered its conception. This edition has remained the definitive one, although in the course of successive reprintings, a few misprints found their way into the text. These were carried over into another bilingual edition published by Présence Africaine in 1968, with the French text accompanied by an English translation prepared by Emile Snyder and based on the earlier New York edition but brought up to date in conformity with Césaire's revisions as contained in the 1956 edition.[19] Finally, in 1983, Présence Africaine brought out a new, corrected

---

[19]It is a matter for regret that these misprints are reproduced in the text of the poem as it appears in *Oeuvres Complètes* published in 1976, which is the basis for the English translation by Clayton Eshelman and Annette Smith in the bilingual volume of *Collected Poems* published in the United States in 1983.

edition of the French text with a slightly altered stanza division; the edition also includes Breton's preface to the 1947 edition as an appendix.[20]

What is striking about this textual history of *Cahier*, its long process of initial composition and continuous revision, is Césaire's concern to achieve a greater degree of formal integration of its structure with the referential function of the poem. For while his revisions were no doubt intended to "firm up" the poem in terms of its expressive means and therefore have a "technical" character, an equally important consideration for him was the need to bring the work into closer relation with the evolving circumstances of its social inspiration. There is internal evidence in the work to suggest a continuing response to events that had a bearing on its theme or confirmed the social and moral preoccupations that govern its articulation.

The essential point that emerges from this textual history is that, in its primary aspect, *Cahier* presents itself as a poem of circumstance, in the best sense of the term: as a poem that registers moments in a dramatic progression of the poet's experience, moments that acquire for him historic significance, which he seeks to endow with an enduring poetic value. The objective reference is not merely the point of departure of a poetic reflection but remains central to its ramifications, functions as the constant focus of its affective moments and as the touchstone of the experience it records. For *Cahier* is eminently a political poem, again in a particularly profound sense of the term: a poem in which the sense of individual destiny is not only located within the framework of a necessary implication in the collective but is also associated with the operative values of human responsibility and moral obligation which flow from that essential relation. These values are affirmed as the basis of a more comprehensive relation of the human estate to nature, as constitutive, in short, of a spiritual imperative.

Given, then, this thematic grounding of *Cahier*, any reading of the poem has to proceed from the external reference to the internal configuration, from its explicit political and social theme as determined by its context of inspiration to its symbolic transpositions in a structure of images that extends its significance beyond the immediate. For if there is any work that can be said, in Sartre's term, to be "overdetermined," none perhaps can be found to qualify more than Césaire's. It is to the global reality of the humiliation of his race that his consciousness is awakened, to an acute sense of epochal catastrophe and of dispossession, a consciousness that proceeds from an encounter with a history that has imprinted on his people the figure of a fallen race. *Cahier* thus derives its primary impulse from the poet's awareness

---

[20]For a fuller discussion of the revisions undertaken by Césaire and the variant versions of passages in the poem, see Thomas Hale, *Les Ecrits d'Aimé Césaire* (section 39/4), and especially Lilian Pestre de Almeida, "Les Versions successives du *Cahier d'un retour au pays natal*" in Ngal and Steins (eds.), *Césaire 70*, 35-90.

of his historicity, of a collective trauma so profoundly internalized as to constitute a fundamental mode of his relation to the world.

To recall these issues that lie at the very surface of what may be
termed the poem's discursive project is both to evoke its background of
inspiration and to define the historical and geographical compass embraced
in the poem, a framework of reference whose import is registered in a key
passage:

> Ce qui est à moi, ces quelques milliers de mortiférés qui tournent en
> rond dans la calebasse d'une île et ce qui est à moi aussi, l'archipel arqué
> comme le désir inquiet de se nier, on dirait une anxiété maternelle pour
> protéger la ténuité plus délicate qui sépare l'une de l'autre Amérique; et
> ses flancs qui secrètent pour l'Europe la bonne liqueur d'un Gulf
> Stream, et l'un des deux versants d'incandescence entre quoi l'Equateur
> funambule vers l'Afrique. Et mon île non-clôture, sa claire audace
> debout à l'arrière de cette polynésie, devant elle, la Guadeloupe fendue
> en deux de sa raie dorsale et de même misère que nous, Haïti où la
> négritude se mit debout pour la première fois et dit qu'elle croyait à son
> humanité et la comique petite queue de la Floride où d'un nègre
> s'achève la strangulation, et l'Afrique gigantesquement chenillant
> jusqu'au pied hispanique de l'Europe, sa nudité où la Mort fauche à
> larges andains.

Cahier requires, then, to be read, at least at a first level of explicit content, as a direct reporting from historical fact and as a kind of mental diary
of the poet's responses to this external determination. The poem assumes a
distinct documentary character as an especially vigorous statement of the
historical grievance of the black race in relation to the specific circumstances of its encounter with the West, a statement that is therefore in the
nature of an outraged deposition at the bar of humanity on the consequences of this encounter. In the strict revolutionary sense of the term, the
poem develops at this level of its expression as a *cahier de doléances*, with the
implication of an imperious demand for redress and justice.

This, then, is poetry that is decidedly "propositional" (in the sense
that Gerald Graff has given to the term[21]); what is more, it is poetry that
assumes a minimal distance between art and life. Although this raises the
question of the nexus between, on one hand, literature as aesthetic phenomenon, with what can be considered its independent, formal status, and on
the other, experience as a lived, discontinuous relation to the world,
Césaire's poem seems to cut through the intractable theoretical hornet's nest
of the question with the very force of its affirmations. A "literal" reading of
the poem clearly accords with this affirmative quality and underscores its
manifest intent as a work of overt social and political protest.

---

[21]See Gerald Graff, *Poetic Statement and Critical Dogma*, Chicago: University of
Chicago Press, 1980.

To approach *Cahier* as an expression of worldly commitment is thus to acknowledge a primary character of the work. For although, as we shall see, the poem provides evidence of its being conscious of itself as a verbal structure—of being to a certain extent self-reflexive—it also deliberately reaches beyond its status as text toward an immediate concreteness of both representation and effect in an outer, extra-textual world of experience. It posits an operative relation between the expression it elaborates and a history that is mirrored in that expression; it is intended to function more as a substantive reconstitution of and reflection upon experience than as a metaphor of that experience. Its structure of language is fashioned both as a representation of a designated reality and as a critical confrontation with that reality. Language here is not merely an inscription of the world, nor does it simply embody a signifying relation that allows a textual gap between the self and the world; it embodies rather an active sense of its potential for the transformation of that world. This sense is not the "residue" of a poetic quality, an element that can be ignored in any meaningful experience of the poem, but is the very core of the poem's thematic development and the conditioning factor of its emotional tone.

But if the poetic attitude in *Cahier* stems directly from Césaire's engagement with the real world, the self that is dramatized in it is a multiple one, extending in directions dictated by the action. The persona who speaks from the center of the poem bears an immediate relation to the biographical self of the poet, a self that is summoned on occasion to bear testimony of a direct, documentary kind upon the argument of the poem, as in the tramway incident recounted in such dramatic detail in the poem. This self is presented as an isolated consciousness that sometimes confronts the collective and at other times merges with it. At the same time, it lends its attributes to the poetic self which is its final projection, along a line that extends from the biographical through the historical to the imaginative.

Cahier is perhaps best envisaged as a sequence of dramatic monologues in which the action is constituted, at one level, by the complex interactions between this composite self and its external solicitations in the real world and, at another level, by the transformations this self undergoes in its adventure toward a form of fulfilment. There is, in other words, a double articulation of the action in the poem, which is propelled by a constantly shifting procession of tableaux and rapid alternation of moods: *Cahier* thus comprises a succession of *affects* rather than of episodes. But if no linear progression as such can be stipulated for the action, its elements do compose a thematic development that follows a classic triadic scheme: the action moves from a situation of alienation through revolt to a new integration.

This development begins with the poet taking the measure of the world as given. *Cahier* presents itself from this perspective as a poetic trans-

position that offers imagistic equivalents of a pathetic imagination, a trans-
position that serves to draw the reality it designates more firmly within the
poet's consciousness. The long evocation of the desolate physical, social,
and moral universe with which the poem opens forms an essential part of
the unfolding process of self-knowledge that the poem adumbrates. The
evocation becomes an act of recognizance: it is by exploring the stark reality
of his native island that he is able to comprehend, in the full sense of the
word, the concrete geography of his intimate self, the bounded horizons of a
landscape that, as we have seen, resonates for him with the echoes of a tragic history. The mood of profound anguish that pervades the evocation is
thus woven with the memory of slavery, which features in several notations
in the poem as a haunting presence and is presented in terms of an experience immediate to the poet's consciousness:

> J'entends de la cale monter les malédictions enchaînées, les hoquette-
> ments des mourants, le bruit d'un qu'on jette à la mer ... les abois d'une
> femme en gésine ... des raclements d'ongles cherchant des gorges ... des
> ricanements de fouet ... des farfouillis de vermine parmi des lassitudes ...

It is within a history set in motion by this original event that the poet
discovers his place in the world or, more precisely, the ambiguous nature of
his mode of insertion in the world. Here we encounter something of a paradox that the very force of conviction of Césaire's work tends to obscure for
us: that of a consciousness turning wholly against all the symbols of its formative context, generated as this is by the rhetoric of an ideal humanism
and universalism, both secular and religious, which nonetheless accommo-
dates itself in practice to the violations involved in the conquest, dispersal,
domination, exploitation, and above all, the ideological devaluation of the
black race. It is this contradiction that the poet denounces in this bitter cry:

> Je salue les trois siècles qui soutiennent mes droits civiques
> et mon sang minimisé.

The quotation underscores the significance of the personal factor in
the poet's commitment, centering as it does on the malaise of assimilation,
the burden of a double consciousness imposed by a situation that denies him
a stable framework of reference for his sense of identity. The psychological
and moral discomforts of this situation become translated into a sentiment
of rootlessness, of separation from a source of being that engenders in the
poet the existential frustration expressed in these lines:

> autour des rocking-chairs méditant la volupté des rigoises
> je tourne, inapaisée pouliche.

The sentiment of spiritual exile arising from an acute sense of personal
predicament thus forms an integral part of the historical consciousness that

underlies the thematic development in *Cahier*. In the primary phase of this development, the poem is a passive registration of a negative situation in the world; it presents a distinct problem, the poet's difficulty of being, a situation that requires to be worked through toward some form of resolution. In the dialectic implicit in the movement of mind charted by the poem, the theme of revolt represents the nodal point that initiates this active phase of its thematic progression.

Cahier is an eminently contestatory poem; it embodies an ideological project: to challenge the historical and socio-political context of its objective reference at its intellectual and mental foundations. Its manifest procedures involve a systematic assault upon the entire structure of ideas and representations that undergird and legitimate this context, whose devastating effects in the real world of events and of a sentient humanity the poem exposes. There is a clarity to the poem's polemical intent about which even the indirections of its expressive modes leave us in no doubt:

> Et la voix prononce que l'Europe nous a pendant des siècles gavés de mensonges et gonflés de pestilence.

The poem's inference of a direct connection between text and world, which we have observed as making for its "propositional" quality, assumes in this respect a contextual significance for the self-awareness of black writers and intellectuals of Césaire's generation that is undeniable. It is of interest, moreover, to observe that the programmatic orientation of Césaire's poem as a revolutionary work is furthered rather than hindered by its aesthetic attributes, a fact that is acknowledged by both Breton and Sartre, despite reservations they are known to have expressed about the direct equivalence between textual values and the political imperatives of writing.

It is nonetheless important to note that this equivalence, as it declares itself in *Cahier*, is not without a number of problems which become evident at the very level of the poem's expression, for there is often a contradiction between the ideological thrust of its discursive content and its exploitation of the connotative values of the reference system that the poem itself is designed to subvert. One might remark, for instance, upon the curious dissonance between the anticlerical posture of the poem and its deployment of liturgical imagery to illuminate the spiritual vision it seeks to project, even when it is recognized that such imagery has been, so to speak, "disestablished" to serve a form of natural religion. We thus have the paradox of an iconoclasm that is mediated by a structure of expression that itself aspires to an iconic status and significance. The contradiction inherent in this paradox is not resolved at the level of content and is only properly engaged at the formal and symbolic level of language.

Be that as it may, this contradiction has a particular interest for understanding the tensions and the deep mechanisms at work in the poem. From this perspective, it is easy to see that the polemical aspect of the poem has as much a personal significance as a collective reference: the tone of bitter invective and angry recrimination that punctuates the poem becomes revelatory of the extensive internalizations which the poem itself is called upon to undo. Its emotional charge plugs, as it were, into a powerful current of resentment accumulated in the poet's mind by the invidious play of contrary impulses, so that the poem comes to serve as a mode through which the turbulence of his soul is externalized. *Cahier* is nothing if not a poem of seething rage:

> Qui ne me comprendrait pas ne comprendrait pas davantage le
> rugissement du tigre

There is thus a real sense in which the poem can be said to have had therapeutic value for the poet himself. We witness in the poem his determined operation upon his own soul as he clears it of the imprint of a system of values he is compelled to turn against, in order to re-inscribe upon it the terms of a new, spiritual vocation. The violence he has to do to himself has an immediate relevance that is far from peripheral to this vocation, for the mood of dissidence that runs through the poem issues out of the disaffection of the assimilated subject toward a framework of references to which he has been conditioned and which he has come to recognize as an insidious but forceful mode of his co-optation into the colonial system. The poet's revolt assumes a moral significance in this light, for it marks his refusal of complicity with a system founded in its very principle upon a denial of justice. The attitude of calculated truculence and the demonstration of perverse wilfulness that go with this revolt represent a distancing of the self from the claims of responsibility the system places upon him, a rejection of the moral burden it imposes upon his lacerated consciousness, and denote a conscious resolve to break with the colonial system in all its implications:

> Accommodez-vous de moi. Je ne m'accommode plus de vous.

The energy with which the theme of revolt is invested in *Cahier* is, thus, clearly a function of the complex mechanisms at work in the poem. What is recognizably a defensive reaction attests to the inner compulsion from which Césaire's expression proceeds. The strategy of provocation which organizes the development of the theme is driven in its elaboration by a relentlessly importunate tone of address. It is a tone that constantly modulates into the categorical accents of an impassioned exhortation, often saved from sinking to the level of a banal platform tirade only by its eloquence. This is of course a feature of the poem imparted by the frank partisanship of its explicit content—the declared aim of the poet is not only to give voice to a collective agony but also to urge into active expression a collective sentiment and resolve. In our experience of the poem, we are required to absorb this feature as an indispensable component of all nationalist literature whose primary design is the enhancement of consciousness with a view to a common project of liberation. *Cahier* belongs to this category of literature, as much in the wider sense of its reference to the historical situation of the black race as in the specific sense of its promotion of a distinct Caribbean sense of nationhood. And Césaire himself has defined this functional role of his work in terms of the poet's responsibility in the colonial context: "Nous sommes les propagateurs d'âmes, les inventeurs d'âmes."

Cahier is intended as a poem of national resurrection and its nationalist focus is implicit in the forceful insistence of its imagery upon the potential of the islands both as landscape and human environment. The inspirational function of the poem comes even more clearly into view in the evocations which mark a series of climaxes on which a heroic note is rung through the poem, a notable instance of which is provided by the justly admired passage devoted to Toussaint L'Ouverture. The demonstrative value of this historical reference is highlighted in a rhetorical flourish that makes its collective significance absolutely clear:

> destin tenace
> cris debout de terre muette la splendeur de ce sang
> n'éclatera-t-elle point?

In an important sense, the dramatic projection of a revolt aboard a slave ship with which the action of the poem culminates provides an answer, albeit in a symbolic mode, to this question. The scene also indicates the progression from revolt to self-affirmation as the logical direction of its thematic development. We arrive here at the point where the poem embraces a whole complex of attitudes that may be subsumed under the term *négritude* which the text itself conveniently supplies for its designation.

In considering this aspect of *Cahier*, it is essential to dissipate a misunderstanding arising from the controversies that have surrounded discussions of the term and its various applications. There has been a tendency in these discussions to make a distinction between what is taken to be the revolutionary négritude of Césaire and its conservative formulation by Senghor. It is apparent, however, from even a cursory reading of *Cahier* that such a distinction is at best a specious one—the nexus between the attitudes Césaire's poem promotes and the ideas of Senghor is too well established to admit of a radical separation between the two, for the emphatic tone of racial celebration in *Cahier* is not only unmistakable, it lends itself in its very terms to an interpretation whose exclusive import cannot be missed. Césaire's négritude as represented in *Cahier* is as much founded on a conception of a racial endowment as Senghor's. This is what prompted Sartre to describe négri-tude as "un racisme anti-raciste," and the very ambiguity of his phrase can only be imputed to the terms in which the concept of négritude is drama-tized, to the form in which Sartre encountered it in Césaire's poem in partic-ular. This ambiguity can be resolved if we take the phrase to mean an open acknowledgment of justified self-consciousness displayed in the works Sartre was examining and for which Césaire's neologism came to stand as a kind of shorthand. Négritude implies in this perspective an effort to rehabilitate the black race, to reverse the ideological denigration it has had to endure—in short, to vindicate the race. There is sufficient consensus on this point to make further discussion unnecessary; indeed, much of the effort to dissociate Césaire from Senghor revolves on this point, on the status of *Cahier* as a poem of racial retrieval in this strictly historical and ideological sense.

Yet it is futile to attempt to winnow this element of the poem from the organicism in which it is enmeshed. The evidence of the text points to a vitalist conception of life, in terms of an effervescence of collective celebra-tion, that saturates the racial sentiment to which the poem gives expression:

véritablement les fils aînés du monde
poreux à tous les souffles du monde
aire fraternelle de tous les souffles du monde
étincelle du feu sacré du monde
chair de la chair du monde palpitant du mouvement même du monde.

Further on in the poem, the poet declares :

Sang! Sang! tout notre sang ému par le coeur mâle du soleil

The controversial nature of this declaration as a formal proposition is evi-dent, even when its polemical context is allowed for, since its meaning can be stretched sufficiently beyond this context to attribute a fundamental biol-ogism to Césaire. It is indeed significant that Césaire himself has had occasion to repudiate such attribution, and it must be said that much of this element of *Cahier* has its source in the fervid sensationalism promoted by writers such as Spengler and Frobenius, who in turn derive from Nietzsche. These references indicate that the poem answers to a specific Western con-vention of sensibility that qualifies as dionysiac, a convention linked to the aesthetic of modernism with which, as we have seen, Césaire was very much in touch in his formative years.

This background partly accounts for what can be described as hyper-romanticism in the poetic formulation of négritude in *Cahier*. There is, however, a further perspective that complements the impact of the intellec-tual and literary influences evoked above and is inherent in the poet's situa-tion and the postures he adopts in reaction to this situation. This has to do with his identification with the common people and the valorization of the simple life associated with them, which he exalts as the antithesis of the inauthentic and regulated existence sanctioned by the established order. The values that the poem celebrates are not simply opposed to this order; they are imagined as genuine in their own right and as pertaining to the peasant folk, described by Césaire in his *L'Etudiant Noir* article as "fils aînés de la terre," a description that reappears as a poetic notation in the passage just quoted. Thus, the organicism that animates the poem's structure of imagery is founded upon the idea of a vital reciprocity between human life and expression, on one hand, and on the other, the rhythms of the natural world, an immediate relation by virtue of which those close to the earth enjoy a particular intensity of experience. This idea is given powerful elaboration as a component of the visionary projections offered by the poem at its symbolic level, but it is derived from what may be considered a populism that represents a moral imperative of its theme, which comes to condition the poet's imagination.

To situate Césaire's négritude in this way is also to account for what appears to be the apologetic stance implied by the celebration of the absence of technological achievement by the black race. Apart from the polemical significance of this celebration as a deliberate valuation of a constant reproach in Western ideology addressed to the race, it represents as well a projection onto the race of the virtues that are deemed by the poet to attach to the natural state, free of the corruptions and complications of a mechanistic civilization that constrain the soul. As in all forms of romanticism, what is at issue here is the dichotomy between nature and artifice, between the spontaneity and moral purity of an immediate connection to the sources of life, on one hand, and, on the other, the interposition between human consciousness and nature of the complex apparatus of modern technological society, with diminished capacity for response to the solicitations of the universe that this is held to imply. In this light, négritude appears as a vision of restitution to wholeness of experience promised by a reconnection to the life-enhancing values of an ideal Africa, the peasant continent par excellence.

It is highly significant in this respect to note that Césaire's poem "A l'Afrique" in the volume *Soleil cou coupé* begins:

Paysan frappe le sol de ton daba
dans le sol il y a une hâte que la syllabe de l'événement ne dénoue pas

and ends:

frappe paysan je suis ton fils
à l'heure du soleil qui se couche le crépuscule sous ma paupière clapote
vert jaune et tiède d'iguanes inassoupis
mais la belle autruche courrière qui subitement naît des formes émues
de la femme me fait de l'avenir les signes de l'amitié.

For Césaire, the Caribbean context gives a particular meaning to this "homecoming" as it is imaginatively realized in *Cahier*. In the nationalist orientation of the poem, it illustrates a case of the "organic intellectual" (to use Antonio Gramsci's expression), making the journey back to the people, as a function both of a revolutionary ideal and of his need to recover a full sense of his identity. Africa as the ultimate reference of his racial conscious-ness introduces a problematic dimension to this process, but if, in the cir-cumstances, the poet's homecoming can be said to be ambiguous, the reference also serves as an expansion of his consciousness. It affords a wider perspective, beyond the negative experience of slavery, to his sense of his-torical being, and gives substance to his exploration of the relationship between the poetic self and its determining environment. For if the persona in *Cahier* is not altogether the biographical self of Césaire, it represents a projection of his preoccupations and of his desires, his predicaments, and his quest for salvation. In its engagement with the actualities of a lived experi-ence, it represents an effort to transform a landscape of historical existence into a universe of rooted being.

What emerges from our consideration of the themes in *Cahier* in their explicit, "discursive" aspect is that, although a political poem, in that the collective situation of the black race is central to its inspiration and devel-opment, it is much more profoundly a personal poem, determined in its whole tone and movement by the responses of a consiousness at odds with its time and place, seeking a new mode of relation to the world. It is a poem of concentrated feeling, bearing the impress of a problematic existence. At the same time, the complexity of the poem's expression alerts us to the fact that the paraphrasable content does not by any means exhaust its full range of meaning, that the poem encloses an internal order of significance that is properly poetic, an order that is structured by language and sustained by the energy of its imagery, whose flow constitutes its informing principle.

Césaire has remarked that he wrote *Cahier* "en tournant le dos à la poésie," adding that he had to "rompre avec la forme régulière du français qui m'étouffait." The abandonment of classical norms which this remark confirms was facilitated for him by developments in French poetry reviewed earlier; they offered precedents that enabled him to forge an individual idiom within the framework of an ongoing tradition, within a contemporary aesthetic more in correspondence with his expressive needs and individual poetic temperament.

It is of interest to note in this regard that we meet in Césaire's work with a constant reflection upon his medium in relation to his situation, his purpose, and his vision, so that his poetry presents itself as the illustration of an *art poétique* that is reiterated within the body of his work, as a poetic lan-guage in continuous interplay with a metalanguage of and in poetry. Again and again, we encounter terms that are made to refer back to themselves as elements within a verbal structure charged with a specific function of signification: thus "langue," "mot," "parole," "vocable" and the like are "foregrounded" as modalities of the same generative principle of language that is manifested in "voix" or "cri," as concrete embodiments of his responses to experience, and which come to define a more than symbolic mode of his apprehension of the world, in both senses of the word. Indeed all his poetry plays upon the intrinsic nature of language to function as a metaphoric designation of reality or experience, upon the slippage between denotation and connotation, upon the inherent ambiguities of meaning that open up an imaginative space for the redirection of the thought processes that language itself initiates and enables, and upon the exploration of their inward sources in a quest for new meanings and new values. As Césaire puts its in a line from the poem "Séisme" in *Ferrements*:

> Essayer les mots? Leur frottement pour conjurer l'informe.

This self-consciousness with regard to language is of course part of the inheritance of the modernist aesthetic that Césaire embraced. It harks back directly to Mallarmé's preoccupation with the purification of conventional forms of French to render them more appropriate to the esoteric design of his poetry ("donner un sens plus pur aux mots de la tribu"), a preoccupation that also compels what T. S. Eliot describes as his "raid on the inarticulate." For the black poet, however, aesthetic and philosophical preoccupation with the nature and possibilities of language has a contextual foundation: it springs directly from the problematic relation of the black self to the speech of the colonial master, which is the linguistic vehicle of his objective and moral subjugation. This situation takes on an especially dramatic dimension in the case of the French-speaking West Indian, the product of an intense process of assimilation by which his mental structure has been constituted. For if, in common with the African—as indeed other colonial subjects in the Third World—he has at his disposal a vernacular in the form of *créole*, it is only in a relative and ambiguous sense that he can claim linguistic independence. In his case, there is no clear-cut opposition between the language of the colonizer and his vernacular, insofar as it is a derivative of French, enclosed in part within the latter's system of designation. The situation of "diglossia" that he lives is thus far from being as radical as it is for the African: if French is not exactly his mother tongue, it is not entirely a foreign language either; it has, moreover, a familiar presence around him as part of his quotidian reality. This is a situation that would have had all the normality of the relation of dialect speakers to a standard national language but for the conflictual nature of the colonial situation. The dominant status of French, with all the historical associations it implies, imposes upon the

French-speaking West Indian the language of the slave master of yesterday, the colonial master of today, and thus favors a feeling of ambivalence towards the language, a sense of its inauthenticity, creative, therefore, of an alienation that manifests itself as a discontinuity between the world as structured by language and the deep places of the self. Yet it is a language from which there is no escape at any level or register of the West Indian's communicative needs; French has become implanted within him as an "intimate enemy"[22]; the political, economic, social, and cultural domination that frames the parameters of his experience becomes translated into a linguistic state of siege upon his consciousness. In these circumstances, language assumes for the French-speaking West Indian an immediate existential import.

For Césaire, the ambiguity of this situation is compounded by the fact that French is the only language in which he can give full expression to his responses as a poet: it is both the determining medium of his historicity and the channel of his effort to unravel the implications of this historicity. For at the level of intensity at which this effort has to be undertaken, créole does not offer the resources adequate to his needs, even if he had been in a position to opt for this vernacular for his writing. He is thus obliged to work out his salvation within the confines of a language in which he is imprisoned. There is also the important consideration that French exerts a normative pressure upon him to demonstrate a mastery of its complexities as a way of validating his discourse at the same time that it offers a resistance he has to overcome in order to make it conform to his particular requirements.

Césaire's approach to the French language obeys this double imperative in what can only be called a project of subjugation of the language in a Promethean appropriation of its structures. His deliberate manipulation of its resources amounts to a highly idiosyncratic usage that results in a recondite idiom, even in its character as poetic language. The unusual profusion of language in this idiom is probably evidence of a self-conscious advance upon a language that is at a remove from what he feels to be his inner self, a language to which he comes as an outside invader imbued with a sense of triumph at his conquest of its treasures. Whatever the case may be, it is essential to observe that the very choice of poetry as a medium predisposes toward the idiosyncratic use of language which Césaire's poetry demonstrates, so that he can be said to be doing no more than playing upon the extended scale offered by the poetic mode. It is no ordinary medium of expression that Césaire employs, but a specialized mode that constitutes an inner coherence within what we have called the system of designation rep-

---

[22]The title of a book by Ashish Nandy, published in 1982 by Oxford University Press.

resented by the French language. Valéry's definition of poetry as "langage dans un langage" takes on a special meaning here: the heightened use of language which poetry involves enables Césaire to reorder the structures of a national tongue to which he stands in something of a marginal position so as to impose upon it the dictates of his individual will and vision. To write in French, to create poetry from its resources becomes for him a way of living through the tensions between language and consciousness to its very limits.

These general considerations, which apply to Césaire's entire poetry, are essential for an understanding of the interplay between the thematic development we have examined in *Cahier* and its language and structure of imagery. The thematic grounding of the poem provides a "semantic anchor" for its expressive procedures which constitute a second order of significance over and above the discursive path of the poem.

Perhaps the most distinctive aspect of this interplay is the connection between the theme of revolt and the dominance of polemical imagery in *Cahier*, a feature which accounts for the poem's most representative mode of activity. The polemical images form a dynamic scheme which stands in opposition to and challenges the implications of the cluster of pathetic images which relate to the poet's initial situation, conditioning a morose order of his imagination. This latter category of images, centered upon the blighted landscape of his native island, coheres as a summation of his tragic apprehension of history. It is impossible not to draw a parallel here between Césaire's *Cahier* and Eliot's *The Waste Land* in their common poetic representation of a physical setting as the equivalent of a moral and spiritual condition, a method that equates their modernism with what Henry James has called "the imagination of disaster." With Césaire, this equation is accentuated by the personal dimension of his imagery that translates a mood of despondency, his sense of a grave diminution of being.

The polemical images, on the other hand, dramatize the unfurling of his consciousness, its activation against resignation and despair. They take charge of his resolve to effect a readjustment of the terms of his relation to the world, a resolve which manifests itself as an operation upon language, as a determined assault upon the universe of discourse which defines his existence.

The first line of attack has perforce to be at the semantic level, for it is in the area of meaning that the black poet encounters the Western language at its most wounding for his self-apprehension. Sartre's remarks (in "Orphée noir") on the consequences for the black poet's expression of the denigration of blackness built into the symbolic system of the European languages are highly pertinent here. The phenomenon he isolates accounts for the systematic reversals of ascribed meanings and associations that characterize Césaire's use of key words and expressions as they affect the symbolic relation of the black race to the French language.

The outstanding example of this procedure is afforded by the evocation of Toussaint L'Ouverture in *Cahier*, in which the negative value attached to whiteness contributes to the sinister atmosphere of the scene setting.[23] The terms of the evocation underscore the discrepancy in the experience of words in the European languages between its original speakers and the black poet. The procedure has a further interest in that it is employed to mark the conflictual relation between master and slave, their antithetical placement in the universal scheme of things:

> chien blanc du nord, serpent noir du midi

The oppositional thrust of this procedure is complemented and emphasized by the revaluation of blackness which his imagery operates in several notations where it is invested with a new energy of meaning summed up in "Soleil noir." Césaire reallocates the meaning of words in the symbolic sphere delineated by the French language in a kind of Nietzschean reversal of their situations: his way with language involves a prior disinvestment of an imposed medium and its transvaluation in the direction of a new and original expressive project.[24] His poetry represents a purposive alienation of French from its native speakers and from its normal context of reference, and its transformation into the antagonistic language of the "Other."

This polemical use of language points to a more general principle at work in Césaire's poetry, amply illustrated in *Cahier*. He plays on the ambiguous relation of language to the reality it is employed to represent in

---

[23]See stanzas 44 and 45, and notes infra.

[24]Consider for example the metatextual terms of the poem "Barbare" in *Cadastre*:

> C'est le mot qui me soutient
> et frappe sur ma carcasse de cuivre jaune
> où la lune dévore dans la soupente de la rouille
>
> les os barbares
> des lâches bêtes rôdeuses de mensonge
>
> Barbare
> du langage sommaire
> et nos faces belles comme le vrai pouvoir opératoire
>
> de la négation.

The poem requires to be taken together with another one in the same volume entitled "Mot" that ends:

> le mot nègre
> dru, savez-vous
> du tonnerre d'un été
> que s'arrogent
> des libertés incrédules.

order to show up its essential contingency. His poetry is thus placed at the very heart of the paradox of meaning, of the process of signification involved in language which can never enable us to mean what we say in any absolute sense. The black poet is especially well placed to grasp the significance of this fact of language, its pure conventionality which denies a unilateral correlation of language to the world. Because language is in essence equivocal, meaning becomes a function not merely of context but of perspective, of the user's orientation of words to a particular purpose. It is this relational and problematic nature of language as a phenomenon that Césaire exploits in his poetry, a medium that is, furthermore, a second order of language and thus permits him such liberties as he needs in order to accommodate his perceptions and responses as a black subject.

Césaire's wilful use of language is most evident in the irony that forms a distinctive element of *Cahier*. If its purpose is obvious—to discredit the entire system of representations that frame the image of the black race in the Western imagination—the range of Césaire's irony is more far-reaching than this limited ideological objective: it is not simply a "tactical" device but an integral part of his approach to language. This complex character of Césaire's irony can be illustrated in the two ways it operates. The first has to do with the changes he rings upon the propositions of the colonial ideology, so as to render manifest their lack of coherence and truth. His intentional parodies of Gobineau, for example, and his mocking allusions to the pieties of the Christian religion form part of a general design—to train a searchlight upon the context and meaning of Western texts in their bearing upon his situation, to show up the contradictions, even at the level of enunciation, between Western humanist discourse and the dehumanization it has been employed to ratify. Irony thus serves Césaire as a means of opening a breach within the system of Western ideology. Césaire's method is a way of "signifying" (to borrow a term given currency by Henry Louis Gates, Jr.) upon this system in order to empty it of meaning, to "unpack" it in its very linguistic foundation.

All this is obvious and straightforward enough, but the full impact of Césaire's irony extends beyond a method of refutation in relation to the black situation. By exposing the Western system of references to the full glare of a critical consciousness, his poetry undertakes, from the vantage point of a besieged humanity, a profound reassessment of the entire structure of ideas and values that is presented as the justifying and ennobling principle of Western civilization. His poetry sets up a counter-discourse to the dominant ideology of the West even in its internal application: it challenges the hegemony it exercises by burrowing into its core and revealing it as a construction, as arbitrary and factitious. In other words, irony determines a mode of "counter-interpellation" (following Althusser's insight) and brings

Césaire's poetry into full contact with the dissident tradition within Western literature and thought.

This observation prompts a consideration of the specific forms taken by the influences from the French literary tradition upon Césaire's work and their impact upon his language in the context of his integration of its contemporary idiom in his poetry. As already noted, Césaire's revolt is founded on the tenor of French modernism that his poetry extends. His work thus represents a major point of intersection between black expression in contemporary times and the modernist movement in French literature and, indeed, in European letters generally. His ironic handling of the literary, cultural, and historical references of his assimilated European inheritance recalls Rimbaud and makes Césaire himself the natural successor, in the fullest sense of the word, to the "nègre" of "Mauvais Sang" and the sardonic observer of colonial exactions in "Démocratie." But while Rimbaud leaves the meaning of his ironies up in the air, so to speak, Césaire brings it down to the ground of a reality and an experience that confer on it its proper contextual value. Césaire thus confirms and authenticates the metaphysical revolt of Rimbaud as a historical proposition.

It is, however, in the relation of Césaire's poetry to Surrealism that his validation of an antecedent movement of dissidence through art is most in evidence. It needs to be emphasized in this connection that Césaire's poetry is not merely tethered to the Surrealist movement, that Césaire is not simply making an opportunistic use of its aesthetic of revolt and liberation, but that his poetry represents a confirmation proceeding from a complete affiliation with the tenets of the movement. The common interest that Breton discerned between himself and Césaire derives from the disaffection they both felt toward a civilization whose foundations they sought to undermine. Breton and his cohorts, operating within this civilization as *franc-tireurs*, represented for Césaire a kind of fifth column with whom it was advantageous to establish a connection, in an eager response to Breton's declaration: "Nous sommes ceux qui donnerons toujours la main à l'ennemi." Césaire brings to Surrealism the "miraculous arms" of black poetic revolt, and irony is a major component of his arsenal, deepened in his case into a "black humor" that is, as it were, a natural reflection of the prominence accorded him by his situation.[25]

The connection between Césaire's poetry and its antecedents in French poetry sheds light on the selective way he relates to the Western frame of reference of his expression. His stance is not so much a global rejection as a discriminating filtering of its aspects, a process that makes

---

[25]The poem "La Tornade" in *Cadastre* affords the best instance of Césaire's "black" humor.

allowance for the integration of those to which he is able to give unqualified assent. This accounts for the peculiar pattern of intertextuality in his poetry. On the one hand, his ironic recall of antecedent texts and consecrated references serves to turn intertextuality on its head, as it were; on the other hand, he makes use of allusions and echoes of other texts as a functional principle of intertextual enforcement of his imagery. They create in his work a network of discrete overtones that together form a resonating scale for his poetic discourse. It remains, nonetheless, a discourse upon which he retains a firm control, paradoxically, through a dislocation of language, through an assault upon the linguistic code itself in a sovereign disposal of its structual elements.

It is a reflection of this subversive use of French in Césaire's poetry that *Cahier* has been called an "anti-poem." The term is inappropriate, for it misses the point of the abrogation of the prose/poetry dichotomy that *Cahier* effectively accomplishes, a point to which we shall return. But it is understandable as an expression of the perplexity that the procedures Césaire adopts are likely to induce at a first approach. That these form part of a deliberate rejection of classical conventions has been commented upon; their positive orientation needs to be appreciated in the light of the compulsions upon the poet for a quickening of his medium. Features such as the disruption of syntax, sudden transitions of thought patterns and direction of imagery, an abundant lexicon enriched by coinages and archaisms that take French back to its Latin origins—all these are intended not only to disconcert but also to shake off the debris of conventional usage from the language and make it gleam afresh with the sharpness of a newly burnished instrument.

These features make for a compactness that produces its effect of hermeticism; yet this is not the negative quality that it seems at first sight—a perverse refusal to communicate—but rather an essential condition of Césaire's way with language, for one of the functions of hermeticism is to create a disjunction between enunciation and an immediately recoverable meaning, precisely to make language yield an enhanced meaning. The point, then, is that Césaire takes language to its full stretch, beyond its functional boundaries, to make it reflect the intense activity of its constitutive parts as they collaborate to produce a new order of significance.

Such an order can only arise from the ruins of the old universe of discourse and the structures of expression by which it is sustained. But the violence done to language in *Cahier* and Césaire's other works also attests to an inner passion that convulses the poet; it is analogous to the passion that suffuses his consciousness. His posture is that of Le Rebelle in *Et Les Chiens se taisaient*, who describes himself as "homme sombre qu'habite la volonté du feu"; thus, in *Cahier*, the poet's brow is bedecked not with laurels associated with the comforting image of a classical tradition but with the wild leaves of a poisonous plant: "sur mon front noir, une couronne de daturas." His savage imagination projects a dream of violence carried through a symbolism of aggression:

> Des mots? quand nous manions des quartiers de monde, quand nous épousons des continents en délire, quand nous forçons de fumantes portes, des mots, ah oui, des mots! mais des mots de sang frais, des mots qui sont des raz-de-marée et des érésipèles et des paludismes et des laves et des feux de brousse, et des flambées de chair, et des flambées de villes...

The imagery here suggests a convocation of the forces of nature, summoned by the voice of the poet as he proffers a menace directed at a world he rejects. The aesthetics of revolt proceeds through images of negation, the elaboration of counter-values in a program of subversion. This context explains the apparent primitivism that gives an air of excess to passages in *Cahier*, as in the vindication of cannibalism to which reference has been made. These passages must be read as deliberate response to the negative terms of Western representations of subjugated cultures, and their transformation by the poet into symbols of force. His identification with these symbols is a way of affirming himself as a factor of disorder within an imposed order, as a dangerous presence; in other words, this is a poetry of terrorism, the mode of a violent disengagement from an intolerable order.

The negation of this order determines an attitude of nihilism that leads to an apocalyptic vision:

> Qu'y puis-je?
>
> Il faut bien commencer.
>
> Commencer quoi?
>
> La seule chose au monde qu'il vaille la peine de commencer
> La Fin du monde parbleu.

Again, it must be made clear that Césaire's nihilism forms part of the Surrealist project, inherited from Dadaism, for the overthrow of the existing social arrangements along with their moral impositions. *Cahier* does not fully exhibit features of Surrealist writing that we find in Césaire's later work, but the gestures it assumes and the outlook it reveals are sufficiently an application of these principles to qualify it as a Surrealist poem. The absence of truly automatic writing notwithstanding, it works up in its imagery a passion that must be interpreted as the poet's wrestling with his demons, and as their conjuration through the medium of poetic language. The polemical images in particular provide an insight into this inner drama of the poem; they restore for us the ordeal of purification the poet undergoes.

This "negative" aspect of *Cahier* is complemented by the vision of reconstruction toward which all his imagery tends. The mood of passionate contestation and the nihilistic stance conveyed by the polemical images represent the reverse of an obstinate aspiration to a sense of accomplishment; they move toward a mythology of conquest grounded in a prophetic vision. *Cahier* presents itself in this light as a poem of transformation in which language comes into its own as "Verbe," as a force in the world, a primordial agent of creation.

Césaire has confirmed in an interview the purposive orientation of his imagery—"Les images ne sont jamais arbitraires," he has declared. For apart from the connotations in which they envelop the designative function of language in its reference to the phenomenal world, they compose an alternative order centered on the poet's insights and intuitions. All of Césaire's imagery is founded upon an immediacy of experience derived from this correspondence, upon an engagement of his consciousness with the structure of apprehension it proposes.

The image of blood provides the focus of the imaginative experience in *Cahier*. It designates the self as organic entity in both its individual and collective reference. The self in this understanding is not so much a unique essence of the individual personality as an instance, a derivation of a collective being in a continuous flow of manifested presence. "Sang" is thus identity defined as a sensual grasp of the self in a bond with community that is vital, in a literal sense; it denotes the collective existence in its extension over time. The themes of *Cahier* lock firmly into the postulation of an association between race and history, an association that turns on the image of blood; in the multiple associations which this image receives in the poem, it builds up a pronounced ancestralism tied to an affective valuation of Africa, the mother continent.

In its immediate aspect, Césaire's ancestralism presents itself as the hankering of a deracinated soul after a sense of origins, as a quest for the truth of his own self. It can be accepted as a form of atavism, which is nothing other than aspiration to a sense of place. This positive orientation emerges from the way in which the temporal dimension of his organic conception of self and community becomes linked in his poetry with the spatial, in which his ancestral sentiment is developed in the telluric scheme of his imagery.

The fundamental proposition of a relation between self and environment has been mentioned as a leading idea of Césaire's Caribbean nationalism. The circumstances of his situation determine, however, that the tellurism which is the poetic expression of this idea cannot be the reflection of a static relation, such as that epitomized in the slogan of Maurice

Barrès, "la terre et les morts," which can only have a grim connotation for Césaire. Césaire's tellurism represents, rather, a dynamic process, a growing with and into the natural environment, its assumption in a kind of Adamite denomination of its properties and qualities:

A force de regarder les arbres, je suis devenu un arbre
et mes longs pieds d'arbre ont creusé dans le sol de larges
sacs à venin

Césaire's tellurism thus has a wider mystic significance, but it also has an immediate one in the Caribbean context. In purely literary terms, it represents a deepening of local color, taking West Indian poetry beyond the facile exoticism of his predecessors. Its symbolic significance is, however, even more important, for it represents a creative animation of the Caribbean consciousness through an invocation of the forces of the land in which it is lodged. The deliberate echo in "pays sans stèle" in *Cahier* of St. John Perse's depiction of the Caribbean as "pays d'herbage sans mémoire" in *Anabase*[26] turns out in this light to be profoundly ironic, for it is meant precisely as a recall of the devastating wash of history over the land and as an indication of the poet's determination to implant the memory of this history in the collective awareness, not, one hardly needs to add, as a form of morbid self-indulgence, but rather as a mode of self-invigoration. To this end, the Caribbean landscape is spiritualized in *Cahier*, transformed into the living symbol of a collective passion, in the religious sense of the word. This sense is apparent in the association between land and mother that also informs Césaire's tellurism. This association is, of course, a commonplace of nationalist discourse, but it is saved in Césaire's case from conventionality by the key role it plays in the more general celebration of the female principle in his poetry.

Césaire's ideal of woman owes something to the Surrealist conception of love and its lyrical reinstatement of sexuality in Western literature, as a direct outgrowth of the focus upon this aspect of human affectivity in Freudian psychoanalysis. The surrealist conception of love corresponds to an advocacy of the "pleasure principle" that acknowledges the positive value of the erotic; it stipulates a transgressive reaction against the sexual code of conventional Western morality, considered as a repressive hold on instinctual tendencies and a confinement of human potentialities, therefore of the general coercive purpose of the dominant morality. It cannot be said, however, that the literature produced by this conception of love advanced very

---

[26]Compare V. S. Naipaul's well-known remark in *The Middle Passage*: "History is built around achievement and creation; and nothing was created in the West Indies."

far beyond an abstract and idealized image of woman, which remains a function of the male writer's repossession of the self in an ecstatic delight of
mind and imagination. However, Césaire restores to the Surrealist conception a quality missing in it, an elemental dimension which Sartre has
described as a pan-sexualism, summed up in *Cahier* in this line:

> terre grand sexe levé vers le soleil.

It seems, therefore, hardly appropriate to speak of eroticism in connection with Césaire's evocation of the female principle. His attachment to
woman in his imagery is expressive rather of the fundamental organicism
that informs his vision, in which sexuality is directly associated with procreation as a principle of the continuity of life. The sexual act thus forms part
of a process of incarnation, involving the intimate collaboration of the male
with the female as equal partners. The erotic aspect of this act indeed fulfils
the requirements of the pleasure principle, but it enters more profoundly
into a union that takes on a sacramental significance:

> le pain et le vin de la complicité,
> le pain, le vin, le sang des épousailles véridiques.

The multiple values of "sang" in this extract, extending from virginal
blood and that of the menstrual cycle to the agony of parturition, relate the
image of woman to the processes of nature and confirm her as a principal
agent of the miracle of life. The image has a relevance to the idea of the
maintenance of the collective being of the race, but this is itself inserted
within the larger organic life of the universe. The procession of vegetal
imagery in the "agro-lunary"[27] scheme of Césaire's poetry serves to establish
the centrality of this conception to Césaire's vision. In *Cahier*, it translates a
dream of regeneration, manifested in the poet's obsession with water as the
element that assures the constant circulation of life in the realm of nature.
Both in its lustral quality and its prophetic significance, water represents the
promise of life:

> viennent les ovaires de l'eau où le futur agite ses petites têtes

The vegetal represents an important dimension of Césaire's telluric
vision and is especially appropriate to the baroque exuberance of the tropical environment. The concept of "réalisme merveilleux" intervenes in
Césaire's poetry in this regard, with specific application to the florid character of his evocations of landscape, which attests to the fascination exerted
upon his imagination by the flourishing of life in all its forms in his environ-

---

[27]The term is borrowed from Mircea Eliade; see his *Traité d'histoire des religions*, Paris,
1962.

ment and the aspect of fantasy this imprints upon the tropical scene. The highly-wrought romanticism of his Surrealist affiliations thus finds a natural setting in this objective correlation of the poetic mind to a native landscape, the spontaneous grasp of an imaginative ideal in the contemplation of a familiar environment.

The complex of agro-lunary images finds its completion in the tree, which functions as a symbol of organic being in all its plenitude; it embraces the earth and everything above it in its representation of the total spatial context of life. The category of space is thus valorized as the realm of fulfil-ment—the bird in flight illustrates Césaire's ideal of freedom—and affirms an expansive vision, an aspiration toward an infinite scope of being. The immediate affective value of the tree as an image of rootedness is thus extended by its messianic import, the connotation it assumes of an exultant upsurge of the life force. It is precisely in terms of this vision of triumphant life that Césaire celebrates his négritude in *Cahier*:

> ma négritude n'est pas une pierre, sa surdité ruée contre la clameur
> du jour
> ma négritude n'est pas une taie d'eau morte sur l'oeil mort de la terre
> ma négritude n'est ni une tour ni une cathédrale
> elle plonge dans la chair rouge du sol
> elle plonge dans la chair ardente du ciel.

The last two lines propose a graphic representation of the totemic pole to enforce the meaning of the collective affirmation the passage proclaims. They illustrate the way in which the image of the tree embodies the play of Césaire's sensibility and imagination around the theme of a vital reciprocity between consciousness and nature. This theme is raised to a level of intensi-ty in the constellation of brilliant images that reflect a poetic awareness of the universe as the domain of existence. As in Whitman's poetry, a "cosmic passion" moves through Césaire's evocations, especially in an imaginative attachment to the sideral sphere. The sun and the stars revolve in his poet-ry as leading lights in a cosmic dance to which his senses and his entire mind relate. The image of the sun in particular gathers up all the tendencies implicit in his structure of imagery: its association with blood gives this image, as we have seen, a polemical reference; its primal attribute as the des-ignation of an ultimate principle of life also links it with the organic concep-tion of sexuality that informs the poet's ideal of woman and constitutes the image as the fundamental reference of a comprehensive vitalism that ani-mates Césaire's poetic universe.

We encounter, then, in *Cahier*, as in Césaire's poetry generally, a pro-cession of images that do not simply reflect a set of objective preoccupations but also structure his inner experience and organize his deepest intuitions into a coherent outlook on the world. If this outlook does not stand apart from the explicit themes of his poetry, it acquires an autonomy of its own that derives from the convergence between the references of his poetry in the real world and their investment by a subjectivity that translates them into poetic terms, and in so doing expands their significance as moments in a spiritual adventure. For *Cahier* develops essentially as a drama of intro-spection, as an adventure whose implications are fully inward. And it becomes clear, as we consider this adventure, that poetry has meaning for Césaire as an act of repletion: the filling of an existential void with the cre-ative possibilities of language.

It is especially in this light that *Cahier* must be considered an epic, that of a consciousness wrestling with the vicissitudes of a prior determina-tion and of its progression toward a new mode of awareness and being. It falls in this respect into the tradition of the long poem of self-reflection in Western literature. Eliot's *The Waste Land* and Whitman's *Song of Myself* have already been evoked, and one could add in English literature such works as Coleridge's *Ancient Mariner* and Hopkins's *Wreck of the Deutschland* as examples of the genre. *Cahier* draws directly, of course, upon this tradition in French, as exemplified by such works as Rimbaud's "Le Bateau ivre," which expands into the sequence that forms his *Illuminations*, Valéry's *Le Cimetière marin*, and especially St. John Perse's *Anabase*, with which it stands in a relation of studied opposition. To place *Cahier* in this tradition is, how-ever, to stress its singularity, not only by reason of its theme and references, but also, and especially, of the very nature of its expression. We might qual-ify this singularity by pointing to the texture and formal design of the poem, to what is clearly a spontaneous recall of the expressive forms and proce-dures of the oral tradition. It seems reasonable to suppose that we are deal-ing here with a factor of Césaire's African antecedents, conveyed through the influence of its survival in the folk culture of his native background.

There is good reason to consider this observation as no mere specula-tion. The formal aspect of *Cahier* has given rise to perplexity only because its distinctive oral quality has rarely been taken into account.[28] It has been per-ceived, from a point of view determined by the conventions of literacy, as a "prose poem," interspersed with passages of verse; this makes for what appears to be an indeterminacy of form that is regularly attributed to its integration of modernist writing. It is much more satisfactory to see this integration itself as an accommodation to a textual framework permissive of an aesthetic dictated by the principles of orality.

The general design of *Cahier* bears out the validity of this approach, for it conforms very closely to the norms of heroic poetry, whose roots in

---

[28]The notable exception to this observation is Zadi Zaourou's *Césaire entre deux cul-tures*.

orality are no longer in doubt. It proceeds through a series of variations on a ground base, furnished by the leading refrain or its derivations, that mark the points of transition in its dramatic development. That these transitions are often abrupt, that they do not follow a linear pattern but move at will across the broad terrain of the poem's field of action suggests an architechtonic design that is expansive and cumulative rather than integrative. This is emphasized by the prominence of such features as enumeration, parallelisms, and insistent repetition that build up the peculiar tension of the poem; these effects of anaphora combine with that of rapid juxtaposition of ideas or images (parataxis) in preference to their controlled connection, to produce the sense of immediacy the poem conveys, of a language of total performance.[29] Indeed, the poem has sometimes been interpreted in terms of Western musical language, although it must be said that its "movements" have less to do with those of a classical symphony than with a set of variations in an immense *passacaglia*.[30]

The formal features we have indicated illuminate the nature of the poem. Its essential modality is that of metonymy, and its poetic status derives not from the Western paradigm instituted by the term "verse," but from an original sense of language as emanation of the voice, the rhythmic and highly stylized disposition of speech in its organic embodiment, oriented, moreover, toward a high register of expression. The conception of poetry as inherent in a particular form of visual representation of language is one that must be considered ultimately superficial, for it reduces the essence of poetry to the convention of literacy. *Cahier* certainly does not conform to this conception, and although it presents itself as a textual object, the false dichotomy imposed by literacy between prose and poetry in imaginative expression is irrelevant to a consideration of its nature. For we are dealing here with a text that embodies an oral conception of poetry as *charged utterance*,[31] in turn narrative, contemplative, incantatory, prophetic, and much else besides—in short, with an expression whose mode of existence restores the immediacies of the imaginative impulse as it moves the poet.

The problem of Césaire's hermetic use of language, in part explained by his need for the renewal of his medium, is also resolved in this perspective offered by the oral tradition. It conforms to the oracular tendency of language in oral cultures, which in its secular applications makes frequent

---

[29]The essentially oral quality of Césaire's poem was verified for the present writer by a powerful recital of *Cahier* he witnessed in 1960, given by the Martinican actress Toto Bissainthe, a performance in which she was accompanied by drums.

[30]Of the kind represented, for example, by the last movement of the Fourth Symphony in E Minor of Johannes Brahms.

[31]The German word *Dichtung*, regularly employed for imaginative expression, retains something of this sense, which is also reflected in the French *le dire*.

use of riddles[32] and in the religious sphere resorts to an esoteric mode. The assimilation of Césaire's poetry to this mode does no more than define the common domain it shares with the language of religion by reason of its visionary purpose.

It is this transcendental quality of language in *Cahier* that Breton hailed as its "ton majeur," reformulated by Sartre as "un superlangage solennel et sacré." No part of the poem illustrates this quality better than the final passage in which the image of the tree intervenes to sustain a double movement of the poet's imagination: an elevation of body and soul in a scene of transfiguration that dramatizes its character as *anabasis*, an upward perspective of its imagery as well as a rising intensity of its rhythm, and a complementary descent that enacts a mystic rite of self-consecration.

Cahier thus intimates a gnostic order of experience in which words are directed toward the recovery of the hidden essence of things. The metaphysical aspiration of the poet takes the form of an envisioned harmony with the life of the universe. This dimension of the poem places it at the confluence of the Surrealist quest for an alternative spirituality to that offered by Western civilization, and the categories of thought and sensibility proposed by cultures still in touch with the dictates of the mythic imagination. For Césaire, this means nothing less than the recuperation of an ancestral inheritance, one that is both a revelation of his being and a privileged mode of access to the profound truth of the universe.

* * * * *

The impact of *Cahier* on the wide circle of readers it has touched is unmatched by that of any of Césaire's other works and accounts for the enormous influence it has exercised in many directions, both literary and ideological, despite the difficulty of the text. It would be a simplification to assume that this impact is due solely or even mainly to its content. Such a view underestimates both the persuasive power of the poem's peculiar eloquence and the receptivity to form in its audience, especially in the francophone African and Caribbean world. This is to forget that this audience, weaned on the classics of French literature, including the rhetorical expressions of the French Revolution, also has a familiarity with the elements of the poem's structure of intertextuality, a familiarity to which the poem appeals for a good part of its effect.

It is of course true that the poem's message has importance for this

---

[32]This feature of the oral tradition has survived in the folk genre known as "cric-crac" in the French West Indies; it is of interest to note that Simone Schwarz-Bart's *Pluie et vent sur Télumée Miracle* builds on this tradition for its narrative structure.

audience, but what drives home this message for them is undoubtedly the exhilaration procured by Césaire's text, the bracing effect his language has on the mind, an effect marvellously captured by Breton in the phrase that concluded his preface to the poem: "La parole d'Aimé Césaire, belle comme l'oxygène naissant."

These considerations take us back to the question with which we started, concerning the relation that obtains between a textual universe projected by the imaginative activity of the poet and the phenomenal world where events occur and consciousness has its activity, a relation that has been enormously complicated by modernist literature. But this relation appears problematic only if a contradiction is assumed between the conventions of modernist writing and an engagement with the world. In fact, the opposite appears to be the case. The moral function of literature has perhaps never been so earnestly confronted and invoked as in the modernist vision and aesthetic: the concern of modernism with the complications in human life brought about by technological organization in industrial society—the historical, cultural, and moral consequences of this development—account for the complex exploration of language that modernism represents, whether this exploration implies a solipsistic recoil from the world or its open confrontation in a literature embodying a public gesture.

More generally still, the view has now come to be accepted that discursive practices generate representations that have a compelling effect on real options in the world. We have seen the way in which *Cahier* operates to reorder the terms of the relation between language and existence in a particular historical context. It may be objected in this connection that the concerns it demonstrates are too limited to this context to have universal relevance. Such a judgment implies, however, a narrow conception of the universal, a restrictive view that excludes the greater part of humanity from its range of reference. For it is precisely in its raising of a powerful voice on behalf of an excluded humanity that *Cahier* qualifies as a work with universal relevance. If it is taken as the master text of decolonization, it is not only in a political sense but also, and more profoundly, in a cultural and moral sense that this must be understood.[33]

Its significance as a poem of cultural affirmation is of course most evident in the Caribbean context, and we have pointed out its nationalist implications in this regard. *Cahier* initiates the exploration of the reaches of the Caribbean mind now being pursued in the work of writers as diverse as Edouard Glissant, René Depestre and Simone Schwarz-Bart working in

---

[33]It is this all-embracing meaning of the poem that has given it an appeal in situations such as in Quebec where the racial factor is not so much an issue as is the question of cultural and linguistic pluralism.

French, and Edward Kamau Brathwaite and Derek Walcott working in English. Theirs is a literature of pilgrimage to the points of the compass and the sources from which the Caribbean self has drawn its shaping influences, a literature that seeks to consecrate the emergence of this self in a new and distinctive relation to the world.

But beyond its local reference and its historical significance, *Cahier* speaks to all humanity, in accents that will no doubt ring most resonantly in the minds of communities who have had the experience of historical suffering, but that have a meaning for all peoples. In this respect, its reference to the "Holocaust"[34] is not merely incidental but consubstantial with its fundamental theme. This theme is none other than what Césaire himself has formulated as "la postulation agressive de la fraternité"—in other words, the passionate insistence upon a humane order of life as a principle of coexistence in an interdependent world.

---

[34]See stanzas 33-35 and notes infra.

CAHIER D'UN RETOUR AU PAYS NATAL

1.

Au bout du petit matin...

Va-t-en, lui disais-je, gueule de flic, gueule de vache, va-t-en je déteste les larbins de l'ordre et les hannetons de l'espérance. Va-t-en mauvais gris-gris, punaise de moinillon. Puis je me tournais vers des paradis pour lui et les siens perdus, plus calme que la face d'une femme qui ment, et là, bercé par les effluves d'une pensée jamais lasse je nourrissais le vent, je délaçais les monstres et j'entendais monter de l'autre côté du désastre, un fleuve de tourterelles et de trèfles de la savane que je porte toujours dans mes profondeurs à hauteur inverse du vingtième étage des maisons les plus insolentes et par précaution contre la force putréfiante des ambiances crépusculaires, arpentée nuit et jour d'un sacré soleil vénérien.

2.

Au bout du petit matin bourgeonnant d'anses frêles les Antilles qui ont faim, les Antilles grêlées de petite vérole, les Antilles dynamitées d'alcool, échouées dans la boue de cette baie, dans la poussière de cette ville sinistrement échouées.

3.

Au bout du petit matin, l'extrême, trompeuse désolée eschare sur la blessure des eaux; les martyrs qui ne témoignent pas; les fleurs du sang qui se fanent et s'éparpillent dans le vent inutile comme des cris de perroquets babillards; une vieille vie menteusement souriante, ses lèvres ouvertes d'angoisses désaffectées; une vieille misère pourrissant sous le soleil, silencieusement; un vieux silence crevant de pustules tièdes, l'affreuse inanité de notre raison d'être.

4.

Au bout du petit matin, sur cette plus fragile épaisseur de terre que dépasse de façon humiliante son grandiose avenir — les volcans éclateront, l'eau nue emportera les taches mûres du soleil et il ne restera plus qu'un bouillonnement tiède picoré d'oiseaux marins — la plage des songes et l'insensé réveil.

5.

Au bout du petit matin, cette ville plate — étalée, trébuchée de son bon sens, inerte, essoufflée sous son fardeau géométrique de croix éternellement recommençante, indocile à son sort, muette, contrariée de toute façons, incapable de croître selon le suc de cette terre, embarrassée, rognée, réduite, en rupture de faune et de flore.

6.

Au bout du petit matin, cette ville plate — étalée...

7.

Et dans cette ville inerte, cette foule criarde si étonnamment passée à côté de son cri comme cette ville à côté de son mouvement, de son sens, sans inquiétude, à côté de son vrai cri, le seul qu'on eût voulu l'entendre crier parce qu'on le sent sien lui seul; parce qu'on le sent habiter en elle dans quelque refuge profond d'ombre et d'orgueil, dans cette ville inerte, cette foule à côté de son cri de faim, de misère, de révolte, de haine, cette foule si étrangement bavarde et muette.

8.

Dans cette ville inerte, cette étrange foule qui ne s'entasse pas, ne se mêle pas : habile à découvrir le point de désencastration, de fuite, d'esquive. Cette foule qui ne sait pas faire foule, cette foule, on s'en rend compte, si parfaitement seule sous ce soleil, à la façon dont une femme, toute on eût cru à sa cadence lyrique, interpelle brusquement une pluie hypothétique et lui intime l'ordre de ne pas tomber; ou à un signe rapide de croix sans mobile visible; ou à l'animalité subitement grave d'une paysanne, urinant debout, les jambes écartées, roides.

9.

Dans cette ville inerte, cette foule désolée sous le soleil, ne participant à rien de ce qui s'exprime, s'affirme, se libère au grand jour de cette terre sienne. Ni à l'impératrice Joséphine des Français rêvant très haut au-dessus de la négraille. Ni au Libérateur figé dans sa libération de pierre blanchie. Ni au conquistador. Ni à ce mépris, ni à cette liberté, ni à cette audace.

10.

Au bout du petit matin, cette ville inerte et ses au-delà de lèpres, de consomption, de famines, de peurs tapies dans les ravins, de peurs juchées dans les arbres, de peurs creusées dans le sol, de peurs en dérive dans le ciel, de peurs amoncelées et ses fumerolles d'angoisse.

11.

Au bout du petit matin, le morne oublié, oublieux de sauter.

12.

Au bout du petit matin, le morne au sabot inquiet et docile — son sang impaludé met en déroute le soleil de ses pouls surchauffés.

13.

Au bout du petit matin, l'incendie contenu du morne, comme un sanglot que l'on a bâillonné au bord de son éclatement sanguinaire, en quête d'une ignition qui se dérobe et se méconnaît.

14.

Au bout du petit matin, le morne accroupi devant la boulimie aux aguets de foudres et de moulins, lentement vomissant ses fatigues d'hommes, le morne seul et son sang répandu, le morne et ses pansements d'ombre, le morne et ses rigoles de peur, le morne et ses grandes mains de vent.

15.

Au bout du petit matin, le morne famélique et nul ne sait mieux que ce morne bâtard pourquoi le suicidé s'est étouffé avec complicité de son hypoglosse en retournant sa langue pour l'avaler; pourquoi une femme semble faire la planche à la rivière Capot (son corps lumineusement obscur s'organise docilement au commandement du nombril) mais elle n'est qu'un paquet d'eau sonore.

16.

Et ni l'instituteur dans sa classe, ni le prêtre au catéchisme ne pourront tirer un mot de ce négrillon somnolent, malgré leur manière si énergique à tous deux de tambouriner son crâne tondu, car c'est dans les marais de la faim que s'est enlisée sa voix d'inanition (un-mot-un-seul-mot et je-vous-en-tiens-quitte-de-la-reine-Blanche-de-Castille, un-mot-un-seul-mot, voyez-vous-ce-petit-sauvage-qui-ne-sait-pas-un-seul-des-dix-commandements-de-Dieu)
car sa voix s'oublie dans les marais de la faim,
et il n'y a rien, rien à tirer vraiment de ce petit vaurien,
qu'une faim qui ne sait plus grimper aux agrès de sa voix
une faim lourde et veule,
une faim ensevelie au plus profond de la Faim de ce morne famélique.

17.

Au bout du petit matin, l'échouage hétéroclite, les puanteurs exacerbées de la corruption, les sodomies monstrueuses de l'hostie et du victimaire, les coltis infranchissables du préjugé et de la sottise, les prostitutions, les hypocrisies, les lubricités, les trahisons, les mensonges, les faux, les concussions — l'essouflement des lâchetés insuffisantes, l'enthousiasme sans ahan aux poussis surnuméraires, les avidités, les hystéries, les perversions, les arlequinades de la misère, les estropiements, les prurits, les urticaires, les hamacs tièdes de la dégénérescence. Ici la parade des risibles et scrofuleux bubons, les poutures de microbes très étranges, les poisons sans alexitère connu, les sanies de plaies bien antiques, les fermentations imprévisibles d'espèces putrescibles.

18.

Au bout du petit matin, la grande nuit immobile, les étoiles plus mortes qu'un balafon crevé,

19.

le bulbe tératique de la nuit, germé de nos bassesses et de nos renoncements.

20.

Et nos gestes imbéciles et fous pour faire revivre l'éclaboussement d'or des instants favorisés, le cordon ombilical restitué à sa splendeur fragile, le pain, et le vin de la complicité, le pain, le vin, le sang des épousailles véridiques.

21.

Et cette joie ancienne m'apportant la connaissance de ma présente misère, une route bossuée qui pique une tête dans un creux où elle éparpille quelques cases; une route infatigable qui charge à fond de train un morne en haut duquel elle s'enlise brutalement dans une mare de maisons pataudes, une route follement montante, témérairement descendante, et la carcasse de bois comiquement juchée sur de minuscules pattes de ciment que j'appelle "notre maison", sa coiffure de tôle ondulant au soleil comme une peau qui sèche, la salle à manger, le plancher grossier où luisent des têtes de clous, les solives de sapin et d'ombre qui courent au plafond, les chaises de paille fantomales, la lumière grise de la lampe, celle vernissée et rapide des cancrelats qui bourdonne à faire mal...

22.

Au bout du petit matin, ce plus essentiel pays restitué à ma gourmandise, non de diffuse tendresse, mais la tourmentée concentration sensuelle du gras téton des mornes avec l'accidentel palmier comme son germe durci, la jouissance saccadée des torrents et depuis Trinité jusqu'à Grand-Rivière, la grand'lèche hystérique de la mer.

23.

Et le temps passait vite, très vite.

Passés août où les manguiers pavoisent de toutes leurs lunules, septembre l'accoucheur de cyclones, octobre le flambeur de cannes, novembre qui ronronne aux distilleries, c'était Noël qui commençait.

Il s'était annoncé d'abord Noël par un picotement de désirs, une soif de tendresses neuves, un bourgeonnement de rêves imprécis, puis il s'était envolé tout à coup dans le froufrou violet de ses grandes ailes de joie, et alors c'était parmi le bourg sa vertigineuse retombée qui éclatait la vie des cases comme une grenade trop mûre.

Noël n'était pas comme toutes les fêtes. Il n'aimait pas à courrir les rues, à danser sur les places publiques, à s'installer sur les chevaux de bois, à profiter de la cohue pour pincer les femmes, à lancer des feux d'artifice au front des tamariniers. Il avait l'agoraphobie, Noël. Ce qu'il lui fallait c'était toute une journée d'affairement, d'apprêts, de cuisinages,

de nettoyages, d'inquiétudes,

de-peur-que-ça-ne-suffise-pas,

de-peur-que-ça-ne-manque,

de-peur-qu'on-ne-s'embête,

puis le soir une petite église pas intimidante, qui se laissât emplir bienveillamment par les rires, les chuchotis, les confidences, les déclarations amoureuses, les médisances et la cacophonie gutturale d'un chantre bien d'attaque et aussi de gais copains et de franches luronnes et des cases aux entrailles riches en succulences, et pas regardantes, et l'on s'y parque une vingtaine, et la rue est déserte, et le bourg n'est plus qu'un bouquet de chants, et l'on est bien à l'intérieur, et l'on en mange du bon, et l'on en boit du réjouissant et il y a du boudin, celui étroit de deux doigts qui s'enroule en volubile, celui large et trapu, le bénin à goût de serpolet, le violent à incandescence pimentée, et du café brûlant et de l'anis sucré et du punch au lait, et le soleil liquide des rhums, et toutes sortes de bonnes choses qui vous imposent autoritairement les muqueueses ou vous les distillent en ravissements, ou vous les tissent de fragrances, et l'on rit, et l'on chante, et les refrains fusent à perte de vue comme des cocotiers :

24.

ALLELUIA

KYRIE ELEISON... LEISON... LEISON,

CHRISTE ELEISON... LEISON... LEISON.

25.

Et ce ne sont pas seulement les bouches qui chantent, mais les mains, mais les pieds, mais les fesses, mais les sexes, et la créature tout entière qui se liquéfie en sons, voix et rythme.

Arrivée au sommet de son ascension, la joie crève comme un nuage. Les chants ne s'arrêtent pas, mais ils roulent maintenant inquiets et lourds par les vallées de la peur, les tunnels de l'angoisse et les feux de l'enfer.

Et chacun se met à tirer par la queue le diable le plus proche, jusqu'à ce
que la peur s'abolisse insensiblement dans les fines sablures du rêve, et l'on
vit comme dans un rêve véritablement, et l'on boit et l'on crie et l'on chante
comme dans un rêve avec des paupières en pétales de rose, et le jour vient
velouté comme une sapotille, et l'odeur de purin des cacaoyers, et les dindons qui égrènent leurs pustules rouges au soleil, et l'obsession des cloches,
et la pluie,
    les cloches... la pluie...
    qui tintent, tintent, tintent...

26.
    Au bout du petit matin, cette ville plate — étalée...
    Elle rampe sur les mains sans jamais aucune envie de vriller le ciel d'une
stature de protestation. Les dos des maisons ont peur du ciel truffé de feu,
leurs pieds des noyades du sol, elles ont opté de se poser superficielles entre
les surprises et les perfidies. Et pourtant elle avance la ville. Même qu'elle
paît tous les jours plus outre sa marée de corridors carrelés de persiennes
pudibondes, de cours gluantes, de peintures qui dégoulinent. Et de petits
scandales étouffés, de petites hontes tues, de petites haines immenses pétris-
sent en bosses et creux les rues étroites où le ruisseau grimace longitudinalement parmi l'étron...

27.
    Au bout du petit matin la vie prostrée, on ne sait où dépêcher ses rêves
avortés, le fleuve de vie désespérément torpide dans son lit, sans turgescence
ni dépression, incertain de fluer, lamentablement vide, la lourde impartialité
de l'ennui, répartissant l'ombre sur toutes choses égales, l'air stagnant sans
une trouée d'oiseau clair.

28.
    Au bout du petit matin, une autre petite maison qui sent très mauvais
dans une rue très étroite, une maison minuscule qui abrite en ses entrailles
de bois pourri des dizaines de rats et la turbulence de mes six frères et sœurs,
une petite maison cruelle dont l'intransigeance affole nos fins de mois et
mon père fantasque grignoté d'une seule misère, je n'ai jamais su laquelle,
qu'une imprévisible sorcellerie assoupit en mélancolique tendresse ou exalte
en hautes flammes de colère; et ma mère dont les jambes pour notre faim
inlassable pédalent de jour, de nuit, je suis même réveillé la nuit par ces
jambes inlassables qui pédalent la nuit et la morsure âpre dans la chair molle
de la nuit d'une Singer que ma mère pédale, pédale pour notre faim et de
jour et de nuit.
    Au bout du petit matin, au-delà de mon père, de ma mère, la case gerçant
d'ampoules, comme un pêcher tourmenté de la cloque, et le toit aminci,
rapiécé de morceaux de bidon de pétrole, et ça fait des marais de rouillure

dans la pâte grise sordide empuantie de la paille, et quand le vent siffle, ces disparates font bizarre le bruit, comme un crépitement de friture d'abord, puis comme un tison que l'on plonge dans l'eau avec la fumée des brindilles qui s'envole... Et le lit de planches d'où s'est levée ma race, tout entière ma race de ce lit de planches, avec ses pattes de caisses de Kérosine, comme s'il avait l'éléphantiasis le lit, et sa peau de cabri, et ses feuilles de banane sechées, et ses haillons, une nostalgie de matelas le lit de ma grand-mère (au-dessus du lit, dans un pot plein d'huile un lumignon dont la flamme danse comme un gros ravet... sur le pot en lettres d'or : MERCI.)

29.
Et une honte, cette rue Paille,

30.
un appendice dégoûtant comme les parties honteuses du bourg qui étend à droite et à gauche, tout au long de la route coloniale, la houle grise de ses toits d'essentes. Ici il n'y a que des toits de paille que l'embrun a brunis et que le vent épile.

31.
Tout le monde la méprise la rue Paille. C'est là que la jeunesse du bourg se débauche. C'est là surtout que la mer déverse ses immondices, ses chats morts et ses chiens crevés. Car la rue débouche sur la plage, et la plage ne suffit pas à la rage écumante de la mer.

Une détresse cette plage elle aussi, avec ses tas d'ordures pourrissant, ses croupes furtives qui se soulagent, et le sable est noir, funèbre, on n'a jamais vu un sable si noir, et l'écume glisse dessus en glapissant, et la mer la frappe à grands coups de boxe, ou plutôt la mer est un gros chien qui lèche et mord la plage aux jarrets, et à force de la mordre elle finira par la dévorer, bien sûr, la plage et la rue Paille avec.

32.
Au bout du petit matin, le vent de jadis qui s'élève, des fidelités trahies, du devoir incertain qui se dérobe et cet autre petit matin d'Europe...

33.
Partir.
Comme il y a des hommes-hyènes et des hommes-panthères, je serais un homme-juif
un homme-cafre
un homme-hindou-de-Calcutta
un homme-de-Harlem-qui-ne-vote-pas

34.
l'homme-famine, l'homme-insulte, l'homme-torture on pouvait à n'importe quel moment le saisir le rouer de coups, le tuer — parfaitement le tuer —

sans avoir de compte à rendre à personne sans avoir d'excuses à présenter à
personne
un homme-juif
un homme-pogrom
un chiot
un mendigot

35.
mais est-ce qu'on tue le Remords, beau comme la face de stupeur d'une dame
anglaise qui trouverait dans sa soupière un crâne de Hottentot?

36.
Je retrouverais le secret des grandes communications et des grandes combustions. Je dirais orage. Je dirais fleuve. Je dirais tornade. Je dirais feuille.
Je dirais arbre. Je serais mouillé de toutes les pluies, humecté de toutes les
rosées. Je roulerais comme du sang frénétique sur le courant lent de l'oeil
des mots en chevaux fous en enfants frais en caillots en couvre-feu en vestiges de temple en pierres précieuses assez loin pour décourager les mineurs.
Qui ne me compendrait pas ne comprendrait pas davantage le rugissement
du tigre.

Et vous fantômes montez bleus de chimie d'une forêt de bêtes traquées de
machines tordues d'un jujubier de chairs pourries d'un panier d'huîtres
d'yeux d'un lacis de lanières découpées dans le beau sisal d'une peau
d'homme j'aurais des mots assez vastes pour vous contenir et toi terre tendue
terre saoule
terre grand sexe levé vers le soleil
terre grand délire de la mentule de Dieu
terre sauvage montée des resserres de la mer avec
dans la bouche une touffe de cécropies
terre dont je ne puis comparer la face houleuse qu'à la forêt vierge et folle
que je souhaiterais pourvoir en guise de visage montrer aux yeux
indéchiffreurs des hommes
il me suffirait d'une gorgée de ton lait jiculi pour qu'en toi je découvre toujours à même distance de mirage — mille fois plus natale et dorée d'un soleil
que n'entame nul prisme — la terre où tout est libre et fraternel, ma terre

37.
Partir.   Mon coeur bruissait de générosités emphatiques.   Partir... j'arriverais lisse et jeune dans ce pays mien et je dirais à ce pays dont le limon
entre dans la composition de ma chair : "J'ai longtemps erré et je reviens
vers la hideur désertée de vos plaies".

Je viendrais à ce pays mien et je lui dirais : "Embrassez-moi sans crainte...
Et si je ne sais que parler, c'est pour vous que je parlerai".

38.

Et je lui dirais encore :

"Ma bouche sera la bouche des malheurs qui n'ont point de bouche, ma voix, la liberté de celles qui s'affaissent au cachot du désespoir".

Et venant je me dirais à moi-même :

"Et surtout mon corps aussi bien que mon âme, gardez-vous de vous croiser les bras en l'attitude stérile du spectateur, car la vie n'est pas un spectacle, car une mer de douleurs n'est pas un proscenium, car un homme qui crie n'est pas un ours qui danse..."

39.

Et voici que je suis venu!

De nouveau cette vie clopinante devant moi, non pas cette vie, cette mort, cette mort sans sens ni piété, cette mort où la grandeur piteusement échoue, l'éclatante petitesse de cette mort, cette mort qui clopine de petitesses en petitesses; ces pelletées de petites avidités sur le conquistador; ces pelletées de petits larbins sur le grand sauvage, ces pelletées de petites âmes sur le Caraïbe aux trois âmes,

et toutes ces morts futiles

absurdités sous l'éclaboussement de ma conscience ouverte

tragiques futilités éclairées de cette seule noctiluque

et moi seul, brusque scène de ce petit matin

où fait le beau l'apocalypse des monstres puis,

chavirée, se tait

chaude élection de cendres, de ruines et d'affaissements

40.

— Encore une objection! une seule, mais de grâce une seule : je n'ai pas le droit de calculer la vie à mon empan fuligineux; de me réduire à ce petit rien ellipsoïdal qui tremble à quatre doigts au-dessus de la ligne, moi homme, d'ainsi bouleverser la création, que je me comprenne entre latitude et longitude!

41.

Au bout du petit matin,

la mâle soif et l'entêté désir,

me voici divisé des oasis fraîches de la fraternité

ce rien pudique frise d'échardes dures

cet horizon trop sûr tressaille comme un geôlier.

42.

Ton dernier triomphe, corbeau tenace de la Trahison.

Ce qui est à moi, ces quelques milliers de mortiférés qui tournent en rond dans la calebasse d'une île et ce qui est à moi aussi, l'archipel arqué comme le désir inquiet de se nier, on dirait une anxiété maternelle pour protéger la ténuité plus délicate qui sépare l'une de l'autre Amérique; et ses flancs qui secrètent pour l'Europe la bonne liqueur d'un Gulf Stream, et l'un des deux versants d'incandescence entre quoi l'Equateur funambule vers l'Afrique. Et mon île non-clôture, sa claire audace debout à l'arrière de cette polynésie, devant elle, la Guadeloupe fendue en deux de sa raie dorsale et de même misère que nous, Haïti où la négritude se mit debout pour la première fois et dit qu'elle croyait à son humanité et la comique petite queue de la Floride où d'un nègre s'achève la strangulation, et l'Afrique gigantesquement chenillant jusqu'au pied hispanique de l'Europe, sa nudité où la Mort fauche à larges andains.

43.

Et je me dis Bordeaux et Nantes et Liverpool et New York et San Francisco
pas un bout de ce monde qui ne porte mon empreinte digitale
et mon calcanéum sur le dos des gratte-ciel
et ma crasse dans le scintillements des gemmes!
Qui peut se vanter d'avoir mieux que moi?
Virginie. Tennessee. Géorgie. Alabama
Putréfactions monstrueuses de révoltes
inopérantes,
marais de sang putrides
trompettes absurdement bouchées
Terres rouges, terres sanguines, terres consanguines.

44.

Ce qui est à moi aussi: une petite cellule dans le Jura,
une petite cellule, la neige la double de barreaux blancs
la neige est un geôlier blanc qui monte la garde devant une prison

45.

Ce qui est à moi
c'est un homme seul emprisonné de blanc
c'est un homme seul qui défie les cris blancs de la mort blanche
(TOUSSAINT, TOUSSAINT LOUVERTURE)
c'est un homme seul qui fascine l'épervier blanc de la mort blanche
c'est un homme seul dans la mer inféconde de sable blanc
c'est un moricaud vieux dressé contre les eaux du ciel
La mort décrit un cercle brillant au-dessus de cet homme
la mort étoile doucement au-dessus de sa tête
la mort souffle, folle, dans la cannaie mûre de ses bras
la mort galope dans la prison comme un cheval blanc

la mort luit dans l'ombre comme des yeux de chat
la mort hoquette comme l'eau sous les Cayes
la mort est un oiseau blessé
la mort décroît
la mort vacille
la mort est un patyura ombrageux
la mort expire dans une blanche mare de silence.

46.
Gonflements de nuit aux quatre coins de ce petit matin
soubresauts de mort figée
destin tenace
cris debout de terre muette
la splendeur de ce sang n'éclatera-t-elle point?

47.
　　Au bout du petit matin ces pays sans stèle, ces chemins sans mémoire, ces vents sans tablette.
Qu'importe?
Nous dirions. Chanterions. Hurlerions.
Voix pleine, voix large, tu serais notre bien, notre pointe en avant.

48.
　　Des mots?
　　Ah oui, des mots!
Raison, je te sacre vent du soir.
Bouche de l'ordre ton nom?
Il m'est corolle du fouet.
Beauté je t'appelle pétition de la pierre.
Mais ah! la rauque contrebande
de mon rire
Ah! mon trésor de salpêtre!
Parce que nous vous haïssons vous et votre raison, nous nous réclamons de la démence précoce de la folie flambante du cannibalisme tenace.

49.
Trésor, comptons :
la folie qui se souvient
la folie qui hurle
la folie qui voit
la folie qui se déchaîne

50.
Et vous savez le reste

51.
Que 2 et 2 font 5
que la forêt miaule
que l'arbre tire les marrons du feu
que le ciel se lisse la barbe
et caetera et caetera...

52.
Qui et quels nous sommes? Admirable question!
A force de regarder les arbres je suis devenu un arbre
et mes longs pieds d'arbre ont creusé dans le sol de larges
sacs à venin de hautes villes d'ossements
à force de penser au Congo
je suis devenu un Congo bruissant de forêts et de fleuves
où le fouet claque comme un grand étendard
l'étendard du prophète
où l'eau fait
likouala-likouala
où l'éclair de la colère lance sa hanche verdâtre et force les sangliers de la
putréfaction dans la belle orée violente des narines.

53.
Au bout du petit matin le soleil qui toussotte et crache ses poumons

54.
Au bout du petit matin
un petit train de sable
un petit train de mousseline
un petit train de grains de maïs

55.
Au bout du petit matin
un grand galop de pollen
un grand galop d'un petit train de petites filles
un grand galop de colibris
un grand galop de dagues pour défoncer la poitrine de la terre

56.
douaniers anges qui montez aux portes de l'écume la garde des prohibitions

57.
je déclare mes crimes et qu'il n'y a rien à dire pour ma défense.
Danses. Idoles. Relaps. Moi aussi

58.
J'ai assassiné Dieu de ma paresse de mes paroles de mes gestes de mes chansons obscènes

59.
J'ai porté des plumes de perroquet des dépouilles de chat musqué
J'ai lassé la patience des missionnaires
insultés les bienfaiteurs de l'humanité.
Défié Tyr. Défié Sidon.
Adoré le Zambèze.
L'étendue de ma perversité me confond!

60.
Mais pourquoi brousse impénétrable encore cacher le vif zéro de ma mendicité et par un souci de noblesse apprise ne pas entonner l'horrible bond de ma laideur pahouine?

61.
    voum rooh oh
    voum rooh oh
    à charmer les serpents à conjurer les morts
    voum rooh oh
    à contraindre la pluie à contrarier les raz de marée
    voum rooh oh
    à empêcher que ne tourne l'ombre
    voum rooh oh
    que mes cieux à moi s'ouvrent

62.
— moi sur une route, enfant, mâchant une racine de canne à sucre
— traîné homme sur une route sanglante une corde au cou
— debout au milieu d'un cirque immense, sur mon front noir une couronne de daturas.

63.
voum rooh
s'envoler
plus haut que le frisson plus haut que les sorcières vers d'autres étoiles exaltation féroce de forêts et de montagnes déracinées à l'heure où nul n'y pense les îles liées pour mille ans!

64.
voum rooh oh
pour que revienne le temps de promission
et l'oiseau qui savait mon nom

et la femme qui avait mille noms
de fontaine de soleil et de pleurs
et ses cheveux d'alevin
et ses pas mes climats
et ses yeux mes saisons
et les jours sans nuisance
et les nuits sans offense
et les étoiles de confidence
et le vent de connivence

65.

Mais qui tourne ma voix? qui écorche ma voix? Me fourrant dans la gorge mille crocs de bambou. Mille pieux d'oursin. C'est toi sale bout de monde. Sale bout de petit matin. C'est toi sale haine. C'est toi poids de l'insulte et cent ans de coups de fouet. C'est toi cent ans de ma patience, cent ans de mes soins juste à ne pas mourir.

rooh oh

66.

nous chantons les fleurs vénéneuses éclatant dans des prairies furibondes; les ciels d'amour coupés d'embolie; les matins épileptiques; le blanc embrasement des sables abyssaux, les descentes d'épaves dans les nuits foudroyées d'odeurs fauves.

67.

Qu'y puis-je?

Il faut bien commencer.

Commencer quoi?

La seule chose au monde qu'il vaille la peine de commencer :

La Fin du monde parbleu.

68.

Tourte
ô tourte de l'effroyable automne
où poussent l'acier neuf et le béton vivace
tourte ô tourte
où l'air se rouille en grandes plaques
d'allégresse mauvaise
où l'eau sanieuse balafre les grandes joues solaires
je vous hais

69.
on voit encore des madras aux reins des femmes des anneaux à leurs oreilles
des sourires à leurs bouches des enfants à leurs mamelles et j'en passe :
ASSEZ DE CE SCANDALE!

70.
Alors voilà le grand défi et l'impulsion
sataniques et l'insolente
dérive nostalgique de lunes rousses,
de feux verts, de fièvres jaunes!

71.
En vain dans la tiédeur de votre gorge mûrissez-vous vingt fois la même pauvre consolation que nous sommes des marmonneurs de mots

72.
Des mots? Quand nous manions des quartiers de monde, quand nous épousons des continents en délire, quand nous forçons de fumantes portes, des mots, ah oui, des mots! mais des mots de sang frais, des mots qui sont des raz-de-marée et des érésipèles et des paludismes et des laves et des feux de brousse, et des flambées de chair, et des flambées de villes...

73.
Sachez-le bien :
je ne joue jamais si ce n'est à l'an mil
je ne joue jamais si ce n'est à la Grande Peur

74.
Accommodez-vous de moi. Je ne m'accommode pas de vous!

75.
Parfois on me voit d'un grand geste du cerveau,
happer un nuage trop rouge
ou une caresse de pluie, ou un prélude du vent, ne vous tranquilisez pas outre mesure:

76.
Je force la membrane vitelline qui me sépare de moi-même,

77.
Je force les grandes eaux qui me ceinturent de sang

78.
C'est moi rien que moi qui arrête ma place sur le dernier train de la dernière vague du dernier raz-de-marée

79.
C'est moi rien que moi

qui prends langue avec la dernière angoisse
C'est moi oh, rien que moi
qui m'assure au chalumeau
les premières gouttes de lait virginal!

80.

Et maintenant un dernier zut :
au soleil (il ne suffit pas à soûler ma tête trop forte)
à la nuit farineuse avec les pondaisons d'or des lucioles incertaines
à la chevelure qui tremble tout au haut de la falaise
le vent y saute en inconstantes cavaleries salées
je lis bien à mon pouls que l'exotisme n'est pas provende pour moi

81.

Au sortir de l'Europe toute révulsée de cris
les courants silencieux de la désespérance
au sortir de l'Europe peureuse qui se reprend et fière
se surestime
je veux cet égoïsme beau
et qui s'aventure
et mon labour me remémore d'une implacable étrave.

82.

Que de sang dans ma mémoire! Dans ma mémoire sont des lagunes. Elles
sont couvertes de têtes de morts. Elles ne sont pas couvertes de nénuphars.
Dans ma mémoire sont des lagunes. Sur leurs rives ne sont pas étendus des
pagnes de femmes.
Ma mémoire est entourée de sang. Ma mémoire a sa ceinture de cadavres!
et mitraille de barils de rhum génialement arrosant nos révoltes ignobles,
pâmoisons d'yeux doux d'avoir lampé la liberté féroce

83.

(les nègres-sont-tous-les-mêmes, je-vous-le-dis
les vices-tous-les-vices, c'est-moi-qui-vous-le-dis
l'odeur-du-nègre, ça-fait-pousser-la-canne
rappelez-vous-le-vieux-dicton :
battre-un-nègre, c'est le nourrir)

84.

autour des rocking-chairs méditant la volupté
des rigoises
je tourne, inapaisée pouliche

85.

Ou bien tout simplement comme on nous aime!

Obscènes gaiement, très doudous de jazz sur leur excès d'ennui.
Je sais le tracking, le Lindy-hop et les claquettes.
Pour les bonnes bouches la sourdine de nos plaintes enrobées
de oua-oua. Attendez...
Tout est dans l'ordre. Mon bon ange broute du néon.
J'avale des baguettes. Ma dignité se vautre dans les dégobillements...

86.

Soleil, Ange Soleil, Ange frisé du Soleil
pour un bond par delà la nage verdâtre et douce des eaux
de l'abjection!

87.

Mais je me suis adressé au mauvais sorcier. Sur cette terre exorcisée,
larguée à la dérive de sa précieuse intention maléfique, cette voix qui crie,
lentement enrouée, vainement, vainement enrouée,

88.

et il n'y a que les fientes accumulées de nos mensonges — et qui ne répon-
dent pas.

89.

Quelle folie le merveilleux entrechat par moi rêvé au-dessus de la bassesse!
Parbleu les Blancs sont de grands guerriers
hosannah pour le maître et pour le châtre-nègre!
Victoire! Victoire, vous dis-je : les vaincus sont contents!
Joyeuses puanteurs et chants de boue!

90.

Par une inattendue et bienfaisante révolution intérieure, j'honore maintenant mes laideurs repoussantes.

91.

A la Saint-Jean-Baptiste, dès que tombent les premières ombres sur le
bourg du Gros-Morne, des centaines de maquignons se réunissent dans la rue
"De Profundis",

92.

dont le nom a du moins la franchise d'avertir d'une ruée des bas-fonds de la
Mort. Et c'est de la Mort véritablement, de ses mille mesquines formes
locales (fringales inassouvies d'herbe de Para et rond asservissement des distilleries) que surgit vers la grand'vie déclose l'étonnante cavalerie des rosses
impétueuses. Et quels galops! quels hennissements! quelles sincères urines!
quelles fientes mirobolantes! "un beau cheval difficile au montoir!" — "Une
altière jument sensible à la molette!" — "Un intrépide poulain vaillamment
jointé!"
Et le malin compère dont le gilet se barre d'une fière chaîne de montre,

refile au lieu de pleines mamelles, d'ardeurs juvéniles, de rotondités authentiques, ou les boursouflures régulières de guêpes complaisantes, ou les obscènes morsures du gingembre, ou la bienfaisante circulation d'un décalitre d'eau sucrée.

93.
> Je refuse de me donner mes boursouflures comme d'authentiques gloires.
> Et je ris de mes anciennes imaginations puériles.

Non, nous n'avons jamais été amazones du roi du Dahomey, ni princes de Ghana avec huit cents chameaux, ni docteurs à Tombouctou Askia le Grand étant roi, ni architectes de Djenné, ni Madhis, ni guerriers. Nous ne nous sentons pas sous l'aisselle la démangeaison de ceux qui tinrent jadis la lance. Et puisque j'ai juré de ne rien celer de notre histoire (moi qui n'admire rien tant que le mouton broutant son ombre d'après-midi), je veux avouer que nous fûmes de tout temps d'assez piètres laveurs de vaisselle, des cireurs de chaussures sans envergure, mettons les choses au mieux, d'assez consciencieux sorciers et le seul indiscutable record que nous ayons battu est celui d'endurance à la chicotte...

94.
Et ce pays cria pendant des siècles que nous sommes des bêtes brutes; que les pulsations de l'humanité s'arrêtent aux portes de la négrerie; que nous sommes un fumier ambulant hideusement prometteur de cannes tendres et de coton soyeux et l'on nous marquait au fer rouge et nous dormions dans nos excréments et l'on nous vendait sur les places et l'aune de drap anglais et la viande salée d'Irlande coûtaient moins cher que nous, et ce pays était calme, tranquille, disant que l'esprit de Dieu était dans ses actes.

95.
Nous vomissure de négrier
Nous vénerie des Calebars
quoi? Se boucher les oreilles?
Nous, soûlés à crever de roulis, de risées, de brume humée
Pardon tourbillon partenaire!

96.
J'entends de la cale monter les malédictions enchaînées, les hoquettements des mourants, le bruit d'un qu'on jette à la mer... les abois d'une femme en gésine... des raclements d'ongle cherchant des gorges... des ricanements de fouet... des farfouillis de vermine parmi des lassitudes...

97.
Rien ne put nous insurger jamais vers quelque noble aventure désespérée.
Ainsi soit-il. Ainsi soit-il.

Je ne suis d'aucune nationalité prévue par les chancelleries
Je défie le craniomètre. Homo sum etc.
Et qu'ils servent et trahissent et meurent
Ainsi soit-il. Ainsi soit-il.
C'était écrit dans la forme de leur bassin.

98.

Et moi, et moi,
moi qui chantais le poing dur
Il faut savoir jusqu'où je poussai la lâcheté.
Un soir dans un tramway en face de moi, un nègre.

99.

C'était un nègre grand comme un pongo qui essayait de se faire tout petit
sur un banc de tramway. Il essayait d'abandonner sur ce banc crasseux de
tramway ses jambes gigantesques et ses mains tremblantes de boxeur affamé.
Et tout l'avait laissé, le laissait. Son nez qui semblait une péninsule en
dérade et sa négritude même qui se décolorait sous l'action d'une inlassable
mégie. Et le mégissier était la Misère. Un gros oreillard subit dont les coups
de griffes sur ce visage s'étaient cicatrisés en îlots scabieux. Ou plutôt,
c'était un ouvrier infatigable, la Misère, travaillant à quelque cartouche
hideux. On voyait très bien comment le pouce industrieux et malveillant
avait modelé le front en bosse, percé le nez de deux tunnels parallèles et
inquiétants, allongé la démesure de la lippe, et par un chef-d'oeuvre caricatural, raboté, poli, verni la plus minuscule mignonne petite oreille de la création.
C'était un nègre dégingandé sans rythme ni mesure.
Un nègre dont les yeux roulaient une lassitude sanguinolente.
Un nègre sans pudeur et ses orteils ricanaient de façon assez puante au
fond de la tanière entrebâillée de ses souliers.
La misère, on ne pouvait pas dire, s'était donné un mal fou pour l'achever.
Elle avait creusé l'orbite, l'avait fardée d'un fard de poussière et de chassie
mêlées.
Elle avait tendu l'espace vide entre l'accrochement solide des mâchoires
et les pommettes d'une vieille joue décatie. Elle avait planté dessus les petits
pieux luisants d'une barbe de plusieurs jours. Elle avait affolé le coeur, voûté
le dos.
Et l'ensemble faisait parfaitement un nègre hideux, un nègre grognon, un
nègre mélancolique, un nègre affalé, ses mains réunies en prière sur un bâton
noueux. Un nègre enseveli dans une vieille veste élimée. Un nègre
comique et laid et des femmes derrière moi ricanaient en le regardant.
Il était COMIQUE ET LAID,
COMIQUE ET LAID pour sûr.

J'arborai un grand sourire complice...
Ma lâcheté retrouvée!
Je salue les trois siècles qui soutiennent mes droits
civiques et mon sang minimisé.
Mon héroïsme, quelle farce!
Cette ville est à ma taille.
Et mon âme est couchée. Comme cette ville dans la crasse
et dans la boue couchée.
Cette ville, ma face de boue.
Je réclame pour ma face la louange éclatante du crachat!...
Alors, nous étant tels, à nous l'élan viril, le genou vainqueur, les plaines à
grosses mottes de l'avenir?
Tiens, je préfère avouer que j'ai généreusement déliré, mon coeur dans ma
cervelle ainsi qu'un genou ivre.

100.
Mon étoile maintenant, le menfenil funèbre.

101.
Et sur ce rêve ancien mes cruautés cannibales :

102.
(Les balles dans la bouche salive épaisse
notre coeur de quotidienne bassesse éclate
les continents rompent la frêle attache des isthmes
des terres sautent suivant la division fatale des fleuves
et le morne qui depuis des siècles retient son cri au dedans de lui-même, c'est
lui qui à son tour écartèle
le silence
et ce peuple vaillance rebondissante
et nos membres vainement disjoints par les plus raffinés supplices
et la vie plus impétueuse jaillissant de ce fumier — comme le corossolier
imprévu parmi la décomposition des fruits du jacquier!)

103.
Sur ce rêve vieux en moi mes cruautés cannibales :

104.
Je me cachais derrière une vanité stupide le destin m'appelait j'étais caché
derrière et voici l'homme par terre, sa très fragile défense dispersée,
ses maximes sacrées foulées aux pieds, ses déclamations pédantesques rendant du vent par chaque blessure.
voici l'homme par terre
et son âme est comme nue
et le destin triomphe qui contemple se muer

en l'ancestral bourbier cette âme qui le défiait.

105.
Je dis que cela est bien ainsi.
Mon dos exploitera victorieusement la chalasie des fibres.
Je pavoiserai de reconnaissance mon obséquiosité naturelle
Et rendra des points à mon enthousiasme le boniment galonné d'argent du
postillon de la Havane, lyrique babouin entremetteur des splendeurs de la
servitude.

106.
Je dis que cela est bien ainsi.
Je vis pour le plus plat de mon âme
Pour le plus terne de ma chair !

107.
   Tiède petit matin de chaleur et de peur ancestrales
je tremble maintenant du commun tremblement que notre sang docile
chante dans le madrépore.

108.
Et ces têtards en moi éclos de mon ascendance prodigieuse!
Ceux qui n'ont inventé ni la poudre ni la boussole
ceux qui n'ont jamais su dompter la vapeur ni l'électricité
ceux qui n'ont exploré ni les mers ni le ciel
mais ils savent en ses moindres recoins le pays de souffrance
ceux qui n'ont connu de voyages que de déracinements
ceux qui se sont assouplis aux agenouillements
ceux qu'on domestiqua et christianisa
ceux qu'on inocula d'abâtardissement
tam-tams de mains vides
tam-tams inanes de plaies sonores
tam-tams burlesques de trahison tabide

109.
   Tiède petit matin de chaleurs et de peurs ancestrales
par-dessus bord mes richesses pérégrines
par-dessus bord mes faussetés authentiques

110.
Mais quel étrange orgueil tout soudain m'illumine?

111.
vienne le colibri

vienne l'épervier
vienne le bris de l'horizon
vienne le cynocéphale
vienne le lotus porteur du monde
vienne de dauphins une insurrection perlière
brisant la coquille de la mer
vienne un plongeon d'îles
vienne la disparition des jours de chair morte dans la chaux vive des rapaces
viennent les ovaires de l'eau où le futur agite ses petites têtes
viennent les loups qui pâturent dans les orifices sauvages du corps à l'heure
où à l'auberge écliptique se rencontrent ma lune et ton soleil

112.
il y a sous la réserve de ma luette une bauge de sangliers
il y a tes yeux qui sont sous la pierre grise du jour un conglomérat frémissant
de coccinelles
il y a dans le regard du désordre cette hirondelle de menthe et de genêt qui
fond pour toujours renaître dans le raz-de-marée de ta lumière
(Calme et berce ô ma parole l'enfant qui ne sait pas que la carte du printemps est toujours à refaire)

113.
Les herbes balanceront pour le bétail vaisseau doux de l'espoir
le long geste d'alcool de la houle
les étoiles du chaton de leur bague jamais vue
couperont les tuyaux de l'orgue de verre du soir puis
répandront sur l'extrémité riche de ma fatigue
des zinnias
des coryanthes
et toi veuille astre de ton lumineux fondement tirer
lémurien du sperme insondable de l'homme la forme
non osée
que le ventre tremblant de la femme porte tel un minerai!

114.
ô lumière amicale
ô fraîche source de la lumière
ceux qui n'ont inventé ni la poudre ni la boussole
ceux qui n'ont jamais su dompter la vapeur ni l'électricité
ceux qui n'ont exploré ni les mers ni le ciel
mais ceux sans qui la terre ne serait pas la terre
gibbosité d'autant plus bienfaisante que la terre déserte
davantage la terre
silo où se préserve et mûrit ce que la terre a de plus terre

115.
Ma négritude n'est pas une pierre, sa surdité ruée
contre la clameur du jour
ma négritude n'est pas une taie d'eau morte sur l'oeil
mort de la terre
ma négritude n'est ni une tour ni une cathédrale
elle plonge dans la chair rouge du sol
elle plonge dans la chair ardente du ciel
elle troue l'accablement opaque de sa droite patience.

116.
Eia pour le Kaïlcédrat royal!
Eia pour ceux qui n'ont jamais rien inventé
pour ceux qui n'ont jamais rien exploré
pour ceux qui n'ont jamais rien dompté
mais ils s'abandonnent, saisis, à l'essence de toute chose
ignorants des surfaces mais saisis par le mouvement
de toute chose
insoucieux de dompter, mais jouant le jeu du monde

117.
véritablement les fils aînés du monde
poreux à tous les souffles du monde
aire fraternelle de tous les souffles du monde
lit sans drain de toutes les eaux du monde
étincelle du feu sacré du monde
chair de la chair du monde palpitant du mouvement
même du monde!
    Tiède petit matin de vertus ancestrales

118.
Sang! Sang! tout notre sang ému par le coeur mâle
du soleil
ceux qui savent la féminité de la lune au corps d'huile
l'exaltation réconciliée de l'antilope et de l'étoile
ceux dont la survie chemine en la germination de l'herbe!
Eia parfait cercle du monde et close concordance!

119.
Ecoutez le monde blanc
horriblement las de son effort immense
ses articulations rebelles craquer sous les étoiles dures
ses raideurs d'acier bleu transperçant la chair mystique
écoute ses victoires proditoires trompeter ses défaites
écoute aux alibis grandioses son piètre trébuchement

Pitié pour nos vainqueurs omniscients et naïfs!

120.
Eia pour ceux qui n'ont jamais rien inventé
pour ceux qui n'ont jamais rien exploré
pour ceux qui n'ont jamais rien dompté

121.
Eia pour la joie
Eia pour l'amour
Eia pour la douleur aux pis de larmes réincarnées.

122.
et voici au bout de ce petit matin ma prière virile
que je n'entende ni les rires ni les cris, les yeux fixés
sur cette ville que je prophétise, belle,
donnez-moi la foi sauvage du sorcier
donnez à mes mains puissance de modeler
donnez à mon âme la trempe de l'épée
je ne me dérobe point. Faites de ma tête une tête de proue
et de moi-même, mon coeur, ne faites ni un père, ni un frère,
ni un fils, mais le père, mais le frère, mais le fils,
ni un mari, mais l'amant de cet unique peuple.

123.
Faites-moi rebelle à toute vanité, mais docile à son génie
comme le poing à l'allongée du bras!
Faites-moi commissaire de son sang
Faites-moi dépositaire de son ressentiment
faites de moi un homme de terminaison
faites de moi un homme d'initiation
faites de moi un homme de recueillement
mais faites aussi de moi un homme d'ensemencement

124.
Faites de moi l'exécuteur de ces oeuvres hautes
voici le temps de se ceindre les reins comme un vaillant homme —

125.
Mais les faisant, mon coeur, préservez-moi de toute haine
ne faites point de moi cet homme de haine pour qui
je n'ai que haine
car pour me cantonner en cette unique race
vous savez pourtant mon amour tyrannique
vous savez que ce n'est point par haine des autres races
que je m'exige bêcheur de cette unique race

que ce que je veux
c'est pour la faim universelle
pour la soif universelle
la sommer libre enfin
de produire de son intimité close
la succulence des fruits.

126.
Et voyez l'arbre de nos mains!
il tourne, pour tous, les blessures incises
en son tronc
pour tous le sol travaille
et griserie vers les branches de précipitation parfumée!

127.
Mais avant d'aborder aux futurs vergers
donnez-moi de les mériter sur leurs ceintures de mer
donnez-moi mon coeur en attendant le sol
donnez-moi sur l'océan stérile
mais où caresse la main la promesse le l'amure,
donnez-moi sur cet océan divers
l'obstination de la fière pirogue
et sa vigueur marine.

128.
La voici avancer par escalades et retombées sur le flot
pulvérisé
la voici danser la danse sacrée devant la grisaille du bourg
la voici barir d'un lambi vertigineux
voici galoper le lambi jusqu'à l'indécision des mornes

129.
et voici par vingt fois d'un labour vigoureux la pagaie
forcer l'eau
la pirogue se cabre sous l'assaut de la lame, dévie un instant
tente de fuir, mais la caresse rude de la pagaie la vire,
alors elle fonce, un frémissement parcourt l'échine de la vague,
la mer bave et gronde
la pirogue comme un traîneau file sur le sable.

130.
    Au bout de ce petit matin, ma prière virile :

131.
donnez-moi les muscles de cette pirogue sur la mer démontée
et l'allégresse convaincante du lambi de la bonne nouvelle!

132.

Tenez je ne suis plus qu'un homme, aucune dégradation, aucun crachat ne le
conturbe,
je ne suis plus qu'un homme qui accepte n'ayant plus de colère
(il n'a plus dans le coeur que de l'amour immense et qui brûle)

133.

J'accepte... j'accepte... entièrement, sans réserve...
ma race qu'aucune ablution d'hysope et de lys mêlés
ne pourrait purifier
ma race rongée de macules
ma race raisin mûr pour pieds ivres
ma reine de crachats et de lèpres
ma reine de fouets et de scrofules
ma reine de squasmes et de chloasmes
(oh ces reines que j'aimais jadis aux jardins printaniers et lointains avec derrière l'illumination de toutes les bougies de marronniers!)
J'accepte. J'accepte.
et le nègre fustigé qui dit : "Pardon mon maître"
et les vingt-neuf coups de fouet légal
et le cachot de quatre pieds de haut
et le carcan à branches
et le jarret coupé à mon audace marronne
et la fleur de lys qui flue du fer rouge sur le gras de
mon épaule
et la niche de Monsieur Vaultier Mayencourt, où j'aboyai six mois de caniche
et Monsieur Brafin
et Monsieur de Fourniol
et Monsieur de la Mahaudière
et le pian
le molosse
le suicide
la promiscuité
le brodequin
le cep
le chevalet
la cippe
le frontal

134.

Tenez, suis-je assez humble? Ai-je assez de cals aux genoux? Des muscles
aux reins?
Ramper dans les boues. S'arc-bouter dans le gras de la boue. Porter.
Sol de boue. Horizon de boue. Ciel de boue. Morts de boue, ô noms à

réchauffer dans la paume d'un souffle fiévreux!

135.

Siméon Piquine, qui ne s'était jamais connu ni père ni mère; qu'aucune mairie n'avait jamais connu et qui toute une vie s'en était allé — cherchant son nom

136.

Grandvorka — celui-là je sais seulement qu'il est mort, broyé par un soir de récolte, c'était parâit-il son travail de jeter du sable sous les roues de la locomotive en marche, pour lui permettre, aux mauvais endroits, d'avancer.

137.

Michel qui m'écrivait signant d'un nom étrange. Michel Deveine adresse *Quartier Abandonné* et vous leurs frères vivants
Exélie Vêté Congolo Lemké Boussolongo quel guérisseur de ses lèvres épaisses
sucerait tout au fond de la plaie béante le tenace secret du venin?

138.

quel précautionneux sorcier déferait à vos chevilles la tiédeur visqueuse des mortels anneaux?

139.

Présences je ne ferai pas avec le monde ma paix sur votre dos.

140.

Iles cicatrices des eaux
Iles évidences de blessures
Iles miettes
Iles informes

141.

Iles mauvais papier déchiré sur les eaux
Iles tronçons côte à côte fichés sur l'épée flambée du
Soleil
Raison rétive tu ne m'empêcheras pas de lancer absurde sur les eaux au gré des courants de ma soif
votre forme, îles difformes
votre fin, mon défi.

142.

Iles annelées, unique carêne belle

143.

Et je te caresse de mes mains d'océan. Et je te vire de mes paroles alizées. Et je te lèche de mes langues d'algues.

Et je te cingle hors-flibuste

144.
O mort ton palud pâteux!
Naufrage ton enfer de débris! j'accepte!

145.
Au bout du petit matin, flaques perdues, parfums errants, ouragans échoués, coques démâtées, vieilles plaies, os pourris, buées, volcans enchaînées, morts mal racinés, crier amer. J'accepte!

146.
Et mon originale géographie aussi; la carte du monde faite à mon usage, non pas teinte aux arbitraires couleurs des savants, mais à la géométrie de mon sang répandu, j'accepte

147.
et la détermination de ma biologie, non prisonnière d'un angle facial, d'une forme de cheveux, d'un nez suffisamment aplati, d'un teint suffisamment mélanien, et la négritude, non plus un indice céphalique, ou un plasma, ou un soma, mais mesurée au compas de la souffrance

148.
et le nègre chaque jour plus bas, plus lâche, plus stérile, moins profond, plus répandu au dehors, plus séparé de soi-même, plus rusé avec soi-même, moins immédiat avec soi-même,

149.
j'accepte, j'accepte tout cela

150.
et loin de la mer de palais qui déferle sous la syzygie suppurante des ampoules, merveilleusement couché le corps de mon pays dans le désespoir de mes bras, ses os ébranlés et, dans ses veines, le sang qui hésite comme la goutte de lait végétal à la pointe blessée du bulbe...

151.
    Et voici soudain que force et vie m'assaillent comme un taureau et l'onde de vie circonvient la papille du morne, et voilà toutes les veines et veinules qui s'affairent au sang neuf et l'énorme poumon des cyclones qui respire et le feu thésaurisé des volcans et le gigantesque pouls sismique qui bat maintenant la mesure d'un corps vivant en mon ferme embrasement.

152.
Et nous sommes debout maintenant, mon pays et moi, les cheveux dans le vent, ma main petite maintenant dans son poing énorme et la force n'est pas en nous, mais au-dessus de nous, dans une voix qui vrille la nuit et l'audi-

ence comme la pénétrance d'une guêpe apocalyptique. Et la voix prononce
que l'Europe nous a pendant des siècles gavés de mensonges et gonflés de
pestilences,
car il n'est point vrai que l'oeuvre de l'homme est finie
que nous n'avons rien à faire au monde
que nous parasitons le monde
qu'il suffit que nous nous mettions au pas du monde

153.

mais l'oeuvre de l'homme vient seulement de commencer
et il reste à l'homme à conquérir toute interdiction immobilisée aux coins de
sa ferveur
et aucune race ne possède le monopole de la beauté, de l'intelligence, de la
force
et il est place pour tous au rendez-vous de la conquête et nous savons maintenant que le soleil tourne autour de notre terre éclairant la parcelle qu'a
fixée notre volonté seule et que toute étoile chute de ciel en terre à notre
commandement sans limite.

154.

Je tiens maintenant le sens de l'ordalie : mon pays est la "lance de nuit" de
mes ancêtres Bambaras. Elle se ratatine et sa pointe fuit désespérément vers
le manche si c'est de sang de poulet qu'on l'arrose et elle dit que c'est du
sang d'homme qu'il faut à son tempérament, de la graisse, du foie, du coeur
d'homme, non du sang de poulet.

155.

   Et je cherche pour mon pays non des coeurs de dattes, mais des coeurs
d'homme qui c'est pour entrer aux villes d'argent par la grand'porte trapézoïdale, qu'ils battent le sang viril, et mes yeux balayent mes kilomètres carrés
de terre paternelle et je dénombre les plaies avec une sorte d'allégresse et je
les entasse l'une sur l'autre comme rares espèces, et mon compte s'allonge
toujours d'imprévus monnayages de la bassesse.

156.

Et voici ceux qui ne se consolent point de n'être pas faits à la ressemblance
de Dieu mais du diable, ceux qui considèrent que l'on est nègre comme commis de seconde classe : en attendant mieux et avec possibilité de monter plus
haut; ceux qui battent la chamade devant soi-même, ceux qui vivent dans
un cul de basse fosse de soi-même; ceux qui se drapent de pseudomorphose
fière; ceux qui disent à l'Europe : "Voyez, je sais comme vous faire des
courbettes, comme vous présenter mes hommages, en somme, je ne suis pas
différent de vous; ne faites pas attention à ma peau noire : c'est le soleil qui
m'a brûlé".

Et il y a le maquereau nègre, l'askari nègre, et tous les zèbres se sécouent à leur manière pour faire tomber leurs zébrures en une rosée de lait frais.
Et au milieu de tout cela je dis hurrah! mon grand-père meurt, je dis hurrah! la vieille négritude progressivement se cadavérise.
Il n'y a pas à dire : c'était un bon nègre.
Les Blancs disent que c'était un bon nègre, un vrai bon nègre, le bon nègre à son bon maître.
Je dis hurrah!
C'était un très bon nègre,
la misère lui avait blessé poitrine et dos et on avait fourré dans sa pauvre cervelle qu'une fatalité pesait sur lui qu'on ne prend pas au collet; qu'il n'avait pas puissance sur son propre destin; qu'un Seigneur méchant avait de toute éternité écrit des lois d'interdiction en sa nature pelvienne; et d'être le bon nègre; de croire honnêtement à son indignité, sans curiosité perverse de vérifier jamais les hiéroglyphes fatidiques.

157.
C'était un très bon nègre

158.
et il ne lui venait pas à l'idée qu'il pourrait houer, fouir, couper tout, tout autre chose vraiment que la canne insipide

159.
C'était un très bon nègre.

160.
Et on lui jetait des pierres, des bouts de ferraille, des tessons de bouteille, mais ni ces pierres, ni cette ferraille, ni ces bouteilles...
O quiètes années de Dieu sur cette motte terraquée!

161.
et le fouet disputa au bombillement des mouches la rosée sucrée de nos plaies.

162.
Je dis hurrah! La vieille négritude
progressivement se cadavérise
l'horizon se défait, recule et s'élargit
et voici parmi des déchirements de nuages la fulgurance d'un signe
le négrier craque de toute part... Son ventre se convulse et résonne...
L'affreux ténia de sa cargaison ronge les boyaux fétides de l'étrange nourrisson des mers!
Et ni l'allégresse des voiles gonflées comme une poche de doublons rebondie, ni les tours joués à la sottise dangereuse des frégates policières ne l'empêchent d'entendre la menace de ses grondements intestins

163.

En vain pour s'en distraire le capitaine pend à sa grand'vergue le nègre le plus braillard ou le jette à la mer, ou le livre à l'appétit de ses molosses

164.

La négraille aux senteurs d'oignon frit retrouve dans son sang répandu le goût amer de la liberté

165.

Et elle est debout la négraille

166.

la négraille assise
inattendument debout
debout dans la cale
debout dans les cabines
debout sur le pont
debout dans le vent
debout sous le soleil
debout dans le sang

   debout

     et

      libre

debout et non point pauvre folle dans sa liberté et son dénuement maritimes
girant en la dérive parfaite
et la voici :
plus inattendument debout
debout dans les cordages
debout à la barre
debout à la boussole
debout à la carte
debout sous les étoiles

   debout

     et

      libre

167.

et le navire lustral s'avancer impavide sur les eaux écroulées.
Et maintenant pourrissent nos flocs d'ignominie!

168.

par la mer cliquetante de midi
par le soleil bourgeonnant de minuit
écoute épervier qui tiens les clefs de l'orient
par le jour désarmé

par le jet de pierre de la pluie

169.

écoute squale qui veille sur l'occident

170.

écoutez chien blanc du nord, serpent noir du midi
qui achevez le ceinturon du ciel
Il y a encore une mer à traverser
oh encore une mer à traverser
pour que j'invente mes poumons
pour que le prince se taise
pour que la reine me baise
encore un vieillard à assassiner
un fou à délivrer
pour que mon âme luise aboie luise
aboie aboie aboie
et que hulule la chouette mon bel ange curieux.
Le maître des rires?
Le maître du silence formidable?
Le maître de l'espoir et du désespoir?
Le maître de la paresse? Le maître des danses?
    C'est moi!

171.

et pour ce Seigneur
les hommes au cou frêle
reçois et perçois fatal calme triangulaire

172.

Et à moi mes danses
mes danses de mauvais nègre
à moi mes danses
la danse brise-carcan
la danse saute-prison
la danse il-est-beau-et-bon-et-légitime-d'être-nègre
A moi mes danses et saute le soleil sur la raquette de mes mains
mais non l'inégal soleil ne me suffit plus
enroule-toi, vent, autour de ma nouvelle croissance
pose-toi sur mes doigts mesurés
je te livre ma conscience et son rythme de chair
je te livre les feux où brasille ma faiblesse
je te livre le chain-gang
je te livre le marais
je te livre l'intourist du circuit triangulaire

dévore vent
je te livre mes paroles abruptes
dévore et enroule-toi
et t'enroulant embrasse-moi d'un plus vaste frisson
embrasse-moi jusqu'au nous furieux
embrasse, embrasse NOUS

173.
mais nous ayant également mordus
jusqu'au sang de notre sang mordus!
embrasse, ma pureté ne se lie qu'à ta pureté
mais alors embrasse
comme un champ de justes filaos
le soir
nos multicolores puretés
et lie, lie-moi sans remords
lie-moi de tes vastes bras à l'argile lumineuse
lie ma noire vibration au nombril même du monde
lie, lie-moi, fraternité âpre
puis, m'étranglant de ton lasso d'étoiles
monte, Colombe
monte
monte
monte
Je te suis, imprimée en mon ancestrale cornée blanche.

174.
monte lécheur de ciel
et le grand trou noir où je voulais me noyer l'autre lune
c'est là que je veux pêcher maintenant la langue maléfique de la nuit en son
immobile verrition!

COMMENTARY AND NOTES

1.

Au bout du petit matin...
Va-t-en, lui disais-je, gueule de flic, gueule de vache, va-t-en je déteste les
larbins de l'ordre et les hannetons de l'espérance. Va-t-en mauvais gris-gris,
punaise de moinillon. Puis je me tournais vers des paradis pour lui et les siens
perdus, plus calme que la face d'une femme qui ment, et là, bercé par les
effluves d'une pensée jamais lasse je nourrissais le vent, je délaçais les monstres
et j'entendais monter de l'autre côté du désastre, un fleuve de tourterelles et de
trèfles de la savane que je porte toujours dans mes profondeurs à hauteur
inverse du vingtième étage des maisons les plus insolentes et par précaution
contre la force putréfiante des ambiances crépusculaires, arpentée nuit et jour
d'un sacré soleil vénérien.

This stanza functions as a prologue to the drama of consciousness enacted by the
poem and as a summation of its development. The opening line serves as a refrain
repeated at key points in the poem and thus provides both a thematic and symbolic
reference for its meaning; standing here at the head of the poem, it registers at once
the essential significance of the dawn (**petit matin**): the slow, hesitant awakening of
the poet's consciousness, personal and racial, which is fundamental to the experience
he is about to relate in the poem. The poet-protagonist thereafter confronts the colonial situation with a gesture of defiance aimed directly at the two figures he considers
its representative agents: the policeman (**flic**) and the priest (**moinillon**). The
peremptory tone of the passage is reinforced by the use of slang and of deliberately
derogatory terms which convey the poet's truculent and dissident mood. The stanza
also suggests an initial confident stance as the poet invokes a racial inheritance from
which he derives the force of his defiance. But although a combative note is struck in
this way at the outset of his adventure, the poet has still to undergo the vicissitudes
of the evolving experience which forms the substance of the poem.

vache: a more forceful variation on **flic**, in line with animal insults (such as "pig")
often employed for policemen.

larbins de l'ordre: "the servants of the established order"; **larbins** is another word
for *valet*, with a more contemptuous connotation.

les hannetons de l'espérance: these agents of the established order are further compared to harmful pests (**hannetons**), destroying a harvest or crop which represents
hope for the future; the image relies for its full effect on the etymology of the French
word **espérance** derived from the Latin *spes*, a word originally enclosed within the
same semantic field as *spica* or *speca*, meaning "an ear of wheat."

mauvais gris-gris: gris-gris is an African term meaning "charms"; the reference is to the priest whose vaunted spiritual powers are dismissed contemptuously.

punaise de moinillon: another derogatory reference to the priest; **moinillon** is a diminutive form for *moine*.

Puis je me tournais…et les siens perdus: the corollary of the poet's determined gesture of refusal is a movement toward a private world of experience closed to the colonial oppressor. Note in passing the allusion to Milton's *Paradise Lost*, with the suggestion of Christian mythology which the poet rejects as an inadequate spiritual resource.

et là, bercé par les effluves: an evocation of an alternative universe to that offered by Western civilization; the poet's deeper self is informed by a ceaseless flow of intense thought (**pensée jamais lasse**, associated with **fleuve** further on in the stanza), by an ideal world of the imagination which is contrasted with the sordid realities evoked at the very end of the stanza.

de l'autre côté du désastre: both in time, before the historical disaster of slavery and colonization, and in space, a possible reference to Africa which stands in the poet's imagination as his spiritual home from which he is now separated, a reading suggested by the word **savane**; the poet's consciousness strains toward this imaginative realm of an anterior state of being.

un fleuve de tourterelles; trèfles de la savane: an evocation of the inner world of the poet's imagination, rendered especially lyrical by the play of alliteration; **tourterelles** (turtledoves) signifies gentleness, while **trèfles** (clover) connotes opulence.

mes profondeurs: an early indication of the ancestralism that underlies the poem and Césaire's expression in general: the reference here is to a racial endowment, conceived as lodged within the depths of the poet's being, which is also a source of poetic intuition; it also suggests a parallel with the system of belief in Haitian Vodun, in which the *loas* (ancestral divinities) are thought to live under the sea, *en bas de l'eau*; the implied image of the sea that underlies the reference in these two senses is made explicit in this extract from *Les Armes miraculeuses*, which expresses the same idea: *les oiseaux chanteront tout doucement dans les bascules du sel la berceuse congolaise que les soudards m'ont désapprise mais que la mer très pieuse des boîtes craniennes conserve sur ses feuillets rituels.*

à hauteur inverse…insolentes: the poet's vision is counterpoised against the achievements of Western technical civilization, symbolized here by the skyscrapers which are seen as an affront to nature. The idea here is that the poet cultivates essential values, elaborated upon later in the poem, that afford a deeper vision and more vivid sense of life and experience.

la force putréfiante des ambiances crépusculaires: strong terms to denote the destructive and corrupting effect of technical civilization. There is possibly here an allusion to Wagner's opera *Götterdämmerung* (in French, *Crépuscule des Dieux*) as a way of characterizing the West, which the poet considers has entered into a phase of moral and spiritual decline, the theme of Oswald Spengler's *Decline of the West*, whose impact in the thirties upon the intellectual atmosphere in Europe was enormous.

sacré soleil vénérien: the colloquial sense of **sacré** ("cursed," "damned") gives a special force to this phrase which sums up the poet's perception of the West: the sun in the temperate zone is seen as afflicted and holding the world in its tenacious and baleful influence (**arpentée nuit et jour**); the epithet **vénérien** is also an anticipation of the next stanza.

2.

> Au bout du petit matin bourgeonnant d'anses frêles les Antilles qui ont faim,
> les Antilles grêlées de petite vérole, les Antilles dynamitées d'alcool, échouées
> dans la boue de cette baie, dans la poussière de cette ville sinistrement
> échouées.

Here begins the series of evocations of the West Indies and of its people whose condition is the central preoccupation of the poem; the evocations run through the work both as comprehensive background to its various developments and as a constant reference for the poet's individual adventure as it unfolds. We must imagine here the poet taking a solitary walk through the land at dawn and registering in his mind the desolate spectacle that meets his eye. The stark and relentless realism of the portrait he offers of the land and of the people, in this and the stanzas that follow, represents, in the moral connotations suggested by the pathological character of the images, an expression of a personal sense of anguish.

anses: creeks; the epithet **frêles** attached to the noun has both a physical reference (the creeks are small inlets of water into the island) as well as a moral one, denoting the fragile spiritual state of the islanders themselves.

grêlées: a word formed from **grêle**, "hail," and referring to the widespread incidence of smallpox (**petite vérole**) among the people; the word appropriately evokes the pock marks which the disease leaves on the skin of its sufferers.

3.

> Au bout du petit matin, l'extrême, trompeuse désolée eschare sur la blessure
> des eaux; les martyrs qui ne témoignent pas; les fleurs du sang qui se fanent et
> s'éparpillent dans le vent inutile comme des cris de perroquets babillards; une
> vieille vie menteusement souriante, ses lèvres ouvertes d'angoisses désaffectées;
> une vieille misère pourrissant sous le soleil, silencieusement; un vieux silence
> crevant de pustules tièdes,
> l'affreuse inanité de notre raison d'être.

The evocation begun in the previous stanza continues with a direct association struck here between the physical misery of the people and their condition of total abjection.

l'extrême, trompeuse désolée eschare sur la blessure des eaux: the island of Martinique in its physical misery is presented as a kind of hideous crust (**eschare**) on an area of the sea, like a scab forming over a wound and concealing its gravity. The condition depicted here is all the more insidious in that its effects are inward; they go into the very soul of the people.

les fleurs du sang qui se fanent: this image reinforces the preceding phrase, **les mar-tyrs qui ne témoignent pas**; the blood that has been shed on this island seems to have had no historical resonance or spiritual significance; **fleurs du sang**, in its liter-al meaning of flower (*flamboyants*), is contrasted here by implication to *fleurs de lys*, the emblem of the Bourbon monarchy in France, with the idea that the historical involvement of France with slavery has left a moral stain on her forever—see also stanza 133 for an explicit reference to this flower. This passage contains the first ref-erence to blood, a dominant image in the poem, on which Césaire rings a number of significant variations. Here, it is used in its fundamental reference to the collective historical being of the West Indian people.

perroquets babillards: "talkative parrots," an image employed to characterize the Martinicans themselves as a superficial people, without a voice of its own.

une vieille vie menteusement souriante: the deceptive postcard image which depicts the Caribbean as a happy place, contrary to the stark reality which the poet is unfolding here; his indignation, barely contained at this point, erupts later into a vehement negation in stanza 69.

pustules: inflamed pimples, often associated with smallpox, already mentioned by the poet in stanza 2 above; this recalls **eschare** earlier in the passage.

l'affreuse inanité de notre raison d'être: a forceful statement in the form of a para-dox which emphasizes the moral and spiritual void of the islanders as the poet sees them: the futility and emptiness (**inanité**) of their lives; the notation returns in a highly significant transformation later in the poem—see stanza 108 and notes.

4.

   Au bout du petit matin, sur cette plus fragile épaisseur de terre que dépasse de façon humiliante son grandiose avenir — les volcans éclateront, l'eau nue emportera les taches mûres du soleil et il ne restera plus qu'un bouillonnement tiède picoré d'oiseaux marins — la plage des songes et l'insensé réveil.

The poet now contrasts the intrinsic forcefulness of the natural environment of Martinique—bordered by the sea and dominated by a volcanic mountain—to the apparent weakness of character, the apparent lack of moral fiber of its inhabitants, in order to point up the tragic irony of their situation: the incomprehensible divorce between their true potential as beings related to this dynamic environment, and the collective apathy they actually display.

les volcans éclateront: the specific reference is to Mont Pélé overlooking the former capital, Saint Pierre; the volcano erupted suddenly and destroyed the city in 1902— see stanza 63 for another reference, even more specific. Mont Pélé links with other evocations of volcanoes in this work—as in Césaire's poetry generally—as a symbol of the poet's imaginative involvement with the forces of nature.

l'eau nue emportera les taches mûres du soleil: water as an agent of purification is another important symbol in Césaire's poetry; the image here, taken with the preced-ing reference to the action of the volcano, marks a double movement indicative of a fundamental principle of harmony in nature: the volcanic explosion is an expression of its destructive possibilities, which is balanced by the restorative powers it also offers.

la plage des songes et l'insensé réveil: the whole stanza leads to this expression of

the poet's imaginative anticipation of a **grandiose avenir** for his people, in consonance with the active qualities of its physical environment.

5.

Au bout du petit matin, cette ville plate — étalée, trébuchée de son bon
sens, inerte, essoufflée sous son fardeau géométrique de croix éternellement
recommençante, indocile à son sort, muette, contrariée de toutes façons, incapable de croître selon le suc de cette terre, embarrassée, rognée, réduite, en
rupture de faune et de flore.

The moral and spiritual prostration of the people is expressed in this stanza in the
physical terms of a city laid low. The greater part of Fort-de-France, to which this
appears to refer in the first instance, is constructed on a hillside overlooking the bay;
the reference thus has a more general application.

cette ville plate: a form of personification which sums up the poet's sense of the
depressed collective awareness of the people; the image is developed at greater length
in stanza 26.

trébuchée de son bon sens: physical and moral attributes clearly associated; in their
collective personality, the islanders seem to stumble, unsure of themselves and
unable to understand their fate.

son fardeau géométrique: a historical burden which seems to increase by geometrical progression, in an ever developing intensity.

croix éternellement recommençante: the historical continuity of the collective
plight of the people, which assumes the quality of an interminable passion, of which
the cross itself is a symbol. Besides the Christian reference, there is a possible allusion
to the fate of Sisyphus, who in Greek myth was condemned by the gods to roll a
boulder up a mountain hill; the boulder rolled back to the valley each time it
reached the summit so that he was obliged to start all over again.

contrariée de toutes façons: frustrated in whatever it undertook; **de toutes façons**
has the meaning here both of "in every way" and "in any case," hinting in this second sense at the fatalistic resignation of the people to their lot.

selon le suc de cette terre: there is a bitter irony in this evocation of a paradoxical
disharmony between the people and their environment which is noted for its production of sugar cane, a natural image, as it were, for what could have been a positive
state of the people themselves.

en rupture de faune et de flore: reinforces the preceding image to mark what the
poet regards as a tragic disconnection of the people from the essential qualities of
their natural habitat; the compulsion towards an organic bond with the land represents a major thematic and symbolic drive in the poem; the phrase here is a negative
formulation of this preoccupation.

6.

Au bout du petit matin, cette ville plate — étalée...

7.

Et dans cette ville inerte, cette foule criarde si étonnamment passée à côté de
son cri comme cette ville à côté de son mouvement, de son sens, sans inquié-

tude, à côté de son vrai cri, le seul qu'on eût voulu l'entendre crier parce qu'on le sent sien lui seul; parce qu'on le sent habiter en elle dans quelque refuge profond d'ombre et d'orgueil, dans cette ville inerte, cette foule à côté de son cri de faim, de misère, de révolte, de haine, cette foule si étrangement bavarde et muette.

8.

Dans cette ville inerte, cette étrange foule qui ne s'entasse pas, ne se mêle pas : habile à découvrir le point de désencastration, de fuite, d'esquive. Cette foule qui ne sait pas faire foule, cette foule, on s'en rend compte, si parfaitement seule sous ce soleil, à la façon dont une femme, toute on eût cru à sa cadence lyrique, interpelle brusquement une pluie hypothétique et lui intime l'ordre de ne pas tomber; ou à un signe rapide de croix sans mobile visible; ou à l'animalité subitement grave d'une paysanne, urinant debout, les jambes écartées, roides.

9.

Dans cette ville inerte, cette foule désolée sous le soleil, ne participant à rien de ce qui s'exprime, s'affirme, se libère au grand jour de cette terre sienne. Ni à l'impératrice Joséphine des Français rêvant très haut au-dessus de la négraille. Ni au libérateur figé dans sa libération de pierre blanchie. Ni au conquistador. Ni à ce mépris, ni à cette liberté, ni à cette audace.

The poet moves from indirect reference through physical terms to consider the people themselves. These four stanzas now dwell on the collective disorientation of the people, producing an impression of incoherence in their personality and their ways. Note the repetition of **dans cette ville inerte**, as an obsessive refrain indicating the poet's concentrated attention on the character and quality of the life that goes on within it, marked by a lack of will and afflicted with a strange inertia. Considered against the background of the people's natural environment, to whose vigor the poet makes constant reference, this collective stupor appears as a paradox—that of a people unaware of its true sources of strength. Furthermore, in stanza 9, in which the historical alienation of the people is presented in precise references to events and personalities which have determined the fortunes of the French West Indies, without the participation of the black population themselves, their passivity appears as a collective gesture of self-negation, as a refusal of history itself.

cette foule criarde: which manifests a superficial liveliness; the notation restates the same idea as in **perroquets babillards** in stanza 4 above; it is further dramatically expressed as a paradox in the phrase **bavarde et muette** that concludes the stanza.

passée à côté de son cri: both in the sense of not having found its true voice, which the poet will give it later in the poem, and also of a passive disregard of its real and profound interests, which the poet spells out in the passage in terms of an impulse to justified revolt.

comme cette ville à côté de son mouvement: ville and people are clearly linked in this evocation to refer explicitly to the social characteristics as opposed to the natural endowments of the people, which are left uncultivated. It is possible that Césaire has in mind here the local middle class of colored and mulatto which tended to distance itself from the rest of the population and whom he specifically attacks later in the poem (see stanzas 18 and 173-74).

quelque refuge profond d'ombre et d'orgueil: cf. **dans mes profondeurs** in stanza 1 above. In an ordinary sense, the phrase refers to the psychological reserves represented by the local aspects of life and culture in the islands; this is linked to the moral and spiritual potential of the people associated with a poetic ideal projected by the poet, designated here by **ombre**; besides the tropical connotation of the word (the sense of relief and ease in the shade), it carries a sense of mystery, which the epithet **profond** serves to underline.

qui ne s'entasse pas: which does not have a collective awareness, despite a common lot and its innate strengths; the situation remains for the poet paradoxical, as indicated in **cette étrange foule.**

le point de désencastration: "of disengagement"; the word **désencastration** is a coinage made up by Césaire from and in opposition to the regular word *encastrer,* "to fit an object neatly into another"; Césaire's term carries a broad hint of emasculation and the whole phrase denotes the total lack of a sense of solidarity in the people.

esquive: the more common occurrence of this word is in the verb *s'esquiver,* meaning "to sidestep"; the people prefer to shirk their historical responsibility rather than assume its burdens; the word thus refers to their moral and spiritual indolence.

à la façon d'une femme...de ne pas tomber: extends the sense of the preceding notation in sexual terms: the poet likens his people to a woman who suddenly abandons the sexual act even at its most intense moment (**cadence lyrique**); they are unable to sustain any undertaking, however engrossing, and for that reason can be said to be disconcerting in their lack of passion or commitment.

l'animalité subitement grave etc.: a realistic touch from direct observation of life in the Caribbean, contrasting with the postcard image of the exotic island woman already hinted at in stanza 4 above.

Joséphine des Français: the first wife of Napoleon Bonaparte was born on the island of Martinique into the white settler class; she became Empress when Napoleon took the title "Emperor of the French" in 1801. Her statue stands in a public square called La Savane overlooking the bay of Fort-de-France, hence **rêvant très haut au dessus de la négraille,** an expression linked directly to **ce mépris** further on in the stanza, by which the poet attributes to her the sentiments that go with her racial and social background. The word **négraille** is an even more contemptuous variant of *nègre,* implying a humanity at the bottom of the heap.

Ni au libérateur: a reference to Victor Schoelcher, who campaigned ceaselessly for the abolition of slavery and is thus the equivalent in French history of the Englishman William Wilberforce. The abolition was finally decreed for all the French colonies in May 1848, and a statue of Schoelcher now stands in a square near the Savanne, hence the apposition **figé dans sa libération de pierre blanchie;** the additional notation conveys the poet's distress at the fact that the name of Schoelcher and his achievement seem to elicit no response from the generality of West Indians. (See also the poem "Statue de Lafcadio Hearn" in *Ferrements* for a similar reference to the indifference of West Indians to the more inspiring aspects of their history.) See also stanzas 148 and 149.

Ni au conquistador: this refers to Bélain d'Esnambuc, who occupied the island of Martinique in 1635 and claimed it for France; **conquistador** is a Spanish word meaning "conqueror," usually applied to the Spanish generals who subdued the local populations in South America and prepared the way for its colonization by Spain. Césaire seems to emphasize in this passage the passive role of the black population in the whole process of conquest and emancipation which constitute the essential elements of colonial history in Martinique and more generally in the West Indies; it should, however, be noted that this is an exaggeration which he has qualified elsewhere in his poetry. (See in particular "Mémorial de Louis Delgrès" in *Ferrements*.)

10.

    Au bout du petit matin, cette ville inerte et ses au-delà de lèpres, de consomption, de famines, de peurs tapies dans les ravins, de peurs juchées dans les arbres, de peurs creusées dans le sol, de peurs en dérive dans le ciel, de peurs amoncelées et ses fumerolles d'angoisse.

The leading refrain of the poem is now taken up and combined with the repeated phrase of the three previous stanzas as a variation of the enumerative procedure. The poet's insistence on **peurs** in this stanza is carried through the device of personification to convey the pervasive atmosphere of demoralization among the people, and serves as a reference point for the transformations that he is later to project in the course of the poem's development.

ses au-delà: this governs the series of morbid evocations in the stanza, giving them something of a metaphysical implication; it establishes a sense of the pathetic horizons open to the people, of their rigorous existential predicament.

de peurs tapies: lying in wait, as if for prey.

de peurs juchées dans les arbres: the personification is rendered even more concrete by this image, which emphasizes the pervasive atmosphere of panic, of a general sentiment of disquiet among the people; there is also an oblique reference here to the practice of runaway slaves of seeking refuge on treetops; the reference is made more directly in stanza 51. (See notes infra.)

peurs amoncelées: piled up, banked up like storm clouds.

ses fumerolles d'angoisses: fumerolle is gas emitted by a dormant volcano; the term here extends the sense of **amoncelées,** and the juxtaposition with **angoisse** has a double function: it not only strengthens the sense of fear experienced by the people (the volcano in their midst is the ultimate threat and source of their fear); it also restates the paradox of their ambiguous relationship to their environment expressed in preceding passages.

11.

    Au bout du petit matin, le morne oublié, oublieux de sauter.

The poet introduces in this single-line stanza another major symbol with an immediate local significance: **le morne** is a little hill or hillock characteristic of the Martinican landscape. The word, which has no real English equivalent, is used here, as in the five stanzas that follow, as a variant of **ville,** with practically the same significance.

oublieux de sauter: a direct reference to volcanic activity in the Caribbean area, the

idea being that the hillock is unaware of its own potential, like the people it symbolizes: the point is shortly to be developed further in stanza 14. There is a possible reference here to *Morne des Sauteurs* in Grenada, where, in 1651, the Carib Indians
committed mass suicide rather than submit to the French, a noble gesture contrasted
with the passivity of the Martinicans. A secondary biblical reference which probably
serves as a grounding for this image recalls the little hills which rejoice in the Book
of Job (65.12) and skipped in the Psalms (114.4, 6), and foreshadows the imagery in
the next stanza.

12.

Au bout du petit matin, le morne au sabot inquiet et docile — son sang
impaludé met en déroute le soleil de ses pouls surchauffés.

There is a transition here in the imagery associated with **morne**. The verb **sauter** in
stanza 11 also suggests the leaping of a horse, which now becomes the implied reference of the metaphor in this stanza.

au sabot inquiet: with hesitant steps, uncertain of its movement, like a horse with a
wounded hoof. (Cf. **trébuchée** in stanza 6.) The characterization of the **morne** as a
disabled horse is particularly significant, since the horse is an archetypal image of
force frequently evoked by Césaire in his poetry - see **chevaux fous** in stanza 36,
where the image has its usual value for Césaire.

son sang impaludé: affected by fever; **impaludé** is a word coined by Césaire from
paludisme (malaria).

de ses pouls surchauffés: the **de** here is adverb of agent.

13.

Au bout du petit matin, l'incendie contenu du morne, comme un sanglot que
l'on a bâillonné au bord de son éclatement sanguinaire, en quête d'une ignition
qui se dérobe et se méconnaît.

The poet returns to the image of the dormant volcano to express once again the
paradox of innate strengths obscured and even negated by apparent weakness.

comme un sanglot: cf. **passée à côté de son cri** in stanza 8 above, for which this
image may provide an explanation: the collective anguish of the people has been so
repressed that they appear like animals who have been muzzled (**bâillonné**); the
image of domestication which the poet elaborates later in the poem is employed here
to suggest those deeper instincts of the people which otherwise would have found
vigorous expression but have been dammed up, so that their affirmative spirit is
crushed.

14.

Au bout du petit matin, le morne accroupi devant la boulimie aux aguets de
foudres et de moulins, lentement vomissant ses fatigues d'hommes, le morne
seul et son sang répandu, le morne et ses pansements d'ombre, le morne et ses
rigoles de peur, le morne et ses grandes mains de vent.

There is a concrete evocation in the present stanza of the economic and industrial
life of the island, dominated by the manufacture of rum at the time when the poem

was written, with its depressing effect on the physical and moral state of the people.

la boulimie aux aguets de foudres et de moulins: foudres are the casks (or tuns) in which rum is stored after distillation, **moulins** the windmills with which the distilleries are worked and which are a prominent feature of the landscape (hence **le morne et ses grandes mains de vents** at the end of the stanza). The casks and the windmills are pictured as ravenous monsters (**boulimie** is excessive hunger, the physical effect of famine) lying in wait (**aux aguets**) for the people, who are cowed into submission by their economic exploitation.

son sang répandu: this alludes primarily to the decimation of the black race during slavery, a reference which forms a constant element of the poet's historical and imaginative awareness, and is given fuller thematic development later in the poem (see stanza 164, where this phrase is repeated in a highly charged context).

ses grandes mains de vent: a direct reference to the windmills as well as a symbolic representation of the island and its people which prefigures the more positive projections which the poet offers in the latter part of the poem, that of an active association with the forces of nature.

15.

  Au bout du petit matin, le morne famélique et nul ne sait mieux que ce morne bâtard pourquoi le suicidé s'est étouffé avec complicité de son hypoglosse en retournant sa langue pour l'avaler; pourquoi une femme semble faire la planche à la rivière Capot (son corps lumineusement obscur s'organise docilement au commandement du nombril) mais elle n'est qu'un paquet d'eau sonore.

The stanza, taken as a whole, provides an insight into the profound mood of despair that their situation has implanted in the deep recesses of the people's mind, and their consequent lack as a collectivity of a will to live.

le morne famélique: a progression from the reference to **boulimie** in the previous stanza, now transferred to the people, to suggest their state of undernourishment.

ce morne bâtard: the cultural ambivalence of the West Indians, and the consequent disorientation this engenders in them, associated directly with the biological fact that a great proportion of the people are racially mixed, and though partly descended from the Europeans, are rejected by them. This is the theme of a novel by the Martinican writer Berthène Juminer, *Les Bâtards*, to which Césaire wrote a preface where he refers to the West Indian as "le bâtard de l'Europe et de l'Afrique, partagé entre ce père qui le renie et cette mère qu'il a reniée."

pourquoi le suicidé s'est etouffé...pour l'avaler: the word **hypoglosse** (from the Greek *hypo*, "under," and *glossa*, "tongue") designates the nerve which lies under the tongue and controls its muscles. The reference is to a well-attested technique employed by slaves to commit suicide by choking on their own tongues, a technique also referred to by the Martinican poet Edouard Glissant in his *Les Indes*, an epic reconstruction of Caribbean history. Here, the poet implies that in their desperate situation, the West Indians of today are well placed to understand their slave forebears' inclination to suicide, even if the heroic significance of the gesture escapes them.

pourquoi une femme semble faire la planche: the same idea of suicide is conveyed here by an indirect reference to the fate of Ophelia in Shakespeare's *Hamlet*, who was borne floating downriver after her suicide; the tone of the evocation brings out more clearly the redemptive value which the poet ascribes to the act of suicide.

la rivière Capot: a stream in the north of Martinique; it becomes torrential and therefore dangerous during the rainy season.

son corps lumineusement obscur: an oxymoron which, in the yoking of contrasting attributes, captures the paradox of the allusion: the glowing body without life, point-ing to the obscure realm of death.

16.

Et ni l'instituteur dans sa classe, ni le prêtre au catéchisme ne pourront tirer un mot de ce négrillon somnolent, malgré leur manière si énergique à tous deux de tambouriner son crâne tondu, car c'est dans les marais de la faim que s'est enlisée sa voix d'inanition (un-mot-un-seul-mot et je-vous-en-tiens-quitte-de-la-reine-Blanche-de-Castille, un-mot-un-seul-mot, voyez-vous-ce-petit-sauvage-qui-ne-sait-pas-un-seul-des-dix-commandements-de-Dieu)
　　car sa voix s'oublie dans les marais de la faim,
　　et il n'y a rien, rien à tirer vraiment de ce petit vaurien,
　　qu'une faim qui ne sait plus grimper aux agrès de sa voix
　　une faim lourde et veule,
　　une faim ensevelie au plus profond de la Faim de ce morne famélique

We have here a specific detail of the effects of their misery on the population: the children at school worn out by hunger are unable to follow their lessons properly, especially as the subjects they are being taught bear no relation to their immediate social and cultural environment. Apart from drawing attention to the alienating effect of colonial education in his country, the stanza also offers a criticism of the insensitive approach and prejudices of those charged with the education of the West Indian child. The evocations here presumably derive from Césaire's own reminis-cences of his early experience in primary school.

négrillon: "picaninny," little black boy (or girl); normally derogatory but used here with a sense of affection.

tambouriner: "persistent drumming"; there is a suggestion that the teacher taps the child on the head in time with his words, in his insistence on getting answers to questions which are incomprehensible to the black schoolchild and therefore cause him considerable mental strain.

un-mot-un-seul-mot: intended to suggest the wearied voice of the history teacher who cannot get a word out of the hungry children.

Blanche-de-Castille: Queen of France in the Middle Ages, remembered as the moth-er of St. Louis, one of the most famous kings of France; the historical reference is of course too remote for the black child to relate to in any meaningful way.

voyez-vous-ce petit-sauvage: the scene has changed from a history class to one in religious instruction; the insensitive attitude of the priest in charge of the class to the particular situation of the children derives from the prejudice noted here and may have been typical, which may account, among other factors, for Césaire's anticlerical attitude already expressed in stanza 2 and given ironic emphasis in stanza 133 (see notes).

aux agrès de sa voix: **agrès** is the French word for "riggings" which sailors had to climb to fasten the sails to the masts in a sailing ship; the child here is so weakened by hunger that his thoughts can no longer climb up his physical frame, as it were, to be voiced.

la Faim de ce morne famélique: the capitalization sums up the tenor of the stanza with its emphasis on hunger as a constant presence and a major preoccupation of the people.

17.

Au bout du petit matin, l'échouage hétéroclite, les puanteurs exacerbées de la corruption, les sodomies monstrueuses de l'hostie et du victimaire, les coltis infranchissables du préjugé et de la sottise, les prostitutions, les hypocrisies, les lubricités, les trahisons, les mensonges, les faux, les concussions — l'essoufle-ment des lâchetés insuffisantes, l'enthousiasme sans ahan aux poussis sur-numéraires, les avidités, les hystéries, les perversions, les arlequinades de la misère, les estropiements, les prurits, les urticaires, les hamacs tièdes de la dégénérescence. Ici la parade des risibles et scrofuleux bubons, les poutures de microbes très étranges, les poisons sans alexitère connu, les sanies de plaies bien antiques, les fermentations imprévisibles d'espèces putrescibles.

This is possibly the most somber of the poem's evocations of the life of the French-speaking West Indies under the colonial dispensation; it brings to a climax the asso-ciation between the physical and the moral with its accumulation of negative images drawn principally from the area of medical pathology, to suggest the total degrada-tion of the people by their historical experience of slavery and their present condi-tion of a dominated and despised race. The moral failings enumerated in this stanza are associated specifically with the colored and mulatto middle classes; they form the subject of an article by Suzanne Césaire in *Tropiques* Number 5 ("Malaise d'une civilisation"); their enumeration here constitutes an indictment, taken up in a more satirical tone in stanza 156.

l'échouage hétéroclite: the West Indian population brought in forcibly as slaves from different places of origin and left stranded on the islands with no sense of a common destiny; **échouage** (substantive of the verb **échouer**, "to be shipwrecked") is linked with the epithet **hétéroclite** to reinforce the idea of **cette foule qui ne sait pas faire foule** in stanza 8, of a haphazard assembly or collection of isolated individuals with no sense of a meaningful relationship with each other, of the need for solidarity.

les sodomies monstrueuses de l'hostie et du victimaire: the master-slave relation-ship presented as an unnatural sexual relationship.

les coltis infranchissables du préjugé et de la sottise: the meaning is that one can-not go further in prejudice and stupidity than is demonstrated by these people; **coltis** is the prow of a ship, the furthermost point, hence **infranchissables**.

les prostitutions: that is, the self-seeking attitude and opportunism of the middle class in the colonial context, often leading to self-abasement before the white mas-ter; the literal sense is also implied.

les concussions: bribery and corruption.

l'enthousiasme sans ahan aux poussis surnuméraires: this expands on the negative attributes of the middle class in a reference to the ambitions of its members for high positions in the colonial civil service, without a corresponding sense of effort to merit them; **ahan** ("panting") is indicative of physical effort; **poussis** is derived from *pousser*, with the derogatory sense of pushiness, of using unscrupulous means for "getting on."

les arlequinades de la misère: comic display put on for reward (from *arlequin*, Harlequin, comic character in pantomine shows.)

les estropiements: crippling or maiming; the word is more normally used in the singular and has an overwhelming moral sense here.

prurits: "pruritus," itching from an infection.

urticaires: rashes on the skin, specifically of the stinging kind (from the Latin *urtica*).

hamacs tièdes de la dégénérescence: hammocks (**hamacs**) suggest an easy and indolent attitude to life; the refusal of effort by the middle class leads to a softening of the moral timbre of its members.

scrofuleux bubons: **scrofuleux** is the adjective of *scrofule*, tuberculosis ("scrofula"); **bubons** is "bubo," a medical term for a swelling or inflammation caused by the plague.

les poutures: culture, in the medical sense of deliberate cultivation of germs (hence **microbes** here).

alexitère: "antidote"; the point is that the collective malady diagnosed by the poet has no known cure.

sanies: "pus"; the **plaies bien antiques** with which the word is joined suggests that the affliction it refers to is a tenacious and moral one, deriving from the historical experience of slavery; see also **vieilles plaies** in stanza 145.

18.

   Au bout du petit matin, la grande nuit immobile, les étoiles plus mortes qu'un balafon crevé,

19.

   le bulbe tératique de la nuit, germé de nos bassesses et de nos renoncements.

These two stanzas present a graphic summing up of the previous negative evocations: the complete alienation of the people assumes for the poet a cosmic dimension.

balafon (also written **balafong**): an African musical instrument similar to a xylophone; the symbolic force of the reference is established even in the negation: the profound self of the race which it evokes is associated with the cosmos.

bulbe tératique: the word **bulbe** has two possible meanings, either as "dome," which seems to be its primary sense here, used to refer to the starless heavens arched menacingly at night over the world, or, in a medical sense, as "swelling," which is also suggested by the participle **germé** in the passage. The two meanings are fused here and in the context appropriately qualified by the epithet **tératique**, "monstrous."

20.

> Et nos gestes imbéciles et fous pour faire revivre l'éclaboussement d'or des instants favorisés, le cordon ombilical restitué à sa splendeur fragile, le pain, et le vin de la complicité, le pain, le vin, le sang des épousailles véridiques.

There is a radical change of tone in this stanza as the poet turns away momentarily from a contemplation of the corrupted world in which his people have their historical being to an imaginative vision of a different reality of their lives; in the rare moments of happiness which shine through their somber existence, he sees pointers to a corporate being informed by essential values. The imagery gives an intensely lyrical as well as tender quality to the passage.

l'éclaboussement d'or des instants favorisés: the vision is presented both as a fleeting reality and as an ideal; **éclaboussements** is another word for *éclat*, hence the qualifier **d'or**.

le cordon ombilical: the organic attachment of the poet to his people, and of the people to their land. Note also that we have here the first direct statement of the essential theme of the poem as suggested by its very title.

le pain, et le vin de la complicité: The imagery here derives from the Christian ritual of Holy Communion, which assumes a literal sense in the word **complicité**, also associated with the poet's deep consciousness of an organic bond with his community, extending to union with nature.

le sang des épousailles véridiques: the virginal blood shed by the new bride on the nuptial night assumes a sacred significance in the act of communion between two souls represented by a healthy sexual union; there is thus an implied contrast here to **sodomies monstrueuses** in stanza 17. The image of blood now takes on an immediate meaning both as a symbol of the biological constitution of a people and of the timeless compact that binds members of a living community from one generation to another in an organic whole.

21.

> Et cette joie ancienne m'apportant la connaissance de ma présente misère, une route bossuée qui pique une tête dans un creux où elle éparpille quelques cases; une route infatigable qui charge à fond de train un morne en haut duquel elle s'enlise brutalement dans une mare de maisons pataudes, une route follement montante, témérairement descendante, et la carcasse de bois comiquement juchée sur de minuscules pattes de ciment que j'appelle "notre maison", sa coiffure de tôle ondulant au soleil comme une peau qui sèche, la salle à manger, le plancher grossier où luisent des têtes de clous, les solives de sapin et d'ombre qui courent au plafond, les chaises de paille fantomales, la lumière grise de la lampe, celle vernissée et rapide des cancrelats qui bourdonne à faire mal...

After the interlude of the preceding stanza, we are taken back in this one to the stark reality of the present. The poet proceeds once more to an evocation of the miserable life of his people with a detailed description of a typical village and neighborhood in the Martinique of his childhood; the graphic character of the description suggests that the details are drawn directly from personal experience. Note the comical tone of the description, touched here and there, however, with bitterness.

cette joie ancienne: a possible echo of Verlaine's line, "Te souviens-tu de notre extase ancienne?" ("Colloque Sentimental"); the phrase harks back to the evocation in the preceding stanza (see commentary above) of that deep layer of the poetic imagination that forms a kind of primordial remembrance, as in **dans mes profondeurs** of stanza 1.

ma présente misère: measured against the poetic ideal; the personal adjective has an obvious collective reference.

une route bossuée: uneven, undulating, therefore deformed; another instance of Césaire's use of physical attributes to characterize moral states : the road itself is symbolic of the inhabitants of the neighborhood.

qui pique une tête: recalls the colloquial expression *piquer une crise* referring to someone seized by hysteria; the road in question seems to have gone mad as it plunges headlong down the hill, scattering the miserable huts before it; further on, it is described as **follement montante** and **témérairement descendante**, as something with a will of its own.

route infatigable: in the sense of continuing its way with the same crazy momentum (**à fond de train**).

maisons pataudes: clumsy, ungainly.

"notre maison": note the ironic tone indicated by the quotation marks; the personal reference and the details of the description that follows give an authentic quality to this recall of the poet's humble background.

solives: beams or rafters of a roof, here made of pine (**sapin**), giving the house a dark, shady interior, hence the epithet **d'ombre**.

pailles fantomales: so worn out as to be mere shades (*fantômes*) of their old self.

la lumière grise...cancrelats: a realistic notation; the dull lamplight occasionally reflects upon the wings of cockroaches which scamper about the house; the epithet **vernissée** describes the glitter of the wings.

22.

> Au bout du petit matin, ce plus essentiel pays restitué à ma gourmandise, non de diffuse tendresse, mais la tourmentée concentration sensuelle du gras téton des mornes avec l'accidentel palmier comme son germe durci, la jouissance saccadée des torrents et depuis Trinité jusqu'à Grand-Rivière, la grand'lèche hystérique de la mer.

The poet's sense of attachment to his country is given a clear affirmation in a tone that is both vigorous and affectionate; the images are appropriately sensual, based as they are on the implied metaphor of a child suckling at its mother's breast, which the poet uses to define his relationship to his native land. A rapid panorama of the landscape of Martinique and of the surrounding sea is also offered in the stanza.

ce plus essentiel pays: that is, to his very being.

gras téton des mornes: the physical aspect of the *mornes* suggests a female breast which is given a maternal significance in this image; the idea is reinforced by the term **la tourmentée concentration sensuelle** which conveys both the picture of a child firmly suckling the breast and the poet's fierce attachment to his native land.

avec l'accidentel palmier: literally, the occasional palm tree, but also with a sense of being part of a rugged landscape (*paysage accidenté*) as its natural outgrowth: this sense is confirmed by **son germe durci,** a notation which, in a variation of **téton,** presents the **morne** as a hard nipple.

la jouissance saccadée: the feminine reference suggests this sexual image.

depuis Trinité jusqu'à Grand-Rivière: the northern part of Martinique where Césaire was born and grew up as a child (see map); the sea is especially rough in the region. The natural vigor of the landscape Césaire was familiar with has left its mark on his poetic temperament as witnessed by the immediate link between landscape and imagery in this passage, which is typical of his style.

la grand'lèche hystérique de la mer: a symbolic rather than geographical notation; the image of the sea crashing on the beach is expressive of the primordial force of nature.

23.

Et le temps passait vite, très vite.

Passés août où les manguiers pavoisent de toutes leurs lunules, septembre l'accoucheur de cyclones, octobre le flambeur de cannes, novembre qui ronronne aux distilleries, c'était Noël qui commençait.

Il s'était annoncé d'abord Noël par un picotement de désirs, une soif de tendresses neuves, un bourgeonnement de rêves imprécis, puis il s'était envolé tout à coup dans le froufrou violet de ses grandes ailes de joie, et alors c'était parmi le bourg sa vertigineuse retombée qui éclatait la vie des cases comme une grenade trop mûre.

Noël n'était pas comme toutes les fêtes. Il n'aimait pas à courir les rues, à danser sur les places publiques, à s'installer sur les chevaux de bois, à profiter de la cohue pour pincer les femmes, à lancer des feux d'artifice au front des tamariniers. Il avait l'agoraphobie, Noël. Ce qu'il lui fallait c'était toute une journée d'affairement, d'apprêts, de cuisinages,
de nettoyages, d'inquiétudes,
de-peur-que-ça-ne-suffise-pas,
de-peur-que-ça-ne-manque,
de-peur-qu'on-ne-s'embête,
puis le soir une petite église pas intimidante, qui se laissât emplir bienveillamment par les rires, les chuchotis, les confidences, les déclarations amoureuses, les médisances et la cacophonie gutturale d'un chantre bien d'attaque et aussi de gais copains et de franches luronnes et des cases aux entrailles riches en succulences, et pas regardantes, et l'on s'y parque une vingtaine, et la rue est déserte, et le bourg n'est plus qu'un bouquet de chants, et l'on est bien à l'intérieur, et l'on en mange du bon, et l'on en boit du réjouissant et il y a du boudin, celui étroit de deux doigts qui s'enroule en volubile, celui large et trapu, le bénin à goût de serpolet, le violent à incandescence pimentée, et du café brûlant et de l'anis sucré et du punch au lait, et le soleil liquide des rhums, et toutes sortes de bonnes choses qui vous imposent autoritairement les muqueueses ou vous les distillent en ravissements, ou vous les tissent de fragrances, et l'on rit, et l'on chante, et les refrains fusent à perte de vue comme des cocotiers :

This stanza provides a general picture of the life of the island, of its rhythm marked by the cycle of the seasons and the succession of characteristic events in nature and in the social and economic life of the people, in very close relation to each other. The year culminates with the feast of Christmas, which affords a reprieve to the misery of the people's lives. The atmosphere of popular joy at this time which the poet presents here not only offers a sharp contrast to his earlier evocations but suggests as well a reserve of moral force in the people to which he appeals later in the poem. There is more than a tinge of nostalgia in this description of the Christmas season which probably represents a high point of Césaire's childhood memories, hence the real feeling of tenderness which pervades the evocation, and determines a sense of identification with the people which he is later to develop in more overtly ideological and symbolic terms in the poem. However, in the long description of the Christmas festivities, the poet also captures, in precise and intimate details, the essential ambivalence of the people's situation, for despite the explosion of popular joy, the impression is still left of an overwhelming sense of a precarious existence; the festivities thus provide only a momentary escape from their condition. Thus, although there is a picturesque note which gives charm to his evocation, the poet never loses sight of his primary intention, which is to provide a realistic picture of the miserable life of the ordinary West Indian in the context of the colonial situation.

Et le temps passait vite, très vite: this line breaks off the evocations in the preceding stanzas and marks a transition in the poem's movement; it thus has the dramatic effect of a pause in a narrative sequence.

pavoisent de toutes leurs lunules: describes the flowering of the mango trees, which seem in August to put out flags (*pavoiser*); **lunules** is a diminutive form of *lune*; the word is normally used to refer to any figure in the shape of a crescent moon and by extension to the white crest at the bottom of the nail in humans.

octobre le flambeur de cannes: the sugar cane plants, flowering at this time and brightening the landscape, seem suddenly to make it come to life; the personifications in the passage receive an active quality with this depiction of October as **flambeur**, "one who sets ablaze."

picotement de désirs: tiny, fleeting sensations of longing, as of a bird pecking, in anticipation of the delights of Christmas.

un bourgeonnement de rêves: the flowering season of the people's dreams.

le froufrou violet de ses grandes ailes: Christmas pictured as a great bird, harbinger of joy and brightness; note the use of synesthesia in the image.

comme une grenade trop mûre: joy bursting forth in its full ripening; the purple color of the pomegranate fruit is anticipated in the **violet** of the preceding image of Christmas; the sensual note is accentuated in the description of the Christmas dinner later in the stanza.

Il n'aimait pas à courir les rues: as during Carnival, which is briefly evoked in the rest of the sentence. The Carnival is an important feature of Caribbean life and takes place around *Mardi Gras* (Shrove Tuesday, immediately before Lent); the personification of Christmas emphasizes its more religious and intimate character.

tamariniers: the tamarind tree, common in the West Indies, gives a fruit with a sharp taste, from which a juice is made.

agoraphobie: "agoraphobia," fear of open spaces (the opposite of claustrophobia), an irrational aversion for crowds or public forums; the point here is that Christmas is not a public occasion (emphasized by **et la rue est déserte** further in the stanza) but rather a family affair (**et l'on est bien à l'intérieur**).

de-peur-que-ça-ne-suffise-pas: this and the two lines that follow express the modest condition of the people.

une petite église...qui se laissât emplir: the village church at which Midnight Mass is celebrated; though modest, it is all-welcoming, as shown by the details that follow of its varied and boisterous congregation.

bien d'attaque: "very vigorously"; the cantor or lead singer (**chantre**) makes up in energy what he lacks in musicality.

luronnes: shameless girls, who are aggressively so (hence **franches**); the masculine form **luron** is not so derogatory in meaning.

et des cases: there is an abrupt change of scene here to a description of the feast at home after the mass; the use of the word **cases** (shacks) is significant; it accords with the poet's earlier description in stanza 21. Cf. the title of Joseph Zobel's classic autobiographical novel, *La Rue Cases-Nègres*.

riches en succulences: the various kinds of food prepared for the feast; there is a boyish note to the description here, appropriate to the reminiscent character of the evocation.

boudin: blood pudding or sausage, a typical item of French West Indian cuisine; the various types are described in the phrases that follow.

qui s'enroule en volubile: "twined like a stalk," in contrast to **large et trapu**, like a thick-set man.

le bénin à goût de serpolet: the mild sort laced with thyme (**serpolet**), in contrast to the heavily spiced one (**le violent à incandescence pimentée**).

l'anis: a spirit made from aniseed.

punch: fruit juice with rum base, a drink common throughout the Caribbean area; the French West Indian variety is often simply white rum with a pinch of lemon. The **lait** here refers to coconut milk.

24.

ALLELUIA
KYRIE ELEISON... LEISON... LEISON,
CHRISTE ELEISON... LEISON... LEISON

This stanza is a throwback to the religious ceremony in the church described earlier, in a recollection of fragments from the Catholic liturgy, now echoing in the neighborhood.

KYRIE ELEISON: "Lord have mercy"; a chant from the first part of the Catholic mass, focused on the Last Supper of Jesus Christ with his Apostles and the Easter proclamation of his resurrection on the third day after his crucifixion, which forms the basis of the Christian religion.

25.

Et ce ne sont pas seulement les bouches qui chantent, mais les mains, mais les pieds, mais les fesses, mais les sexes, et la créature tout entière qui se liqué-fie en sons, voix et rythme.

Arrivée au sommet de son ascension, la joie crève comme un nuage. Les chants ne s'arrêtent pas, mais ils roulent maintenant inquiets et lourds par les vallées de la peur, les tunnels de l'angoisse et les feux de l'enfer.

Et chacun se met à tirer par la queue le diable le plus proche, jusqu'à ce que la peur s'abolisse insensiblement dans les fines sablures du rêve, et l'on vit comme dans un rêve véritablement, et l'on boit et l'on crie et l'on chante comme dans un rêve avec des paupières en pétales de rose, et le jour vient velouté comme une sapotille, et l'odeur de purin des cacaoyers, et les dindons qui égrènent leurs pustules rouges au soleil, et l'obsession des cloches, et la pluie,

les cloches... la pluie...

qui tintent, tintent, tintent...

The self-abandon displayed by the people goes with an exuberance that the poet is later to present as an expression of their essential vitality; there is already in this stanza an insistence on the sense of rhythm as a black racial endowment. The delib-erate anti-climax of the second paragraph dramatizes the fragile nature of the peo-ple's reprieve and the desperateness of their predicament described as l'enfer; the term itself is not only an inversion of the meaning of Christmas but also anticipates the sense of heroic mission involved in the poet's return, conceived as a descent into the hell of his native land, the central theme of the poem, underlined by the title of Jean-Paul Sartre's essay, "Orphée noir." The stanza ends on a note which conveys the people's resignation to their lot, the weariness of their soul from which their fan-tasies cannot deliver them; they inevitably return to the dreary monotony of their miserable lives, emphasized by the repetition of rêve, which gives an ironic as well as tragic tone to the evocation.

les chants etc.: a note of anguish is introduced into the evocation in almost ono-matopoeic terms to suggest the same sense of insecurity conveyed by sabot inquiet in stanza 12.

le diable le plus proche: the word enfer suggests this play on the familiar expression *tirer le diable par la queue*, meaning "to be hard up," " to subsist on meagre means"; this sense underlies the implication here of a collective desperation which forces everyone to look for an expedient as a form of escape from the general lot.

sablures: a word coined by Césaire from *sables*; the dreams with which the people bury their fears are like the fine soft sand of the seashore.

paupières en pétales de rose: an expressive variation on the colloquial expression *la vie en rose*, "daydreaming."

sapotille: sapodilla, a plum-like fruit with velvety skin, commonly found in the West Indies.

purin: manure.

pustules: descriptive of the bare red skin of the turkey's neck, which is rough, as if covered with pimples.

26.

> Au bout du petit matin, cette ville plate — étalée...
> Elle rampe sur les mains sans jamais aucune envie de vriller le ciel d'une stature de protestation. Les dos des maisons ont peur du ciel truffé de feu, leurs pieds des noyades du sol, elles ont opté de se poser superficielles entre les surprises et les perfidies. Et pourtant elle avance la ville. Même qu'elle paît tous les jours plus outre sa marée de corridors carrelés de persiennes pudibondes, de cours gluantes, de peintures qui dégoulinent. Et de petits scandales étouffés, de petites hontes tues, de petites haines immenses pétrissent en bosses et creux les rues étroites où le ruisseau grimace longitudinalement parmi l'étron...

The poem's leading refrain is now employed to announce a return to the catalogue of misery interrupted by the evocation of the Christmas season. The opening line serves once again as a dramatic device: it returns our attention to the town, the **Elle** that is the focus of the stanza. This stanza as well as the next one, which continues its tenor, are dominated by images of prostration and humiliation, in addition to the familiar ones of disease encountered in previous evocations. There is a concrete quality to the details with which the poet presents the physical environment of the people, and the corresponding moral atmosphere of their existence.

vriller: to turn rapidly on oneself in an upward movement or to pierce or drill an object; both senses are fused in the use of the word here to suggest some kind of forceful manifestation, such as is required in a gesture of protest, with an effect of moral elevation (**stature de protestation**), which the poet demands of his people.

ciel truffé de feu: the brilliance of the sky (as in the Caribbean) seems to cow the houses (symbolic of the people who live in it) into a passive mood; **truffé** in the sense of "studded with" conveys the intensity of the scene as determined by its complement.

leurs pieds des noyades du sol: a description of the neighborhood in which the houses are erected on piles barely above ground covered by water; they are therefore not firmly rooted, hence **superficielles**.

Et pourtant elle avance la ville: the tone is ironic; the town is expanding into the countryside in a disorderly fashion; its unruly expansion is compared a little further on to the swelling of a tide.

même qu'elle paît tous les jours: like a hungry ruminant; note the familiar tone of the phrase to reinforce the irony.

plus outre: beyond (from Latin *ultra*); the idea is that the countryside itself is being engulfed in the **marée** of sordid houses.

persiennes pudibondes: an intriguing detail: the shuttered houses are depicted as prudish, in violent contrast to the filth and obscenity of the **cours gluantes** that surround them.

en bosses et creux: cf. **route bossuée** in stanza 21; the physical image is used to sum up the mediocrity and narrowness of the lives of the people enumerated in descriptive terms earlier.

le ruisseau grimace longitudinalement: the open drainage running with filth forms a rivulet that stretches like a line down the street; **longitudinalement** carries the additional connotation of prostration.

étron: human waste.

27.

Au bout du petit matin la vie prostrée, on ne sait où dépêcher ses rêves avortés, le fleuve de vie désespérément torpide dans son lit, sans turgescence ni dépression, incertain de fluer, lamentablement vide, la lourde impartialité de l'ennui, répartissant l'ombre sur toutes choses égales, l'air stagnant sans une trouée d'oiseau clair.

The terms **ruisseau** and **étron** at the end of the previous stanza now supply motifs for the imagery in the present one: the dull and uninspiring current of life in this environment suggests the metaphor of a turgid and polluted river. The sensation of stagnation is conveyed through morbid images which express the poet's deep sense of moral disgust at the mean quality of life of the people.

rêves avortés: cf. stanza 25 and note; there is a suggestion also that aborted fetuses, dropped in the gutter, are like dreams dropped in the river of life.

torpide: lethargic, dull.

turgescence: swelling up or increasing in volume, as opposed to **dépression,** "sinking," both said of a river; the total immobility represented by the images symbolizes the lifelessness of the people.

fluer: to flow; the word has the same root as English "flux," borrowed from Latin.

l'ombre sur toutes choses: a uniform dullness of existence.

l'air stagnant: the suffocating atmosphere.

trouée d'oiseau clair: the bird in flight seen as piercing clean through the air.

28.

Au bout du petit matin, une autre petite maison qui sent très mauvais dans une rue très étroite, une maison minuscule qui abrite en ses entrailles de bois pourri des dizaines de rats et la turbulence de mes six frères et soeurs, une petite maison cruelle dont l'intransigeance affole nos fins de mois et mon père fantasque grignoté d'une seule misère, je n'ai jamais su laquelle, qu'une imprévisible sorcellerie assoupit en mélancolique tendresse ou exalte en hautes flammes de colère; et ma mère dont les jambes pour notre faim inlassable pédalent de jour, de nuit, je suis même réveillé la nuit par ces jambes inlassables qui pédalent la nuit et la morsure âpre dans la chair molle de la nuit d'une Singer que ma mère pédale, pédale pour notre faim et de jour et de nuit.

Au bout du petit matin, au-delà de mon père, de ma mère, la case gerçant d'ampoules, comme un pêcher tourmenté de la cloque, et le toit aminci, rapiécé de morceaux de bidon de pétrole, et ça fait des marais de rouillure dans la pâte grise sordide empuantie de la paille, et quand le vent siffle, ces disparates font bizarre le bruit, comme un crépitement de friture d'abord, puis comme un tison que l'on plonge dans l'eau avec la fumée des brindilles qui s'envole...Et le lit de planches d'où s'est levée ma race, tout entière ma race de ce lit de planches, avec ses pattes de caisses de Kérosine, comme s'il avait l'éléphantiasis le lit, et sa peau de cabri, et ses feuilles de banane sechées, et ses haillons, une nostalgie de matelas le lit de ma grand-mère (au-dessus du lit, dans un pot plein d'huile un lumignon dont la flamme danse comme un gros ravet...sur le pot en lettres d'or : MERCI.)

The poet returns to his childhood memories with a special focus upon his personal family background, to establish his credentials as spokesman for his people: his sense of a common lot with the rest of the black population of the islands derives from this background. The details he provides, though graphic, cannot be taken as strictly autobiographical; the possessive adjectives have less a personal than a collective reference. These details have a significance, however, as an indication of his humble origins which qualify him to speak for the people; having known at first hand their life of poverty and misery, he belongs among them, so that his poetry represents an authentic testimony of their condition.

une autre petite maison: the parents' home, as distinct from that of his grandfather, described in stanza 21.

dont l'intransigeance affole nos fins de mois: this phrase is a strong variation on the meaning of *tirer le diable par la queue* echoed in stanza 25 to underline the permanent anxiety of the poet's poor family, presumably heightened at the end of the month by the need to pay the rent.

et mon père fantasque: both as he appears in the awed imagination of the young boy and as a realistic description of the father's condition responsible for the sudden changes of humor graphically presented here.

grignoté: "slowly eaten up"; the **misère** which is the cause may refer either to a physical ailment or to the father's mental strain caused by poverty; the child is unable to fathom its nature.

et ma mère: there is a note of affection and retrospective commiseration in this evocation of the almost heroic struggle of the poet's mother to provide for her children; this image of the mother forms part of the larger significance of the female principle in Césaire's poetry.

dont les jambes pour notre faim inlassable pédalent: the epithet **inlassable**, qualifying **faim**, serves already here as a transferred epithet, before it is applied directly to the mother's feet, working incessantly on the pedals of the old-style sewing machine (**une Singer**) in her effort to meet the family's constant need for food.

la morsure âpre: the immediate reference is the grinding sound and the stabbing action of the sewing machine as heard in the night, with the added sense of the pain it inflicts on the mother, suggested indirectly by **la chair molle**.

la case gerçant d'ampoules: the family house compared to a body covered with blisters (**ampoules**); **gercé** means "cracked" and refers to the wooden material of the structure. Note the use of **case** to qualify **maison** once again.

cloque: infection on the leaves of a peach tree (**pêcher** in the passage).

rapiécé de morceaux de bidon de pétrole: the roof of the house is held together with bits of rusted petrol cans, which explains **des marais de rouillures** that follows; the use of cans for improvised buildings in slum areas gave the word *bidonville* in French.

disparates: normally an adjective, used here as a noun to describe the odds and ends that make up the house.

font bizarre le bruit: the unusual construction emphasizes the strangeness of the different sounds made by the wind as it blows through the flimsy roof, with its mixture of various materials; these sounds are described in graphic terms in the notations that follow.

brindilles: twigs.

Et le lit de planches d'où s'est levée ma race: "the grandparents' bed in which my race was engendered"; a bitter exclamation, which also announces the poet's developing sense of identification. This is the first explicit reference to the notion of race in the poem, anticipating the more pointed references in the latter part of the poem.

pattes de caisses de Kérosine: boards laid on kerosene tins serving as the four feet (**pattes**) of the bed.

l'éléphantiasis: a disease that makes the sufferer's limbs swell, especially the legs. The disease was fairly common until very recently in the Caribbean—in the English-speaking areas, it is known as "big foot"—and in other tropical countries; the imagery here is descriptive but also recalls the terms of the poet's earlier pathological evocations.

sa peau de cabri: refers to a mat made from the dried skin of a goat, a household item like the others enumerated in the passage.

une nostalgie de matelas: cf. **les chaises de pailles fantomales** in stanza 21.

lumignon: diminutive of *lumière*: refers to the weak light of the lamp.

ravet: cockroach; an assimilation is implied in the comparison which has been anticipated in stanza 21.

MERCI: presumably, "Thanks be to God"; the poet draws out the unintended irony of the inscription.

29.

> **Et une honte, cette rue Paille,**

30.

> **un appendice dégoûtant comme les parties honteuses du bourg qui étend à droite et à gauche, tout au long de la route coloniale, la houle grise de ses toits d'essentes. Ici il n'y a que des toits de paille que l'embrun a brunis et que le vent épile.**

Beyond the family house, the poet now considers in these two stanzas the whole street and entire neighborhood, composed of houses roofed with straw (hence the name of the street), with the same insistent realism as in previous evocations.

les parties honteuses: normally a euphemism for the private parts of the human body, used here to mean the secret recesses of the village; the literal sense of **honteuses** is of course primarily intended.

la houle grise: the succession of roofs forms a kind of wave whose meanness is emphasized by the epithet. Ordinarily, the image of the sea wave has a positive significance in Césaire's poetry; its inversion here into a negative image is therefore significant.

essentes: shingles; bits of wood used for roofing.

embrun: sea-spray.

31.

Tout le monde la méprise la rue Paille. C'est là que la jeunesse du bourg se débauche. C'est là surtout que la mer déverse ses immondices, ses chats morts et ses chiens crevés. Car la rue débouche sur la plage, et la plage ne suffit pas à la rage écumante de la mer.

Une détresse cette plage elle aussi, avec ses tas d'ordures pourrissant, ses croupes furtives qui se soulagent, et le sable est noir, funèbre, on n'a jamais vu un sable si noir, et l'écume glisse dessus en glapissant, et la mer la frappe à grands coups de boxe, ou plutôt la mer est un gros chien qui lèche et mord la plage aux jarrets, et à force de la mordre elle finira par la dévorer, bien sûr, la plage et la rue Paille avec.

Another realistic portrayal, with the focus here on a typical beach in the northern part of Martinique, where there are many, some with black sand and others with blackened gravel stones, like the one described in this stanza. The morbid images are derived directly from the unsanitary habits of the people themselves.

ses croupes furtives: of people relieving themselves, assimilated to the beach itself.

et le sable est noir: due to its volcanic origin.

la mer est un gros chien qui lèche: cf. **la grand'lèche hystérique de la mer** in stanza 22.

elle finira par la dévorer: the poet indirectly invokes the cleansing power of the sea against the physical corruption he has just described.

32.

Au bout du petit matin, le vent de jadis qui s'élève, des fidelités trahies, du devoir incertain qui se dérobe et cet autre petit matin d'Europe...

This stanza marks a major transition in the development of the poem. Its immediate reference is to Césaire's actual departure from Martinique to France, and his confused sentiment as he leaves the closed and squalid environment of his native island for the wider world represented by France and Europe. The change of scene introduced by the stanza thus brings with it a new sentiment as the poet becomes aware of the wider dimensions of the collective situation of his people, which he has presented so far only in its immediate Caribbean context, but is about to project over a broader canvas, in line with his actual experience of moving out into the wider world. As he looks back on his early experience of life on the island and considers his sense of relief at escaping from it (denoted here by the phrase **le vent de jadis**), he comes to grasp its moral significance for himself, the flight from responsibility and commitment implied by an earlier attitude of detachment from the reality of his people's life, and the sense of betrayal which this provokes in him (**des fidélités trahies, du devoir incertain qui se dérobe**). This rigorous self-assessment now provides the emotional and moral perspective for the drama of consciousness which begins to unfold as he confronts the Western world (**cet autre petit matin d'Europe**) and begins to detail the historical grievance of his race. Note in passing the echo of a line - *le vent se lève* - of Paul Valéry's *Le Cimetière marin*, which also enacts a psychological and spiritual adventure.

33.

Partir.
Comme il y a des hommes-hyènes et des hommes-panthères, je serais un
homme-juif
un homme-cafre
un homme-hindou-de-Calcutta
un homme-de-Harlem-qui-ne-vote-pas

34.

l'homme-famine, l'homme-insulte, l'homme-torture on pouvait à n'importe
quel moment le saisir le rouer de coups, le tuer — parfaitement le tuer — sans
avoir de compte à rendre à personne sans avoir d'excuses à présenter à
personne
un homme-juif
un homme-pogrom
un chiot
un mendigot

At a first level of meaning, these stanzas have an autobiographical significance, as Césaire's recollection of his sense of relief on leaving his native island for the first time. In the context of the poem, and against the background of the misery that he has evoked all through the preceding stanzas, provoking a profound revulsion in him, his departure takes on in his mind the character of a flight; in this sense, the stanzas connect with the one immediately preceding to convey a retrospective sense of guilt. At the same time, we witness here the active development of the poet's sense of identification which leads to his resolve to return to his people and to take up their cause. The allusions in these stanzas to the historical situation of oppressed minorities throughout the world place the particular situation of the black race in a comprehensive context and offer an insight into the widening sense of injustice from which his particular identification proceeds. There is in these allusions a conflation of two series of evocations—that of the horror of slavery peculiar to the experience of the black race, with that of the atrocities visited upon other racial minorities, especially the Jews, during the Second World War, which brought home to Europeans the evil of racism. The procedure is intended not only to establish a parallel between the historical experience of blacks and that of other persecuted races, but also the continuity of evil as a feature of universal history. Although the poet details only a few representative examples of these minorities and their condition, this stanza indicates the all-inclusive character of his reaction to oppression, a point he makes even more explicit further on in the poem (see **faim universelle, soif universelle** in stanza 125.) There is thus a dramatic anticipation here of stanza 39 where the poet's new-found resolve is elaborated upon in terms that are both poignant and ironic (see notes infra). The intervening stanzas depict the political and social context of the poet's developing awareness as well as the poetic motivations of this resolve.

Partir: the departure is to Europe and marks a movement outwards, into an existential exile, which is often represented in black literature by the theme of separation from an original homeland. However, a certain ambivalence attaches to this theme in its statement here, due to the specific context explained above.

des hommes-hyènes et des hommes-panthères: African totemism, in which human beings are placed in an essential relation with other living beings (often animals), supplies the foundation for the poet's expression here of a sense of identification with all oppressed peoples. The terms employed have other associations as well: the animals designated—scavengers and predators—allude to the image of savagery held up by Europe of so-called primitive peoples; at the same time, the allusion functions for the poet as a mode of assuming an aggressive posture, which becomes explicit in the notation **le rugissement du tigre** in stanza 36.

un homme-juif: the experience of the Jews, among the most persecuted of all the races of mankind, has been similar in some important respects to that of black people; it designates them as an obvious reference for the poet's identification in this stanza and the next.

un homme-cafre: a reference to the black population in South Africa who used to be contemptuously referred to by the whites as "Kaffirs," of which **cafre** is the French equivalent; the term is derived from an Arabic word meaning "pagan."

un homme-hindou-de-Calcutta: a reference to the miserable condition of the Indian population under colonial rule. Calcutta is in the eastern part of India and was noted for the abject poverty of its inhabitants. Note that the French word *hindou* is regularly employed for an Indian, though its strict application is to the Hindu religion.

un homme-de-Harlem-qui-ne-vote-pas: in the thirties when the poem was written, and up until the late fifties, black people were deprived of political and civic rights in most parts of the United States and subjected nearly everywhere in the country to severe racial discrimination. Harlem, the black ghetto of New York and the center of black life in America, thus becomes an appropriate reference for the deprived and oppressed black population with which the poet's people in many ways share a common historical condition; this he dwells upon a little further on in the poem (see stanza 42).

l'homme-famine, l'homme-insulte, l'homme-torture: the racial minorities singled out for mention by the poet are seen as incarnations of the states to which they are reduced, in order to emphasize the sense of outrage which runs through the poet's account of the injustices and atrocities visited upon them.

un homme-pogrom: another reference to the historical experience of the Jews, as a parallel to that of the black race; **pogrom** is a Russian word for the habitual organized attack on Jewish communities in Czarist Russia; the word has come to have the wider meaning of collective harassment and massacre of minority groups.

un chiot: literally, "puppy"; used here in the general sense of "dog," or animal, and indicating the contemptuous treatment to which racial minorities were liable.

un mendigot: "a beggar"; oppression involves material deprivation and moral degradation.

35.

mais est-ce qu'on tue le Remords, beau comme la face de stupeur d'une dame anglaise qui trouverait dans sa soupière un crâne de Hottentot?

The oppression of minorities and the forms of social injustice which they have to endure, and which the poet evokes in the previous stanzas, represent a pattern of inhumanity in which the atrocities that often accompanied colonial conquest stand out prominently; whole populations were decimated, as in the case of the Hottentots, an ethnic group in South Africa, referred to here. The systematic extermination of native populations as a method of colonial conquest is a theme which Césaire was later to develop in *Discours sur le colonialisme*, in which he cites numerous examples of the brutality with which the French established their colonial empire in Africa and other parts of the world.

le Remords: this refers in the first place to the poet, suddenly assailed by remorse for his flight from homeland; the remorse turns out, however, to be salutary (hence **beau**), since it leads to a serious examination of conscience on his part, a process we are soon to witness (see stanzas 39 and 40).

la face de stupeur d'une dame anglaise: the simile links the poet's personal dilemma with the moral issue involved in colonialism: the English lady who is forced to recognize that her life is based on oppression represents what Césaire regards as the collective responsibility of the white races for the crimes committed in their name during colonial conquest, a responsibilty which remains as a kind of historical skeleton in their racial cupboards. Compare the following lines from *Cadastre*: *Arrêtez cet homme innocent: / il porte mon sang dans son nez, il colporte mon sang dans ses souliers*. Note too that the simile derives from the poetic manner of Lautréamont, whose influence on Césaire was determinant.

36.

Je retrouverais le secret des grandes communications et des grandes combustions. Je dirais orage. Je dirais fleuve. Je dirais tornade. Je dirais feuille. Je dirais arbre. Je serais mouillé de toutes les pluies, humecté de toutes les rosées. Je roulerais comme du sang frénétique sur le courant lent de l'oeil des mots en chevaux fous en enfants frais en caillots en couvre-feu en vestiges de temple en pierres précieuses assez loin pour décourager les mineurs. Qui ne me compendrait pas ne comprendrait pas davantage le rugissement du tigre.

Et vous fantômes montez bleus de chimie d'une forêt de bêtes traquées de machines tordues d'un jujubier de chairs pourries d'un panier d'huîtres d'yeux d'un lacis de lanières découpées dans le beau sisal d'une peau d'homme j'aurais des mots assez vastes pour vous contenir et toi terre tendue terre saoule
terre grand sexe levé vers le soleil
terre grand délire de la mentule de Dieu
terre sauvage montée des resserres de la mer avec
dans la bouche une touffe de cécropies

terre dont je ne puis comparer la face houleuse qu'à la forêt vierge et folle que
je souhaiterais pouvoir en guise de visage montrer aux yeux indéchiffreurs des
hommes
il me suffirait d'une gorgée de ton lait jiculi pour qu'en toi je découvre toujours
à même distance de mirage — mille fois plus natale et dorée d'un soleil que
n'entame nul prisme — la terre où tout est libre et fraternel, ma terre

The theme of revolt which underlies and sustains the whole poem now comes to the
fore in this stanza, at the same time that a new and determined accent becomes
noticeable in the poet's language. The stanza itself is made up largely of indirect evocations of the elements through which the poet identifies with the world of nature as
a preparation for his poetic project of universal renewal. The social and moral levels
of his revolt as it begins here to unfold (note the use of the conditional in the verbs)
are thus subsumed within the poetic and the symbolic. The memory of slavery is
brought into prominence in this stanza for the first time; it determines not only a
personal level of experience, expressed as an individual rage in relation to a specific
historical condition, but also a broader consciousness of human suffering: the poet's
expression begins to acquire a prophetic element, thus assuming a universal reference
and dimension.

le secret des grandes communications: the intimate communion with the hidden
energies of the forces of nature envisioned by the poet represents a form of access to a
profound source of strength that he draws upon in order to carry out his mission, one
that is both secular and spiritual.

Je dirais orage: the invocation begins appropriately with the affirmation of the poet's
faith in the power of poetic utterance and develops as a vision of turbulence in
nature - and perhaps in the poet himself—in conformity with his dream of a reordering of the universe itself; the succession of images that make up the invocation in the
first part of the stanza suggests a ritual cleansing, leading to the lyrical statement of
an ideal of rejuvenation, expressed in the phrases **humecté de toutes les rosées** and
enfants frais further in the stanza.

Je roulerais comme du sang frénétique: despite the conditional tense of the verb,
the simile presents in the form of a dramatic statement the poet's active being as his
senses become heightened and his whole frame is enlivened for the momentous
enterprise he sets out to accomplish.

le courant lent de l'oeil des mots: the poet situated at the very heart of language, in
an implied metaphor related to "the eye of the hurricane" (alluded to in **orage**), the
calm center of a general commotion of the elements; the phrase thus expresses the
poet's dissatisfaction with ordinary language which, in its normal reference to everyday experience, proves inadequate for the poet's task and needs to be given a new
impulse to render it capable of conveying the scope and intensity of the poet's emotions and vision. The images that follow enact this process of the poet's quickening
of language and prepare us for Césaire's development of a poetics of revolt stated
more fully in stanzas 65 and 66.

en chevaux fous: the language of revolt as the expression of an indomitable spirit;
the poet's earlier identification with the forces of nature is here given an aggressive
significance through the archetypal symbol of natural force represented by the horse,
a symbol that occurs frequently in Césaire's poetry and finds its most forceful expression in the poem "Les Pur-Sang" (in the volume *Les Armes miraculeuses*), a poem

which opens with the lines: *Et voici par mon ouïe tramée de crissements / et des fusées syncoper des laideurs rêches / les cent pur-sang hennissant du soleil / parmi la stagnation.* Note further that in Haitian Vodun, the devotees are said to be "mounted" by the *loas* when they fall into a trance.

en enfants frais: this image connects with the earlier images of transformation, expressing an ideal of regeneration.

en caillots: i.e., of blood; the phrase may be taken either as an epithet of **enfants**, suggesting a latent state of being as new life begins to be elaborated, or as a complement to **sang**, denoting an essential vitality.

en couvre-feu: besides the revolutionary significance of the poet's expression in its historical and social reference, the theme of revolt which it sustains also implies a state of emergency signified by a curfew in the spiritual order.

en vestiges de temples: the visionary import of the poet's language gives it a sacred quality and relates it to an order of reality which is inaccessible to ordinary experience, hence **pierres précieuses** in the expression that follows, suggesting a quality both distant and difficult to attain, but of an inestimable value. The image recalls both Rimbaud's phantasmagorias in *Les Illuminations* and Mallarmé's habitual metaphorical assimilation of poetry to the essence of jewels.

Qui ne me comprendrait pas...le rugissement du tigre: animal imagery, constituting a whole "bestiary," plays a central role in Césaire's poetics of revolt.

Et vous fantômes: an invocation to the ghosts of the poet's dead slave ancestors who haunt his racial memory; they are called upon to rise from the depths of historical time in order to testify to the cruelties perpetrated against them.

bleu de chimie: in apposition to **fantômes**; the ancestors are recalled by the agency of the poetic word, whose transmuting power constitutes a form of "chemistry" or alchemy (cf. *l'alchimie du verbe* of Rimbaud). The ancestors reappear shaded in the mystical color of blue, endowed therefore with the spectral and supernatural quality of ghosts; there is an obvious element of African belief here.

d'une forêt de bêtes traquées: an allusion to the practice of hunting down runaway slaves like wild beasts; the notation also recalls **des hommes-hyènes et des hommes-panthères** in stanza 33.

des machines tordues: the slaves were broken on machines of torture, some of which are enumerated later in the poem (see stanza 133); note the transfer, for effect, of the epithet **tordues** from the slaves to the instruments on which they were broken.

d'un jujubier de chairs pourries: the meaning of this phrase is that of natural growth perverted; **jujubier** is a tree cultivated in Southern France which produces a red fruit.

d'un panier d'huîtres d'yeux: a precise reference to the atrocities committed by the Nazis during the Second World War in concentration camps where millions of Jews were systematically exterminated and their bodies desecrated in various ways, as in this example of human eyes gathered in baskets like oysters.

d'un lacis de lanières découpées dans le beau sisal d'une peau d'homme: another reference to a form of Nazi atrocity in which human skins were used as vellum to make lampshades or as leather to make shoes; the notation **beau sisal** adds a sardonic tone to this evocation of human depravity.

J'aurais des mots assez vastes pour vous contenir: the poet's testimony is both a comprehensive denunciation of evil in the world and the expression of a universal hope for its containment.

et toi terre tendue: there is a rapid transition here to an intense invocation of cosmic forces which represent the poet's ultimate reference for his project of universal renewal. Césaire's pan-sexualism and tellurism receive here a forceful expression whose general tenor is the profound integration of the poet's consciousness and whole disposition into the animating principle of the cosmic order, as a condition for true poetic expression.

terre grand sexe levé vers le soleil: in most mythologies, the earth, represented as the mother of all creation, is the very embodiment of the feminine principle, while the sun symbolizes the male principle of fecundation; earth and sky thus form the primordial couple.

grand délire de la mentule de Dieu: reinforces the previous line; **mentule** is the male organ, ascribed here to the sun, imaged as sovereign deity, in its copulation with the earth. The overt sexual imagery merges with a vast telluric evocation to suggest the spiritual dimension of the life of the universe.

montée des resserres de la mer: the basis of this image is the deep human intuition, now more or less confirmed by modern science, that all forms of life originated from the sea; the earth itself is figured here as having emerged from the hidden recesses (**resserres**) of the sea, carrying the germ of life which was later to flourish over its vast expanses.

une touffe de cécropies: the milky sap of the cecropia tree, a species of the fig family characteristic of the West Indies, suggests this association of the earth with the tree and by extension with the female principle itself. Césaire's use of the natural environment of his native land in his imagery functions here as a mode of identification, as the lines that follow make clear.

terre dont je ne puis comparer la face houleuse: this is a direct allusion to the poet's island home, in which the movement of the sea, reproduced in the undulating landscape marked by the hills (*mornes*), is an ever-present reality; thus, in this image which recalls the earlier evocation of Martinique in stanza 22, the earth itself takes on the character of the sea and makes one with it in an intimate union of the elements.

forêt vierge et folle: a literal description of a tropical forest, extending the identification of land and sea in the previous line in a somewhat conventional comparison with the rolling vegetation of a tropical scenery to the turbulent waves of the sea. The standard expression **forêt vierge** both denotes the primeval quality of the land evoked and associates its untamed and fierce aspect to the aggressive disposition of the poet. Note also the compaction of the image obtained by the oblique reference to the foolish virgins of the New Testament (Matthew 25.1-13).

que je souhaiterais en guise de visage montrer: the most savage and triumphant aspect of nature becomes symbolic of the poet's stance in his confrontation with an unacceptable order of life.

yeux indéchiffreurs des hommes: specifically of the colonizer, who despite his vaunted science, is presented as being limited in his understanding of the true inner reality of things (cf. **nos vainqueurs omniscients et naïfs** in stanza 119).

il me suffirait de ton lait jiculi: this introduces another evocation of Martinique, in terms of a lyrical ideal, as a promised land; we have here an amplification of previous brief evocations of the island in positive terms; **lait jiculi** is the juice of a tropical plant producing a hallucinatory effect; the image implies the idea of possession in both the sense of the poet being given over to his land in body and soul, and of a mystic union with that land transformed by his vision.

toujours à même distance de mirage: an indication that the Martinique evoked here is indeed symbolic of a poetic ideal.

mille fois...nulle prisme: this phrase in parenthesis refers to **terre**; it describes the poet's vision of his island home restored to a pristine purity. Note the force of the image of light—the island of the poet's vision is bathed in a pure radiance, symbolic both of its physical beauty as a tropical gem and of spiritual illumination.

37.

 Partir. Mon coeur bruissait de générosités emphatiques. Partir...j'arriverais lisse et jeune dans ce pays mien et je dirais à ce pays dont le limon entre dans la composition de ma chair : "J'ai longtemps erré et je reviens vers la hideur désertée de vos plaies".
 Je viendrais à ce pays mien et je lui dirais : "Embrassez-moi sans crainte... Et si je ne sais que parler, c'est pour vous que je parlerai".

38.

 Et je lui dirais encore :
"Ma bouche sera la bouche des malheurs qui n'ont point de bouche, ma voix, la liberté de celles qui s'affaissent au cachot du désespoir".
 Et venant je me dirais à moi-même :
"Et surtout mon corps aussi bien que mon âme, gardez-vous de vous croiser les bras en l'attitude stérile du spectateur, car la vie n'est pas un spectacle, car une mer de douleurs n'est pas un proscenium, car un homme qui crie n'est pas un ours qui danse..."

The theme of return to the homeland on which the whole poem revolves receives explicit statement in these stanzas. **Partir** now suggests the journey back: the memory of his people's plight haunts the deracinated poet who, in his European sojourn, now sees himself as a prodigal son. This inspires his resolution to return to his homeland, as a first step towards both taking up their cause and self-realization. However, this resolve is presented as a youthful impulse, still requiring proper reflection as to its mode of action. The use of the conditional indicates that the project which begins to form in his mind is as yet hesitant, undefined, until his actual arrival, announced in stanza 39, when he reunites with his people and witnesses once again the concrete reality of their lives.

Mon coeur bruissait: the agitation in the poet's mind, which produces a rush of indistinct emotions; **bruissait** is from the infinitive *bruire*, "to make a low confused sound."

générosités emphatiques: his youthful heart is filled with extravagant thoughts of a heroic mission awaiting him; the antithesis between the verb and its complement adds a touch of irony to Césaire's presentation of what seems to him in retrospect to have been his state of mind at the time of the experience he now describes.

j'arriverais lisse et jeune: the verbs here and in the passages that follow are in the conditional tense of reported speech, in the so-called "style indirect libre"; these are the thoughts that fill the poet's youthful imagination. At the same time, there is a connection with **enfants frais** in stanza 36, making for a double suggestion of imagined project and authentic ideal.

je lui dirais; J'ai longtemps erré: phrases which recall the words with which, in the Bible (Luke 15: 18-20), the prodigal son of the parable announces his resolve to return to his father's home.

ce pays dont le limon entre dans la composition de ma chair: a variation in emphatic terms on the theme of the poet's organic attachment to his native land.

Ma bouche sera la bouche des malheurs: this often-quoted passage continues in reality the ironic recall of the poet's state of mind at an earlier time; nonetheless, they do provide a clear statement of the unfolding of his commitment to the cause of his people.

une mer de douleurs: an apt image for the condition of the islands, in which the sea forms an intimate element of the total environment and features as a backdrop to the tragic drama of the population; see stanza 150 for an even more graphic development of this image.

proscenium: a stage platform; complements **spectacle.**

un ours qui danse: as in a circus show; the enumeration which ends on this note is based on a rhetorical device which is a kind of litotes, emphasis by understatement or double negative.

39.

Et voici que je suis venu!
De nouveau cette vie clopinante devant moi, non pas cette vie, cette mort, cette mort sans sens ni piété, cette mort où la grandeur piteusement échoue, l'éclatante petitesse de cette mort, cette mort qui clopine de petitesses en petitesses; ces pelletées de petites avidités sur le conquistador; ces pelletées de petits larbins sur le grand sauvage, ces pelletées de petites âmes sur le Caraïbe aux trois âmes,
et toutes ces morts futiles
absurdités sous l'éclaboussement de ma conscience ouverte
tragiques futilités éclairées de cette seule noctiluque
et moi seul, brusque scène de ce petit matin
où fait le beau l'apocalypse des monstres puis,
chavirée, se tait
chaude élection de cendres, de ruines et d'affaissements

This stanza introduces us to the central section of the poem. Although it occurs well before the passages in which the full import of its meaning is presented—the poet has still to return, in several stanzas that follow, to an earlier state of his experience—it records the decisive factor in the transformation of the poet's consciousness to which the remaining part of the poem is largely devoted and thus in a way anticipates the real "action" of the poem.

De nouveau...devant moi: the poet imagines himself back again in his homeland, confronted once more with the misery of the islands, in which nothing seems to have changed since his departure to Europe. Although the details are presented in practically the same terms as in previous evocations, a new introspective note is introduced as the poet considers afresh the scene of material and moral desolation before him and works through its impact on his mind to its significance for himself.

clopinante: "awkward," "limping"; cf. **sabot inquiet** in stanza 12.

ces pelletées de petites avidités: the demoralized state of the people, whose condition is notable for its great mass (**pelletées**) of limited ambitions which together amount to nothing but rather weaken their impulse to revolt against the white master (**conquistador**); the idea is developed through the rest of the passage by repetition and alliteration, weaving a kind of counterpoint through the evocation.

Caraïbes aux trois âmes: the triple heritage of the West Indies deriving from the indigenous Caribs, Africans, and Europeans. Although the Caribs have been practically eliminated as a distinct racial group, their physical features are still to be seen in people of mixed descent in Martinique and other parts of the West Indies.

absurdités sous l'éclaboussement de ma conscience ouverte: though we have had its development intimated from the very beginning of the poem, the awakening of the poet's consciousness to the tragic situation of his people is depicted here as a sudden explosion of feeling and a sudden access of insight.

éclairées de cette seule noctiluque: in the dark night of the collective alienation (see stanza 18), the poet is alone in his awareness of its true dimensions and its implications; his consciousness is thus the only light in this area of moral darkness; it is likened to the feeble light of a glowworm (**noctiluque**) in the night.

et moi seul: connects with the previous line which it governs by inference; the emphasis is on the momentary separation of the poet from the scene he contemplates and meditates upon; the meditation leads to a self-scrutiny in the rest of this stanza and in the stanza that follows, giving a touch of irony to the extreme self-consciousness displayed by the poet.

brusque scène de ce petit matin: recalls his attitude at the very beginning of the poem, echoed in the refrain; the point is developed in the rest of the passage.

où fait le beau...se tait: the line enacts a drama of self-doubt: as the poet considers the scale of his people's plight and the enormity of the task of deliverance he has set for himself, he begins to entertain doubts about the adequacy of his own powers and of his mental disposition. In this compact image, the principal reference is to the poet himself who is the subject of the phrase **où fait le beau**; he chides himself for his presumption in an immature parading of his powers (as in **je delaçais les monstres** of stanza 1, echoed here in the ironic reference to himself as **l'apocalypse des monstres**, that is, as a kind of heroic slayer of dragons). He realizes that his attitude comes from a superficial understanding of his mission and results in an unsteady resolve which is engulfed like a boat capsizing—indicated by **chavirée**, qualifying **apocalypse**—so that he is reduced to a humiliating silence.

chaude élection...d'affaissement: the somewhat deprecatory tone of the previous line is qualified in this line; though his zeal is momentarily dampened by a sober realization of his present inadequacy, the poet retains the warmth of his enthusiasm, which is compared to the ashes after a fire; the suggestion in the line of an original catastrophe—in the words **ruines** and **affaissements**—applies both to his moral situation as depicted in the stanza and to the general historical situation of his people. We have here another example of Césaire's method: the image of a boat sinking in the previous line is rapidly transformed to that of water poured over burning wood, and its meaning enlarged to suggest a comprehensive moral drama.

40.

— Encore une objection! une seule, mais de grâce une seule: je n'ai pas le droit de calculer la vie à mon empan fuligineux; de me réduire à ce petit rien ellipsoïdal qui tremble à quatre doigts au-dessus de la ligne, moi homme, d'ainsi bouleverser la création, que je me comprenne entre latitude et longitude.

This stanza continues the poet's self-scrutiny, which now takes the form of a soliloquy as he debates within himself the proper scope of his mission in relation to what seems the utter insignificance of his island home in the universal scheme: the heroic adventure he contemplates seems to bear no relation to the meanness and narrowness of this environment, presented here in precise geographical terms. He has yet to achieve a real sense of place secured by an awareness of the meaning to himself and to the world of his island.

empan fuligineux: empan is the "span," the distance between the thumb and the little finger; **fuligineux** means "covered with soot," therefore black; as the black poet considers the span of the fingers on his hand, they describe an arc that resembles the spread of the islands in the Caribbean Sea (see map); it is this limited horizon that he seeks to transcend. The poet's sense of confinement by his island background which inspires this reflection is developed in the next stanza.

ce petit rien ellipsoïdal: i.e., Martinique, which has the shape of an oval (*ellipse*), as is evident from the map.

à quatre doigts au-dessus de la ligne: Martinique lies close to the Equator, between latitudes 14 and 18 degrees North; **doigts** recalls **empan**, and forms with it a uniform scheme of imagery, though it also carries the specific meaning here of "at a little distance from...," as in the colloquial expression *être à deux doigts de...*, "to be close to."

moi homme, d'ainsi bouleverser la création: the presiding idea of the stanza is now given full expression: the poet's understanding of his mission as comprehensive in scope, going beyond the limited boundaries (**latitude et longitude**) of his native island. Although there remains a trace of irony here, implied in the self-questioning of the passage, the tone has become affirmative, leading to the intense aspiration expressed in the next stanza.

41.

Au bout du petit matin,
la mâle soif et l'entêté désir,
me voici divisé des oasis fraîches de la fraternité
ce rien pudique frise d'échardes dures
cet horizon trop sûr tressaille comme un geôlier.

The return of the refrain testifies to the growing awareness that is beginning to take shape in the poet's consciousness, as he moves towards an understanding of the particular relation of his island to the wider historical experience of the race, which he is to state in the next stanza. Here, the desire for a greater destiny, sharpened by his confinement within the narrow limits of his little island and by his acute sense of separation from his own people—of his psychological and moral solitude described earlier in stanza 39—impels him, despite his sense of inadequacy already described, towards a gesture of self-affirmation which would elevate him and his people above the sordid and harrowing circumstances of their lives.

le mâle soif et l'entêté désir: i.e., for a spiritual connection as well for liberation generally. Compare the declaration of "le Rebelle" in Césaire's dramatic poem *Et Les Chiens se taisaient: Je suis un homme de bonne soif qui circule fou autour de mares empoisonnées.*

oasis fraîches de la fraternité: his singularity and his resultant solitude engender the aspiration to a new community of fulfilled individuals.

ce rien pudique: Martinique, which seems to the poet an insignificant place tucked away shyly in a corner of the earth.

frise d'échardes dures: the poet's impatience with his island people whose ways gall him, as one is pricked by thorns (**échardes**), used in particular of those that have got under the skin; **frise**, in apposition here to **rien**, is a word borrowed from architecture and normally designates a sculptured plane in a building (frieze); the **de** is complement of agent. The whole phrase has the meaning of "hedged round with thorns"; thus, there is possibly an indirect reference to the crown of thorns worn by Jesus Christ during his Passion.

cet horizon trop sûr: the idea of confinement running through the stanza now leads to this image of the island as a prison. The poet's horizon is so well defined (**trop sûr**) as to be limiting, and the moral atmosphere within it is so pervaded with an existential fear (hence **tressaille** - consider the signficance of **peurs** in stanza 11) as to breed disaffection between the colonized and the colonizer, the latter pointedly designated as **geôlier**. Note the complex imagery employed by Césaire here. The verb **tressaillir** has two meanings, fused here: in the sense of "to shimmer," as of a distant horizon in the glare of the sun, it forms part of the stream of associations indicated by **oasis** above; in the other sense of "to shiver with fear," there is a transfer of its immediate reference from the colonized subject himself to the colonizer, to suggest a general implication of both parties involved in the colonial relationship in the tensions bred by their uneasy relationship, a key idea in Césaire's analysis of the colonial situation in *Discours sur le colonialisme.*

42.

Ton dernier triomphe, corbeau tenace de la Trahison.
Ce qui est à moi, ces quelques milliers de mortiférés qui tournent en rond dans la calebasse d'une île et ce qui est à moi aussi, l'archipel arqué comme le désir inquiet de se nier, on dirait une anxiété maternelle pour protéger la ténuité plus délicate qui sépare l'une de l'autre Amérique; et ses flancs qui secrètent pour l'Europe la bonne liqueur d'un Gulf Stream, et l'un des deux versants d'incandescence entre quoi l'Equateur funambule vers l'Afrique. Et mon île non-clôture, sa claire audace debout à l'arrière de cette polynésie, devant elle,

la Guadeloupe fendue en deux de sa raie dorsale et de même misère que nous,
Haïti où la négritude se mit debout pour la première fois et dit qu'elle croyait à
son humanité et la comique petite queue de la Floride où d'un nègre s'achève la
strangulation, et l'Afrique gigantesquement chenillant jusqu'au pied hispanique
de l'Europe, sa nudité où la Mort fauche à larges andains.

The poet turns his gaze outward to consider the objective situation of the black
world in its present circumstances of general desolation and historical determina-
tions: the geographical and historical perspectives combine to afford him an enlarged
vision of himself and that of his island, and to establish a wider sense of his identification with the race in its world-wide dispersion. There is a progression of the geographical scene-setting as the poet's vision moves out from his native island to
encompass the entire black world defined by a common historical experience of
domination and exploitation. This stanza represents a forthright statement of the
historical grievance of the black race in modern times, deriving from the common
experience of slavery, colonialism, and racism.

corbeau tenace de la Trahison: this concludes the poet's introspection on a somber
note; as he examines himself and his attitude to his native island and its people, his
alienation seems complete, marking the triumph of his conditioning which leads to a
self-hatred that he comes to realize is a veritable betrayal of his people. The sentiment expressed here is illustrated in the tramway incident recounted later in the
poem (see stanza 99). It is also possible to read **Trahison** here as an anticipation of
the betrayal and imprisonment of Toussant L'Ouverture, soon to be evoked in stanza
44.

Ce qui est à moi: the entire black world as the universe of the poet's ideological and
moral concerns.

dans la calebasse d'une île: a reference once again to Martinique expressed in an apt
image of confinement, with the secondary idea of moral and spiritual disorientation,
represented in the phrase **qui tournent en rond**; **calebasse** (calabash) is a gourd.

l'archipel arqué: the collection of islands (archipelago) in the Caribbean Sea, spread
out like an arc, with the idea also of a tension, as of a bow.

désir inquiet de se nier: cf. **habile à découvrir le point...d'esquive** in stanza 8.

la ténuité plus délicate: the image is based on the geographical position of the
Caribbean islands in relation to the mainland continent; the islands form a half circle separating the Atlantic Ocean from the Caribbean Sea, and seem to serve as a
protective shield for Central America, situated in a thin strip (**ténuité**) between the
two land blocks of North and South America.

et ses flancs qui secrètent pour l'Europe la bonne liqueur: beneath the reference to
the Gulf Stream (see the next note), there is a covert reference to rum, an important
product of the West Indies, which was exported mostly to Europe at the time the
poem was written. There is a suggestion in the word **flancs** (loins) both of maternal
feeling (**anxiété maternelle**) and of the male physical labor involved in the cultivation of the sugar cane from which rum is made. The whole phrase is reminiscent of
Voltaire's celebrated indictment of slavery in *Candide*: "C'est à ce prix que vous
mangez du sucre en Europe."

Gulf Stream: a warm current which flows from the West Indies to the North
Atlantic and has a tempering effect on the climate of Western Europe; this geo-phys-
ical phenomenon is associated with the warming effect of rum.

l'un des deux versants d'incandescence: i.e., the West Indies, which are on the American side of the tropical zone, characterized by the blazing sun (hence **incandescence**), with Africa on the Eastern Atlantic representing the other side of the same zone; the expression alludes to the presence of the black race in the two hemispheres and carries a connotation of the heightened disposition of the race.

l'Equateur funambule vers l'Afrique: a development of the preceding expression: the Equator is figured as a thin line stretching like a tightrope (**funambule**—normally a noun but used here as a verb) between the West Indies and Africa; the notation succinctly establishes the racial and historical connection between the two areas.

Et mon île non-clôture: halfway through the stanza, the poet makes a dramatic return to his point of departure in order to describe a new outward movement, in a progression similar to the earlier evocation; **non-clôture** refers both to the shape of the island (cf. **ellipsoïdal** in stanza 40) and to the fact of its being opened out on all sides to the sea, thus employed as an image both of the poet's point of anchor as well as of an all-embracing vision of the black world expressed in the stanza.

la Guadeloupe fendue en deux: the other French colony in the West Indies at the time the poem was written, with the same conditions (**de même misère que nous**). Guadeloupe, which lies to the north of Martinique and is now, like its sister island, a department of France, is composed in fact of two islands lying closely together, Basse Terre and Grande-Terre; hence the decription here. (See map.)

Haïti où la négritude se mit debout pour la premiére fois: The republic of Haiti, which occupies the Western half of the same island with the Dominican Republic (see map) has a special significance in Césaire's work for the reason stated here. The poem will shortly proceed (in stanzas 44 and 45) to a celebration of the memory of Toussaint L'Ouverture, the hero of the Haitian revolution; meanwhile, the poet presents Haiti here as a symbol of black affirmation associated explicitly with the idea of négritude in this passage. This is the first occurrence of the word, employed in this particular context to designate the black world in its collective aspect and to sum up the meaning of the *tour d'horizon* of this world which the poet undertakes in this section of the poem.

la comique petite queue de la Floride: the State of Florida in the southeastern extremity of the United States is made up of a peninsula jutting out into the Caribbean Sea just north of the Caribbean; on the map it resembles a tail attached to the rest of the union. Florida, like other southern states (mentioned in the next stanza), was notorious for the lynching of blacks; hence the tragic complement **où d'un nègre s'achève la strangulation**.

Et l'Afrique: Africa is presented in this evocation as a lumbering giant caterpillar (**chenille**—the word, normally a noun, is used here as verb), and its people as disarmed and defenceless against colonial exactions which reap a copious harvest (**andains**) of desolation and death. The reference to Africa as the ultimate point of the poet's racial and historical consciousness completes the process, dramatized in this stanza, of the poet's discovery of his personal world of affiliations and enables him to enter fully into his theme in the stanza that follows.

43.

Et je me dis Bordeaux et Nantes et Liverpool et New York et San Francisco
pas un bout de ce monde qui ne porte mon empreinte digitale
et mon calcanéum sur le dos des gratte-ciel et ma crasse
dans le scintillements des gemmes!
Qui peut se vanter d'avoir mieux que moi?
Virginie. Tennessee. Géorgie. Alabama
Putréfactions monstrueuses de révoltes
inopérantes,
marais de sang putrides
trompettes absurdement bouchées
Terres rouges, terres sanguines, terres consanguines.

The poet is now able to speak for his people with all the assurance with which his previous meditation has empowered him. It is significant that he begins in this stanza by presenting the economic aspect of slavery and colonialism as a crucial element of the historical grievance of the black race. The theme of the exploitation of the black man's labor for the development of the Western world recurs constantly in black protest literature; this stanza is representative of this theme which receives an equally somber expression in stanza 134.

Et je me dis...San Francisco: Bordeaux and Nantes in France, and Liverpool in England were the principal European ports involved in the triangular circuit between Europe, Africa, and America through which the economic system based on the slave trade operated; these cities reaped immense prosperity from the trade which, as has been argued by the late Eric Williams in his *Slavery and Capitalism*, laid the basis for the full development of capitalism, especially with relation to banking and finance. New York on the eastern seaboard of the United States and San Francisco on the west coast are mentioned as cities whose development was largely due to the exploitation of cheap labor, especially that of black workers.

mon empreinte digitale: the stamp of the black man's labor in the construction of universal civilization; the singular personal adjective has an obviously collective meaning in this and the lines that follow.

mon calcanéum: i.e., "heel."

et ma crasse...gemmes: a reference to the mines in South Africa where black labor is employed in the physical process of extracting the precious minerals for which the country is reputed and on which its prosperity is based; the line presents an arresting contrast between the miserable condition of the black miners (**crasse**) and the brilliance of the gems which they bring up from the earth, leading to the bitter irony expressed by the line. The resentment contained in this line is more fully expressed by Césaire in the poem "Ex-voto pour un naufrage" in the volume *Soleil cou coupé*.

Virginie etc.: these are the states in the south of the United States where black slaves were concentrated in large numbers and compelled to work on the tobacco or cotton fields organized in extensive plantations; **révoltes inopérantes** refers to the numerous unsuccessful slave revolts which took place in these states, notably that led by Nat Turner; **trompettes bouchées** is a literal allusion to the muted trumpet often used to accompany the blues, the form of black music which in its lyrics and melodic structure captures most poignantly the unhappy condition of the black community in North America.

Terres rouges...consanguines: the fact that the four states mentioned here have a near tropical climate suggests this series of somber evocations; the first term denotes the physical aspect of their soil which is red, as in most parts of Africa; the second extends this meaning to symbolize the tragic experience of its black slaves; and the third provides appropriate emphasis of their common significance for black historical experience. Note, however, that the image of red earth acquires a positive connotation in other contexts, especially in the celebrated passage where Césaire proclaims his négritude (stanza 115).

44.

Ce qui est à moi aussi: une petite cellule dans le Jura,
une petite cellule, la neige la double de barreaux blancs
la neige est un geôlier blanc qui monte la garde devant une prison

45.

Ce qui est à moi
c'est un homme seul emprisonné de blanc
c'est un homme seul qui défie les cris blancs de la mort blanche
(TOUSSAINT, TOUSSAINT LOUVERTURE)
c'est un homme seul qui fascine l'épervier blanc de la mort blanche
c'est un homme seul dans la mer inféconde de sable blanc
c'est un moricaud vieux dressé contre les eaux du ciel
La mort décrit un cercle brillant au-dessus de cet homme
la mort étoile doucement au-dessus de sa tête
la mort souffle, folle, dans la cannaie mûre de ses bras
la mort galope dans la prison comme un cheval blanc
la mort luit dans l'ombre comme des yeux de chat
la mort hoquette comme l'eau sous les Cayes
la mort est un oiseau blessé
la mort décroît
la mort vacille
la mort est un patyura ombrageux
la mort expire dans une blanche mare de silence.

These two stanzas, linked to the previous two by the refrain **ce qui est à moi,** compose a eulogy in heroic and mythic terms to the memory of Toussaint L'Ouverture, already indirectly evoked in the earlier reference to the Haitian revolution. The stanzas are a factual recall of the tragic fate of this significant figure in black history as well as a symbolic presentation of the historical passion of the black race which he embodies; taken together, they contain one of the most moving evocations in the poetry of Césaire. The presentation of Toussaint L'Ouverture's solitary confrontation with death is given dramatic intensity not only by the parallelism which sustains a structure of variations on the single theme of the hero's ordeal but also by the graphic quality of the images: the repetitions, especially the insistence on the words **blanc** and **mort**, and the shifting interplay between these words and the ideas they evoke contribute to the complex of effects which point up the moral implication the poet is at pains to enforce. Césaire was later to document Toussaint's career in his biography

of the Haitian leader published in 1961. The terms in which he characterizes the
subject of his study have a direct bearing upon the poetic evocation we have here:

> Toussaint Louverture est l'une des plus magnifiques forces qui ait jamais jailli des
> profondeurs ignorées d'une race. Pour des raisons que nous ne connaîtrons jamais,
> le Destin a voulu qu'il surgisse de notre peuple.... Phénomène de la nature qui
> dépasse notre faible raison, nos incertaines connaissances. Il reste une surprise et
> demeure inexpliqué.

Césaire's attachment to the figure of Toussaint L'Ouverture is representative of its
hold on the minds of other West Indian writers and intellectuals such as Edouard
Glissant of Martinique and René Depestre of Haiti. It is also of interest to note
Toussaint's impact on the feelings and imagination of his contemporaries in Europe,
as demonstrated by the sonnet dedicated to him by the English poet William
Wordsworth.

une petite cellule dans le Jura: the evocation begins with a piece of scene-setting, in
a precise reference to the fortress of Joux in the Jura mountains in Eastern France
where Toussaint was held under extremely harsh conditions, dramatically presented
in the lines that follow.

la neige la double de barreaux blancs: apart from the descriptive value of this line—
the graphic picture of the bars on Toussaint's prison cell frozen over by the icy
weather—the image of snow prepares for the intense dramatic and symbolic evocation in the next stanza; note also the associations suggested by the play on words and
the alliteration, made more explicit in the next line of this stanza and developed
throughout the next. It is more than likely that the frigid atmosphere and associated
vocabulary of Mallarmé's poem "Le Vierge, le vivace et le bel aujourd'hui" have
exerted a direct influence on Césaire's poetic writing in these two stanzas.

un homme seul emprisonné de blanc: Toussaint's solitude in his snow-bound prison
associated with his stoic acceptance of his impending end.

TOUSSAINT, TOUSSAINT LOUVERTURE: This serves as an anguished apostrophe to the spirit of the great man; the capitalization indicates the heroic and near-
mythic dimension he has assumed in the poet's imagination.

l'épervier blanc: Toussaint's capture and imprisonment were ordered by Napoleon
Bonaparte, whose imperial emblem was the eagle, seen here as a bird of prey in an
image in complete character with theme and setting.

la mer inféconde de sable blanc: the landscape around the fortress presents the desolate prospect of a snowclad wasteland; there is a deliberate reversal here of the conventional association of whiteness with goodness and positive values.

moricaud vieux: "an old black man"; the term **moricaud** is normally pejorative but is
used here positively, to stress the pathos of Toussaint's experience.

les eaux du ciel: the heavens represented as falling, frozen as snow, and Toussaint as
heroically facing up to the cataclysm.

La mort décrit un cercle brillant: like a saint's halo in Christian iconography.

la mort étoile doucement: this both refers to the silent falling of the snow portend-
ing advancing death for Toussaint and develops the implication of an apotheosis in
the previous line: the word *étoiler*, which normally takes an indirect object with the

complement *de*, is used here as an intransitive verb to reinforce the idea of the hero transformed into a constellation at his death, an idea which may have been borrowed from Mallarmé.

cannaie mûre de ses bras: Toussaint's physical frame is represented here in the Caribbean terms of a sugar field (**cannaie**), as a landscape over which a forceful wind of death is blowing; his stoic acceptance of his martyrdom is suggested in the epithet **mûre.**

La mort galope: a reference to "Baron Samedi," arch-spirit of death in the folk mythology of the Haitian peasantry, also evoked for dramatic effect in the final scenes of Césaire's play *La Tragédie du Roi Christophe.* In the syncretic system of the Vodun cult with which this mythology is associated, such a spirit (also called *guédé*) is sometimes represented as mounted on a horse. Note too that death is often portrayed in Western iconography as likewise mounted on a horse; the combined force of the two conventions is used to particular effect here to give a sense of urgency to the drama depicted.

la mort hoquette: the dying rasps of Toussaint; a striking example of transferred epithet.

Cayes: coral reefs in the Caribbean Sea.

patyura: a little animal whose presence is said to presage death, hence **ombrageux.**

la mort expire: this refers primarily to Toussaint himself in another example of transferred epithet; the phrase carries with it, however, an additional force of meaning in its suggestion of a metaphysical dimension to the death of the hero, belying its apparent finality: the **silence** with which the evocation of Toussaint's drama ends may thus be likened to that in Mallarmé's *Hommage* (to Wagner), with the immediate silence of the hero's death represented as the prelude to eternal fame; this significance is stated in the next stanza.

46.

Gonflements de nuit aux quatre coins de ce petit matin
soubresauts de mort figée
destin tenace
cris debout de terre muette
la splendeur de ce sang n'éclatera-t-elle point?

This stanza serves as a coda to the eulogy in the previous two stanzas, a concluding statement on the martyrdom of Toussaint L'Ouverture, of his heroic sacrifice which stands as one of the greatest moments in the somber history of the black race. The poet insists on the transformation of will and consciousness that the example of Toussaint's passion and death achieved for the Haitian people and which he now hopes will remain as inspiration to his own people and the rest of the black race.

Gonflements de nuit: Even in his death, Toussaint represents a promise of life, a welling up of hope in the breasts of his people in the midst of their seemingly impossible situation.

aux quatre points de ce petit matin: the cardinal points, which mark the length and breadth of the land; note the recall of the poem's governing refrain, taken up in the next stanza where it leads to a new movement in its development.

soubresauts de mort figée: Toussaint's death, by making him immortal, has given a surprising turn to history; the poet hopes that it will also presage a movement of mind in his own people, one that will reverse their passive attitude in a new collective will; the oxymoron (combination of contrasting ideas or images), employed here to particular effect, carries the full burden of meaning in the image.

cris debout de terre muette: the same idea; this line, with its variation on the previous one, foreshadows the scene of liberation that is given dramatic representation towards the end of the poem (see stanzas 164 ff.).

47.

  Au bout du petit matin ces pays sans stèle, ces chemins sans mémoire, ces
vents sans tablette.
Qu'importe?
Nous dirions. Chanterions. Hurlerions.
Voix pleine, voix large, tu serais notre bien, notre pointe en avant.

The evocation of Toussaint leads to a new movement in the poem, a new beginning, as it were, marked by the return of the original refrain. The poet begins to discern the revolutionary potential of his people to which he proceeds to give voice in the elaboration of a distinctive mode of expression.

ces pays sans stèle: without their own funeral monuments (**stèle**), testimonies of particular heroes in a glorious history.

Nous dirions etc.: the revolutionary potential of the poetic word which has the power to change the world; as in stanza 36, the poet uses the conditional, to signify that the transformation he wishes to accomplish is still at this stage a project; nonetheless, it is one invested with a personal faith and passion.

48.

  Des mots?
  Ah oui, des mots!
Raison, je te sacre vent du soir.
Bouche de l'ordre ton nom?
Il m'est corolle du fouet.
Beauté je t'appelle pétition de la pierre.
Mais ah! la rauque contrebande
de mon rire
Ah! mon trésor de salpêtre!
Parce que nous vous haïssons vous et votre raison, nous nous réclamons de la
démence précoce de la folie flambante du cannibalisme tenace.

49.

Trésor, comptons :
la folie qui se souvient
la folie qui hurle
la folie qui voit
la folie qui se déchaîne

The polemical intent of the poem is now explicitly affirmed in these two stanzas. The black poet calls into question the values which have been presented in colonial ideology as not only distinctive of Western civilization, but also as normative references for the rest of humanity. For the black poet, however, these values are correlative with colonial oppression and the cultural alienation that is its inevitable consequence; his poetry therefore assumes the character of a formal repudiation of these values. These stanzas provide both an instance of the poet's gesture of refusal and the characteristic modes it involves. Stanza 49 elaborates on the previous one, in a series of verses linked by parallelism into a general statement that provides, as it were, a ground for the poet's movement of negation, developed further in the next two stanzas.

Raison, je te sacre vent du soir: discursive reason, codified in the rules of formal logic, is dismissed by the poet as powerless to provide any significant insights into experience, and recourse to it must therefore appear as an impoverishment of the human mind. (Cf. *Et Les Chiens se taisaient: Le monde assassiné d'ambages, pris dans le filet de ses propres parenthèses*.) The poet's scornful rejection is emphasized by the ironic contrast between the verb *sacrer*, which connotes reverence, and the dismissive complement **vent du soir**, which portends the death of the spirit.

Bouche de l'ordre...corolle du fouet: these two lines continue the tenor of the previous one. For the black poet, Western rationalism, held as the key principle for the orderly organization of thought and of political life, signifies rather the intellectual instrument for the domination and oppression of his race. There is a play on the literal meaning of **corolle**, petals of a flower, used here to depict the strands of the whip commonly used on slaves, but also suggesting the word **corollaire** ("corollary"), a technical term in logic ("entailment"). In the phrase **bouche de l'ordre**, we have an echo of lines from Apollinaire's *La Jolie Rousse*, whose theme captures the pervasive mood of disenchantment with Western civilization in the wake of the First World War from which much of modern expressionism derives.

Beauté...pétition de pierre: a reference to the classical ideal of beauty in Western civilization, represented by Greek art, generally considered to have found its highest expression in stone and marble statues; the black poet rejects this ideal as a universal aesthetic norm, seeing in it rather the expression of an unmoving and lifeless principle. There is an implied contrast to African art, whose more forceful style had gained recognition in the West at the time the poem was written. The phrase **pétition de pierre** both echoes Baudelaire's line "Je suis belle, ô mortels, comme un rêve de pierre" in "La Beauté" and also contains a play on the term *pétition de principe*, a literal translation into French of the Latin *petitio principii*, used in logic to describe an argument that does not advance beyond its premise (in English, "begging the question").

Mais ah! la rauque contrebande de mon rire: note the expressive onomatopoeia: the black poet's subversion of Western values is enforced mainly through the derisive tone of his repudiation of them, given expression in a deliberate infraction of the rules of the master's language. (The same idea is conveyed by the line *trouée de parole dans le gosier d'un bègue* in *Les Armes miraculeuses*.)

mon trésor de salpêtre: the force of the poet's revolutionary project derives from the earth itself; **salpêtre** (saltpeter or potassium) is a mineral explosive compound used in the manufacture of gunpowder.

Parce que nous vous haïssons...cannibalisme tenace: for the strictly polemical significance of this passage, see the remarks in the Introduction, p. lx. Also compare the
following opening lines of the poem "Corps perdu" in *Cadastre*, in which the reference takes on its full meaning as the conversion of an imposed negativity into a principle of strength: *Moi qui Krakatoa / moi qui tout mieux que mousson / moi qui poitrine
ouverte / moi qui laïlape / moi qui bêle mieux que cloaque / moi qui hors de gamme / moi qui
Zambèze ou frénétique ou rhombe ou cannibale / je voudrais être de plus en plus humble et
plus bas / toujours plus grave sans vertige ni vestige / jusqu'à me perdre tomber / dans la
vivante semoule d'une terre bien ouverte.*

démence précoce: "dementia praecox"; a term in medical language for a form of
insanity that afflicts heavy drinkers in the later stages of their addiction, and whose
onset is characterized by violent trembling; **folie flambante** is a rewording of the
same term in ordinary language.

la folie qui se souvient: taken in a literal sense, this line refers to the tenacious
memory of the poet concerning the wrongs endured by his race over the centuries;
the lines that follow reinforce this sense in their expression of the violent response of
the oppressed black subject to his condition. But the glorification of madness in
these lines is also consistent with the creative principles and conceptions of the
human mind embraced by the Surrealists, who placed a premium on abnormal states
of consciousness, including that of insanity, considered as privileged means of insight
and illumination; as André Breton declared, "Ce n'est pas la crainte de la folie qui
nous forcera à laisser en berne le drapeau de l'imagination." This secondary reference
is indicated by **la folie qui voit.**

50.

Et vous savez le reste

51.

**Que 2 et 2 font 5
que la forêt miaule
que l'arbre tire les marrons du feu
que le ciel se lisse la barbe
et caetera et caetera...**

The black poet's rejection of the colonial order and of the cultural values that go
with it, especially Western rationalism, leads him, as a "logical" consequence of his
posture (**Et vous savez le reste**) to embrace an alternative order of values, marked by
the pure irrationalism expressed here. As explained in the notes below, the lines
contain references to the methods employed by runaway slaves for seeking refuge
from their lot, a fact which establishes a formal correspondence between their gesture of refusal and that of the poet. This provides the poet's expression with a basis in
the reality of black experience. Although the poet's words appear as a series of riddles, their meaning becomes comprehensible to those familiar with the system of references from which the poet proceeds to develop, at another level of apprehension,
an autonomous system of counter-values.

Que 2 et 2 font 5: a proposition that seems to go against common sense, but which
has for the poet, attuned to a deeper level of reality, an uncommon truth value.

que la forêt miaule: the animal noises which runaway slaves made as signals to each other gives to the forest a sinister "voice" (cf. **la mort luit...comme des yeux du chat** in stanza 45) which the black poet appropriates for his own expression in order to confound the colonial master.

l'arbre tire les marrons du feu: a precise reference to the practice of runaway slaves who used to hide from their pursuers on treetops; *marron* was the standard word for runaway slave, giving the verb *marronner*. The reference itself is an ironic play on a French colloquial expression, equivalent to the English "pulling chestnuts out of the fire," or, "snatching victory from the jaws of defeat."

le ciel se lisse la barbe: an allusion to the indifference of the Catholic Church to the lot of the slaves, and by extension, that of heaven itself.

52.

> Qui et quels nous sommes? Admirable question!
> A force de regarder les arbres je suis devenu un arbre
> et mes longs pieds d'arbre ont creusé dans le sol de larges sacs à venin de hautes villes d'ossements
> à force de penser au Congo
> je suis devenu un Congo bruissant de forêts et de fleuves
> où le fouet claque comme un grand étendard
> l'étendard du prophète
> où l'eau fait
> likouala-likouala
> où l'éclair de la colère lance sa hanche verdâtre et force les sangliers de la putréfaction dans la belle orée violente des narines.

The opening question is addressed more to the poet himself than to any audience; it provides an occasion for the poet's self-definition in terms that are both historical and symbolic, expressive of an organic connection with Africa (of which the Congo becomes a kind of metonym) and represented in its aspect of a wild and untamed environment—as the expression, therefore, of a natural force appropriate to the recalcitrant and violent mood of his revolt.

je suis devenu un arbre: the fundamental reference of Césaire's vegetal imagery.

de larges sacs à venin: the image here forms part of Césaire's symbolism of aggression elaborated more fully in stanza 66.

de hautes villes d'ossements: the poet's thoughts turn to the death of innumerable black people during slavery and as a result of colonial exactions in Africa; the mention, in the next line, of the Congo, which was the theater of some of the worst colonial abuses, is a pointed reference to these exactions.

un Congo bruissant de forêts et de fleuves: the Congo River Basin is formed by the vast area of Central and Equatorial Africa and is well known for its dense tropical forests and its many rivers; the phrase itself both recalls the collocation in the administrative term **eaux et forêts** and refers back to **forêt vierge et folle** in stanza 36, in an emphatic restatement of the primeval attributes of the poet's landscape of original being.

où le fouet claque: a reference to the exactions visited upon Africans in the Congo Free State established by King Leopold of Belgium in the early years of this century; the abuses committed were so extensive that they provoked an international outcry; they were the subject of André Gide's *Voyage au Congo*, which appeared about the time Césaire's poem was in gestation. Joseph Conrad's fictional depiction of the ravages of Belgian colonialism in the Congo in *Heart of Darkness* also comes to mind.

l'étendard du prophète: the messianic import of colonial revolt: the whip waving over the victims' backs is transformed into the banner of self-liberation in a dramatic reversal of situations, an example of the rhetorical device of prolepsis.

où l'eau fait likouala-likouala: onomatopoeia in an African register, suggestive of turbulent movement and announcing the action in the rest of the stanza. The Likouala is a river in the interior of the present-day Republic of the Congo.

où l'éclair de la colère...narines: the extremely condensed character of the imagery in this passage is due to a complex play of transferred epithets, but the meaning is clear - the justified resentment of the oppressed Africans will lead to a movement of revolt that will purify and renew their collective being; **hache verdâtre** designates the violent but salutary reaction of the oppressed, acting in alliance with a beneficent nature, alluded to in the notation **verdâtre**, which links with the poet's earlier self-indentification with the vegetal realm; **les sangliers de la putréfaction** is a characteristic description of the colonizers, likened to predatory animals - in this case, wild boars - laying waste all before them: they are, however, to be held at bay before being forcefully expelled from the collective body of the colonized. The whole passage is a poetic valorization of revolt as a positive mode of self-assertion.

53.

Au bout du petit matin le soleil qui toussotte et crache ses poumons

This single-line stanza expands on the notation **le soleil vénérien** in stanza 1: the sun is coughing up its infection; the association carries forward the imagery that concludes stanza 52, giving it a cosmic dimension.

54.

Au bout du petit matin
un petit train de sable
un petit train de mousseline
un petit train de grains de maïs

55.

Au bout du petit matin
un grand galop de pollen
un grand galop d'un petit train de petites filles
un grand galop de colibris
un grand galop de dagues pour défoncer la poitrine de la terre

These two stanzas, with their contrasted leitmotifs (**un petit train** in the one and **un grand galop** in the other), require to be taken together; they project a vision of a possible revolt of the West Indian in a development from an evocation of the banal and everyday reality of their lives to an invocation of elemental forces, rising to a crescendo of cosmic proportions; the incantatory style suggests a predication or magical operation, in which the poet wilfully identifies himself with the forces of the universe in his vision of a reordering of the processes of nature and of the entire realm of life.

un petit train de mousseline: designates the female population—see **petit train de petites filles** in the next stanza—in solidarity with their men; **mousseline** (muslin) is light material used by women for clothing.

un grand galop de pollen: marks a natural development, as it were, from the organic image of **grain de maïs** in the previous stanza; in the simultaneous evocation of the subtle process of pollination in the initiation of growth and the externalized strength of the horse, the image depends for its appeal on a sense of the tremendous force of nature in all aspects of its manifestation.

un grand galop...petites filles: a pure oxymoron, employed once again in a dramatic combination of contrasted images for emphasis; the idea here is an amplification of the reference to the role of women in the previous stanza, and amounts to a poetic valorization of the feminine principle associated with procreation and renewal of the species.

un grand galop de colibris: **colibri** is the Caribbean term for *oiseau-mouche* (hummingbird), a brightly plumed bird with a long sharp beak with which it sucks flowers and also protects itself. A prominent feature of the Caribbean fauna and flora, it functions in Césaire's poetry primarily as a central symbol of his native land in its natural aspect and, in poetic terms, of its aggressive potential and thus as a kind of personal tutelary or totemic animal for the poet (see **l'oiseau qui savait mon nom** in stanza 64, and also the invocation in stanza 106). This significance of the bird is made clear in Caliban's song in the third act of Césaire's *Une Tempête* which contains the line: *l'incisif colibri au fond d'un corrole s'ejouit*.

un grand galop de dagues...la terre: this line expresses in a forceful metaphor the idea of a redemptive act of aggression linked to the normal processes of nature; in the same way that the tilling of the earth for sustenance is both a violation of nature and a necessary human need, the recourse to violence by the oppressed appears as a spiritual imperative; in both cases, a harmony with nature is restored at a higher level.

56.

douaniers anges qui montez aux portes de l'écume la garde des prohibitions

This stanza marks another transition in the poem. We are now to be presented with a catalogue, running over the next five stanzas, in which the poet details the negative qualities attributed to the African and, by extension, the black race, in the colonial ideology; this stanza serves, in an apostrophe addressed to the white man, as a preface to the catalogue whose deliberately sarcastic and ironic tone in the poet's rehearsing of its elements is intended to underline the self-serving character of the denigration of Africa and the black race which it purveys.

douaniers anges: the phrase is a transformation of a line from Apollinaire's poem "Arbre" in which the "naive" painter, Le Douanier Rousseau is referred to as *ange*; the reference is given a negative turn here in a kind of antiphrasis presenting the colonial master as an evil angel, the diabolical embodiment of repression, mounting guard - in both a literal and metaphoric sense—at the very borders of the collective life of the people; connect this phrase with **larbins de l'ordre** in stanza 1 and **la rauque contrabande de mon rire** in stanza 48.

aux portes de l'écume: a particularly expressive image denoting Martinique—and by extension the whole of the Caribbean area—habitually associated with the sea in the more positive references of the poem and seen here as the gateway to the open expanses of the waves; the image dwells on the folly of the colonizer in presuming to maintain any form of control (**la garde des prohibitions**) over this natural element of Caribbean life. There is possibly an oblique reference here to the ineffectual attempt to control the distribution of alcohol and the government's intrusion upon private lives in the United States during the era of Prohibition.

57.

je déclare mes crimes et qu'il n'y a rien à dire pour ma défense.
Danses. Idoles. Relaps. Moi aussi

58.

J'ai assassiné Dieu de ma paresse de mes paroles de mes gestes de mes chansons
obscènes

59.

J'ai porté des plumes de perroquet des dépouilles de chat musqué
J'ai lassé la patience des missionnaires
insultés les bienfaiteurs de l'humanité.
Défié Tyr. Défié Sidon.
Adoré le Zambèze.
L'étendue de ma perversité me confond!

The mood of self-recrimination in these three closely linked stanzas is of course affected, and the tone sarcastic; the terms are those by which Africans were denigrated in the colonial ideology.

Danses. Idoles. Relaps: The usual "charges" against the African and, by extension, the black race, which in Western discourse have often taken the form of objections to the modes of cultural and spiritual expression of the continent, considered incompatible with the norms of civilization; **relaps** means "heresy"; the sense here is of a deviation from an accepted norm which thus places one outside the pale of consideration.

J'ai assassiné Dieu: an allusion to the phrase "Dieu est mort" derived from the writings of the German philosopher Nietzsche and the Russian novelist Dostoevsky; the ironic intent of the allusion is evident from the connection of this phrase with **Moi aussi**, which precedes it, and from the rest of the passage.

dépouilles de chat musqué: the ceremonial garb made of animal skin often worn by the officiating priest in African religious rituals; **chat musqué** is a kind of antelope.

Défié Tyr. Défié Sidon: Tyre and Sidon were commercial ports of great importance to ancient Phoenicia; the black poet, aware of their significance for Western historiography, takes his cultural distance from these references inculcated into him by his colonial education.

Adoré le Zambèze: the Zambesi River in Southern Africa. African religion has been disdainfully termed "animism" by Western anthropologists who consider it merely a worship of natural phenomena—a river, in the present allusion—to which the natives are supposed to attribute a soul; such a procedure cannot, therefore, in their view, qualify as a genuine form of religion, which implies the abstract idea of divinity.

L'étendue de ma perversité me confond: this sums up the very basis of the indictment of the African in the colonial ideology which denies the very humanity of the race. The strong charge of irony in this line is based on the rhetorical device of antiphrasis, stating the opposite of what one intends.

60.

Mais pourquoi brousse impénétrable encore cacher le vif zéro de ma mendicité et par un souci de noblesse apprise ne pas entonner l'horrible bond de ma laideur pahouine?

The poet's dissident mood is further expressed in this stanza in which he assumes the negative image foisted on the black race both as a form of counter-attack, underlined by irony, and as a mark of strength appropriate to his revolt.

brousse impénétrable: the expression serves both as an irritated expletive and as an indirect statement of the poet's cultural allegiances (cf. **forêt vierge** above).

le vif zéro de ma mendicité: the negative image of the black man in the colonial ideology is based on a hierarchy which assigns him the lowest place in the order of being; at best, he stands in need merely of charitable consideration by the white race; **mendicité** recalls **mendigot** in stanza 34.

souci de noblesse apprise: derived from Western culture; the sarcasm of the passage is obvious.

ma laideur pahouine: the Pahouins in this reference are an ethnic group in present-day Gabon, although the lower case indicates a more general meaning of Africans, or someone with negroid features. The phrase **l'horrible bond** to which this serves as complement is intended to carry a sense of menace. Note the way sound values are employed to emphasize the point being made.

61.

> voum rooh oh
> voum rooh oh
> à charmer les serpents à conjurer les morts
> voum rooh oh
> à contraindre la pluie à contrarier les raz de marée
> voum rooh oh
> à empêcher que ne tourne l'ombre
> voum rooh oh
> que mes cieux à moi s'ouvrent

In another remarkable transition, the black poet now enters his role as a magician of words who employs language to transform the world. The incantatory character of the lines is a further development of the procedure observed in stanzas 54 and 55.

voum rooh oh: a magical formula, sung or chanted.

à charmer les serpents: this is to be taken as an indication of the poet's orphic attributes, his familiarity with and power over the elements of the natural world, even in its most hazardous aspect. Note, however, that snake-charming is more usually associated with India.

à conjurer les morts: as in the recall of the slave ancestors in stanza 36.

à contraindre la pluie: it is often claimed that this can be done by African rainmakers.

à contrarier les raz de marée: the poet claims a power specific to the Caribbean, an area of the world especially subject to sea swells.

à empêcher que ne tourne l'ombre: probably a reference to the situation in Martinique during the Second World War during most of which the island was under the control of the Vichy regime, a situation that Césaire described in the journal *Tropiques* as a period of darkness.

que mes cieux à moi s'ouvrent: the quest for identity in spiritual terms receives here its clearest expression in the poem. Compare the following lines from the poem "Visitation" in *Les Armes miraculeuses*: *pour moi je n'ai rien à craindre je suis d'avant Adam / je ne relève ni du même lion ni du même arbre je suis / d'un autre chaud et d'un autre froid.*

62.

> —moi sur une route, enfant, mâchant une racine de canne à sucre
> —traîné homme sur une route sanglante une corde au cou
> —debout au milieu d'un cirque immense, sur mon front noir une couronne de daturas.

This stanza marks an interlude which presents in three brief evocations the poet's personal relation to the collective experience of the race. A detail from his memory of his childhood is juxtaposed with a distant vision of a captured slave, leading to another statement of his mission as a black poet.

une racine de canne à sucre: the sugar cane is a constant reminder both of the slave past and of the economic bondage of the islands.

corde au cou: the memory of slavery as a theme in the poetry of Césaire is carried by a cluster of images which recur throughout the entire *Cahier* as well as in the rest of his poetry; we have here a characteristic element of this cluster.

une couronne de daturas: **datura** is an extremely poisonous plant. Césaire may also have had in mind here other poisonous plants found in Martinique and known by such local names as *herbe poison, bois-poison* and *oregine*. The use of poison from plants on the white population is a well-attested mode of operation by the black slaves, and is used to great narrative effect by Alejo Carpentier in his historical novel *El reino de este mundo* (*The Kingdom of this World*) based on events in Haiti. The dramatic context here of this notation (**au milieu d'un cirque immense**, which recalls stanza 38) emphasizes its ominous import as a powerful element of the poet's symbolism of aggression.

63.

voum rooh
s'envoler
plus haut que le frisson plus haut que les sorcières vers d'autres étoiles exalta-
tion féroce de forêts et de montagnes déracinées à l'heure où nul n'y pense
les îles liées pour mille ans!

The poet now resumes his incantation on an even more energetic note, invoking once again the primal forces of nature for the restoration of his native land to a pristine state of grace.

plus haut que le frisson: aspiration to the sacred delirium of possession, even in its most intense manifestation.

vers d'autres étoiles: the poet's aspiration for himself and his people to a new destiny, a new orientation of being; a restatement of the same idea as in **que mes cieux à moi s'ouvrent** (in stanza 61), but given here a clearly collective significance.

des montagnes déracinées à l'heure où nul n'y pense: this links with **les volcans éclateront** in stanza 4, in a specific reference to the sudden eruption of Mont Pélé.

les îles liées pour mille ans: this is less the expression of a political ideal than a prophetic vision of the restored spiritual harmony of the West Indian, founded on an organic compact of the people of all the islands in the Caribbean; the millenary character of the entire passage is rendered literally by this phrase upon which it converges.

64.

voum rooh oh
pour que revienne le temps de promission
et l'oiseau qui savait mon nom
et la femme qui avait mille noms
de fontaine de soleil et de pleurs
et ses cheveux d'alevin
et ses pas mes climats
et ses yeux mes saisons
et les jours sans nuisance
et les nuits sans offense
et les étoiles de confidence
et le vent de connivence

This evocation, expressing a calm and confident vision of restoration and reconciliation with nature, comes as a moment of respite in the turbulent progression of the poem. The note which pervades the series of predications which compose it is more lyrical, due both to the suggestive appeal of the imagery, centered on a female figure, and the use of parallelism and assonances, leading up to the near rhymes of the final lines.

le temps de promission: like the prophet of the Old Testament, the poet foresees a new era of grace for his people; **promission** is a coinage of Césaire's, from the Latin *promitto*, with the meaning of "covenant."

l'oiseau qui savait mon nom: most likely the hummingbird (*colibri*), which would confirm the association noted in stanza 55.

la femme qui avait mille noms: there is probably a conflation here of an ideal image of Martinique with that of the poet's wife, represented as a mythical female figure and celebrated later (in stanzas 112 and 113); also, as a possible extension, the notation might represent Africa in her inscrutable character.

de fontaines de soleil et de pleurs: a new set of attributes for the **femme** referred to in the previous line; she is associated with the positive images of light and water, endowed with a mysterious quality, further emphasized by the terms of her evocation in the next line.

et ses cheveux d'alevin: the female figure is now presented as a sea goddess, with hair made of small fishes (**alevins**); the notation is almost certainly based on the Haitian divinity known as "la Sirène," equivalent to the Yoruba goddess of the sea *Yemoja* ("Mother of Fishes"), also found under this name in the African-derived religions of the Brazilian *candomblé*. The West African concept of "Mammy Water" is a generalized representation of the same figure.

et ses pas...mes saisons: these two lines appear to confirm the multiple associations of the female figure: in their reference to the poet's wife, they indicate a sense of intimate union with a female partner, while in their reference to the poet's native island, envisioned as restored to its true essence, they express the hope of an attachment which will henceforth govern the poet's sensibility.

et les jours...vent de connivence: the parallel structure of these four lines is reinforced by the incidence of associated images of nature; **le vent de connivence** expresses the idea of total integration with the world stated more fully at the end of the poem. (See stanzas 172-74.)

65.

Mais qui tourne ma voix? qui écorche ma voix? Me fourrant dans la gorge mille crocs de bambou. Mille pieux d'oursin. C'est toi sale bout de monde. Sale bout de petit matin. C'est toi sale haine. C'est toi poids de l'insulte et cent ans de coups de fouet. C'est toi cent ans de ma patience, cent ans de mes soins juste à ne pas mourir.
rooh oh

Once again, the poet abandons his ideal vision to confront the present reality of his situation. This stanza is thus a restatement of the historical resentment of the black race, which the poet presents in a counter-accusation of the oppressor in order to establish the justification for the poetic revolt that is to receive earnest elaboration in the stanzas that follow.

qui écorche ma voix?: the poetic voice exacerbated into a raucous cry; link with **la rauque contrebande de mon cri.**

Mille pieux d'oursin: sea urchins (**oursins**) are typical of the Caribbean Sea; they have skins covered with tiny prickly protrusions like needles (**pieux**). Note the aggressive connotation of the image here, which contrasts with its purely exotic appeal in José-Maria Hérédia's "Le Récif de Corail."

sale bout de monde: the continuation of **de petit matin** indicates that the reference is to the Martinique of the opening stanzas.

cent ans de coups de fouet: poetic term for a whole historical epoch; in reality, slavery lasted in the Western hemisphere on the whole for some four hundred years.

cent ans de ma patience: the word **patience** is employed here in its etymological meaning of "suffering" (Latin *patior*, from which both English and French have derived the cognate word "passion" in the sense of a long endurance). The Christian idea of the Passion relating to the suffering of Jesus Christ, culminating in his crucifixion, is based on this meaning. See also stanza 115, where the phrase is dramatically transformed in the poet's triumphant declaration of his négritude.

66.

> nous chantons les fleurs vénéneuses éclatant dans des prairies furibondes; les ciels d'amour coupés d'embolie; les matins épileptiques; le blanc embrasement des sables abyssaux, les descentes d'épaves dans les nuits foudroyées d'odeurs fauves.

The evocation of general disorder in the natural world, to which this stanza is devoted, represents another sequence in the projection of the poet's apocalyptic vision associated with his poetic revolt and the symbolism of aggression through which it is channeled.

fleurs vénéneuses: this forms with **couronne de daturas** in stanza 62 and similar references to poisonous plants a distinctive schema parallel to the more positive vegetal imagery within the poem's symbolic structure.

matins épileptiques: denoting extreme agitation, and possibly a carry-over of the idea contained in the reference to **démence précoce** in stanza 48.

le blanc embrasement des sables abyssaux: the creative disorder projected by the poet will reach right down and set aflame the very depths of the sea (**abyssal** is an adjective for "pertaining to the sea bed"); **blanc embrasement** suggests the white incandescence of an extremely hot agent; its conjunction with **sables abyssaux**, denoting the imagined sandy wastes that form the sea bed, is another instance of an oxymoron, in an image which emphasizes the collaboration of all the elements of the natural world in the poet's project of revolt.

les descentes d'épaves...d'odeurs fauves: the poet now transforms the picture of the wretched condition of new slaves as they disembark from the ships that have brought them across the ocean from Africa into an image of strength; the newly arrived slaves are famished and physically degraded, they are described as **épaves**, a word that is often used in this figurative sense in common parlance in French to refer to human beings who have degenerated into a miserable condition. They still have clinging to them the strong smell of the hold in which they have been confined like wild animals (**odeurs fauves**) during the voyage from Africa. Their animal-like state is enlisted in this passage to create an appropriate concluding image of ferocity for the stanza.

67.

Qu'y puis-je?

Il faut bien commencer.

Commencer quoi?

La seule chose au monde qu'il vaille la peine de commencer :

La Fin du monde parbleu.

These five lines, though separated in the text, form a kind of dramatic monologue and are to be taken as composing a single stanza. The final emphatic line, with its truculence set off by the colloquialism **parbleu**, sums up the import of the previous stanza.

68.

Tourte
ô tourte de l'effroyable automne
où poussent l'acier neuf et le béton vivace
tourte ô tourte
où l'air se rouille en grandes plaques
d'allégresse mauvaise
où l'eau sanieuse balafre les grandes joues solaires
je vous hais

The poet now turns once again to his island home in order to present yet another evocation of the moral limitations of his people; his disgust is expressed in terms which also combine with his disaffection towards Western civilization in its moral and spiritual effects.

l'effroyable automne: autumn and the associated image of twilight have a negative connotation in Césaire's poetry; compare Baudelaire's "Chant d'automne" with its similar association of autumn as harbinger of death.

l'acier neuf; béton vivace: symbols of industrial civilization; for the poet, soul-deadening.

où l'air se rouille: suggested by **acier** above; the browning of vegetation in autumn is also implied in the image, in a surprising reversal of the conventional associations of autumn with peace and bounty; for the black poet, the onset of this season indicates a comprehensive degradation of nature, projected in the strongly negative images in the rest of the stanza.

l'eau sanieuse: a strong image of revulsion, in keeping with previous references to the unhealthy condition of the island; **sanieuse** derives from *sanie*, fluid from a running wound or infection.

69.

on voit encore des madras aux reins des femmes des
anneaux à leurs oreilles des sourires à leurs bouches
des enfants à leurs mamelles et j'en passe :
ASSEZ DE CE SCANDALE!

Against the background of the physical and moral misery of his Caribbean environment which the poet has so extensively explored in his previous evocations, he now presents the typical postcard image with which the outside world is most familiar, in order to stress its falsehood. The capitalization of the violent exclamation at the end of the stanza is a mark of strong indignation at the deceit involved in the projection of this exotic and happy image of Caribbean life.

des madras aux reins des femmes: the "national" costume of the Martinican woman is made up of a long colorful dress with a scarf of fine madras material wound around the waist; contrast with the more realistic image of the rustic female in stanza 8.

des sourires à leurs bouches: cf. **une vieille vie menteusement souriante**, stanza 3.

70.

Alors voilà le grand défi et l'impulsion
sataniques et l'insolente
dérive nostalgique de lunes rousses,
de feux verts, de fièvres jaunes!

This stanza derives its essential inspiration from the Surrealist cult of the diabolic, as a negation of accepted Western values.

dérive nostalgique de lunes rousses: in the superstitions of the French peasantry, the appearance of a reddish moon is considered an ill omen; note the way in which color notations beginning here run through the rest of the stanza.

de feux verts: green traffic lights, giving free passage to the violent impulses of the poet in his revolt.

de fièvres jaunes: suggestive of both a feverish excitement and a deadly intent.

71.

En vain dans la tiédeur de votre gorge mûrissez-vous vingt fois la même pauvre
consolation que nous sommes des marmonneurs de mots

72.

Des mots? Quand nous manions des quartiers de monde, quand nous épousons
des continents en délire, quand nous forçons de fumantes portes, des mots, ah
oui, des mots! mais des mots de sang frais, des mots qui sont des raz-de-marée
et des érésipèles et des paludismes et des laves et des feux de brousse, et des
flambées de chair, et des flambées de villes...

These two stanzas are linked, the one developing from the other. They provide the clearest statement of the nature and purpose of the black poet's relation to language. Stanza 72 breaks into two distinct parts: the first details the objective of the poet's revolt, which assumes a cosmic dimension; the second, introduced by the echo of the leading phrase (**des mots**, encountered earlier at the head of stanza 61 and expanding on it) presents a new conception of poetic language as a negation of the conventional diction and accepted classical norms, in order to stress its revolutionary potential. The poet's concern with the elaboration of a poetics appropriate to his dissident mood finds here perhaps its most forceful statement, achieved in the special tension produced throughout the stanza by the play of sonorities and, in particular, of effects of alliteration.

marmonneurs de mots: a reference to the prejudiced conception of African languages as being no more than inarticulate stutter, less than human.

des continents en délire: a variation on and expansion of the idea of **fièvres jaunes** above.

de fumantes portes: as in an assault on a stronghold, here cultural and symbolic.

des mots de sang frais: recalls **en caillots** in stanza 36; there is the same atmosphere here as in the previous stanza of general turbulence in the universe.

érésipèles: an inflammation of the skin.

flambées de villes: a forceful complement to **fumantes portes**; setting an enemy's town on fire is the ultimate act of human violence.

73.

Sachez-le bien :
je ne joue jamais si ce n'est à l'an mil
je ne joue jamais si ce n'est à la Grande Peur

The preceding evocations of disaster culminate in this stanza in which the black poet proffers a menace of epochal dimensions. The psychological mechanism involved here is well brought out in Césaire's self-presentation in the opening line of the poem "Marche des pertubations" in *Cadastre*: *un coup de foudre en menace sur le front le plus intouchable du monde*. Note the symmetry of this stanza, with the second line reinforced in the third by the parallelism.

l'an mil: in early Christendom, the year 1000 A.D. was considered a fateful one which would see the end of the world, as predicted in the Book of the Apocalypse (Book of Revelation); this belief determined a widespread fear throughout Europe as the year approached. The reference to this phenomenon of the European subconscious is intended to make clear the apocalyptic significance of the black poet's revolt.

74.

Accommodez-vous de moi. Je ne m'accommode pas de vous!

75.

Parfois on me voit d'un grand geste du cerveau,
happer un nuage trop rouge
ou une caresse de pluie, ou un prélude du vent, ne vous tranquilisez pas outre mesure:

The poet's familiarity with nature in its multiple manifestations enables him to move at ease within its entire realm and to adopt various postures appropriate to his requirements; the emphasis remains on his harnessing of its forces to sustain his revolt.

76.

Je force la membrane vitelline qui me sépare de moi-même,

77.

Je force les grandes eaux qui me ceinturent de sang

Though each of these two lines, thrown into sharp relief by the preceding stanza, stands separately, they are closely linked in their import: taken together, they provide a profound insight into the wrenching nature of the process of disalienation upon which the poet is engaged; the organic imagery contributes to the force of the statement.

membrane vitelline: the membrane which serves as a protection for the fetus in the mother's womb; the imagery implies the idea of a willed rebirth of the poet to his essential self.

Je force les grandes eaux...sang: this line reinforces and expands the field of allusion of the image in the preceding line: **les grandes eaux** refers in the first instance to the water in which the fetus floats in the womb and which is normally released at the onset of labor; this "breaking of water" is associated with blood, which accompanies delivery of the baby. This meaning is extended into a recollection of the forced voyage of the poet's ancestors across the ocean and their subsequent ordeal under slavery, events which are the immediate historical antecedents to his present existence and consciousness, and represent therefore the genesis of his historical being. The poet both assumes and counters this significance in this and the previous line.

78.

C'est moi rien que moi qui arrête ma place sur le dernier train de la dernière vague du dernier raz-de-marée

The Surrealist cast of this stanza is evident, but it carries a precise meaning in consonance with the dictates of the poet's revolt: the poet takes his stand (**ma place sur le dernier train**) at the threshold of a new order as he directs an energetic movement *against* an old order.

79.

C'est moi rien que moi
qui prends langue avec la dernière angoisse
C'est moi oh, rien que moi
qui m'assure au chalumeau
les premières gouttes de lait virginal!

A development of the previous stanza with a reversal leading to a transition.

avec la dernière angoisse: the pathetic character of the poet's situation reflected in the very tone of his language.

qui m'assure au chalumeau: a characteristic use of vegetal imagery to signify regeneration; **chalumeau** is a reed; a secondary reference to the musical instrument (woodwind) makes the word an allusion to poetry.

lait virginal: cf. **lait jiculi**, stanza 36 and note.

80.

Et maintenant un dernier zut :
au soleil (il ne suffit pas à soûler ma tête trop forte)
à la nuit farineuse avec les pondaisons d'or des lucioles incertaines
à la chevelure qui tremble tout au haut de la falaise
le vent y saute en inconstantes cavaleries salées
je lis bien à mon pouls que l'exotisme n'est pas provende pour moi

The entire environment of Martinique is embraced in this evocation in natural terms, terms which also suggest its ambiguous status and upon which the poet centers his own situation, involving a double movement of rejection and affirmation.

un dernier zut: a deliberate crassness of expression, giving vent to the poet's intense irritation.

au soleil: which dominates the tropical landscape but is here presented as effete compared to the poet's burning temperament (**il ne suffit pas à soûler ma tête trop forte**); this negative transformation of the image of the sun is uncharacteristic and is reversed later in the poem with great effect in the exultant lines of stanza 118.

à la nuit farineuse: the tropical night studded with stars, giving the sky a powdery aspect.

pondaisons d'or des lucioles incertaines: the indirect allusion to the stars suggests this picture of glowworms as they twinkle at night like suspended points of gold; the epithet **incertaines** indicates the intermittent action of the insects who therefore seem hesitant, unsure of themselves.

à la chevelure...falaise: a realistic depiction of the Martinican scenery with the palm trees, whose fronds stand out like hair waving in the strong wind, lining the elevated beaches at the seaside.

cavaleries salées: violent gusts of wind carrying sea-spray through the vegetation; connect with **la grand'lèche hystérique de la mer** in stanza 22.

je lis bien...pour moi: the very pulse of the poet beating in unison with the agitated landscape he has just presented assures him that he is not made for facile exoticism, qualified here as **provende** (animal feed) a term which carries the further suggestion of domestication. The poet's rejection of the exotic image of his native land leads to a half-ironic, half-triumphant affirmation of his true essence, implied all along in the strong quality of the imagery employed throughout the stanza.

81.

Au sortir de l'Europe toute révulsée de cris
les courants silencieux de la désespérance
au sortir de l'Europe peureuse qui se reprend et fière
se surestime
je veux cet égoïsme beau
et qui s'aventure
et mon labour me remémore d'une implacable étrave.

This stanza complements the phrase **Partir** in stanza 37 with which the poet announces his intention to return to his native land. It is not only a statement of his disaffection towards Europe, which determines his movement outwards in a gesture of revolt, but also of a focused quest for fulfilment.

toute révulsée de cris: a reference to the profound malaise in Europe, marked in particular by the outbreak of the Spanish Civil War in 1936, an event that was to quicken the pace of events leading to the Second World War; **les courants de désespérance** and **l'Europe peureuse** refer to the general sense of apprehension, amounting to despair, about the approaching general conflict. Cf. Senghor's *Hosties noires* for a similar reference to events of the day.

qui se reprend et fière se surestime: a comment on the spiritual arrogance of Europe, undermined by events just alluded to; this phrase prepares the even more forthright irony of **maîtres omniscients et naïfs** in stanza 119.

je veux cet égoïsme beau: a positive attachment to the collective self, in contrast to what the poet sees as the neurotic nationalism and collective narcissism displayed during the 1930s in European mass movements of the fascist kind.

et qui s'aventure: "which is daring"; first, in the sense of challenging the colonial order, and further, capable of moving towards new perspectives of the self and of being.

et mon labour: the ploughing here is primarily psychological, the tremendous effort of the mind involved in the process of disalienation, which immediately calls up from the depths of the poet's consciousness the memory of slavery—also suggested by **labour** taken in the physical sense—elaborated upon in the next stanza.

d'une implacable étrave: the dogged movement of the slave ship's prow (**étrave**) as it cuts its way through the sea transporting the Africans into captivity, evoked as symbolic of an implacable historical destiny. The latter sections of the poem enact a symbolic reversal of this image, first in stanzas 127-29 and more forcefully in stanzas 162-67.

82.

Que de sang dans ma mémoire! Dans ma mémoire sont des lagunes. Elles sont couvertes de têtes de morts. Elles ne sont pas couvertes de nénuphars. Dans ma mémoire sont des lagunes. Sur leurs rives ne sont pas étendus des pagnes de femmes.
Ma mémoire est entourée de sang. Ma mémoire a sa ceinture de cadavres!
et mitraille de barils de rhum génialement arrosant nos révoltes ignobles, pâmoisons d'yeux doux d'avoir lampé la liberté féroce

This stanza contains perhaps the most dramatic evocation in the poem of the memory of slavery, which represents one of the central themes of Césaire's poetry. The evocation here connects directly with that in stanzas 111 and 112 (see notes infra).

Dans ma mémoire sont des lagunes: It is possible to read here a play on the word **lagunes** to mean *lacunes*, blanks in the poet's racial memory as a Caribbean whose distinctive history begins with slavery; the gap between this history and the earlier African existence of the race is appropriately described as being filled with only the harrowing memory of suffering and death; the tragic hold of this experience upon the poet's consciousness is conveyed in the stanza by the repetition of **mémoire** with its varied complements, and **entourée de sang** which functions as an insistent refrain.

têtes de morts: a double reference to those who died during the great crossing of the ocean and to the skull and crossbones banner of pirate ships, to which the poet assimilates the slave ships.

nénuphars: waterlilies, which are round and white like skulls but have conventional romantic associations; the poet insists rather on the stark truth of the historical reality recalled by his memory.

Sur leurs rives...pagnes de femmes: the notation here continues the bitter irony of the preceding phrase. In her commentary on *Cahier* in the Collection "Comprendre" (p. 66), Lilyan Kesteloot has suggested that this image is a reminiscence from Césaire's reading of *L'Ame nègre* by Maurice Delafosse, where the same image occurs in an extract, in a French translation, from the Pular (Fulani) epic *Silamaka et Poulorou*, an extract that describes the scene of a great massacre during a war; the image apparently stuck in Césaire's mind, to reappear in this passage which evokes an epochal conflict between Europe and the black race.

ceinture de cadavres: of the poet's forebears.

et mitraille de barils de rhum: this recalls **Les Antilles dynamitées d'alcool** in stanza 2, to which it gives a historical extension; the poet's anguished scrutiny of history takes in the record of failed revolts, which he attributes to the disabling effect of alcohol cunningly supplied in liberal quantities by the white masters to the slaves in order to weaken their resolve.

pâmoisons d'yeux doux: cf. **les paupières en pétales de rose** in stanza 25; **pâmoison** (substantive of the verb *se pâmer*, "to swoon") denotes the false sense of rapture induced by drink.

d'avoir lampé la liberté féroce: *lamper* is to drink excessively; the sense of the verb is transferred here, with the suggestion that the people are so absorbed in the consumption of alcohol that they are diverted from the pursuit of their true objective of liberation, which they can only dream of.

83.

(les nègres-sont-tous-les-mêmes, je-vous-le-dis
les vices-tous-les-vices, c'est-moi-qui-vous-le-dis
l'odeur-du-nègre, ça-fait-pousser-la-canne
rappelez-vous-le-vieux-dicton :
battre-un-nègre, c'est le nourrir)

A recitation of some of the standard prejudices of the whites concerning the black Caribbean population; this recalls stanza 16, cast in the same form.

84.

autour des rocking-chairs méditant la volupté
des rigoises
je tourne, inapaisée pouliche

This short stanza is a graphic representation of the master-slave relationship. The picture presented is that of the slave master seated in the rocking chair fondling a bundle of whips (**rigoises**) in a sadistic anticipation (**méditant la volupté**) of their use on the slave. The picture is completed by the slave prancing around the master like a colt (**pouliche**); the poet turns his identification with the slave thus reduced to the level of a domestic animal into an expression both of an immediate colonial resentment and of a larger existential frustration (**je tourne, inapaisée pouliche**).

85.

Ou bien tout simplement comme on nous aime!
Obscènes gaiement, très doudous de jazz sur leur excès d'ennui.
Je sais le tracking, le Lindy-hop et les claquettes.
Pour les bonnes bouches la sourdine de nos plaintes enrobées
de oua-oua. Attendez...
Tout est dans l'ordre. Mon bon ange broute du néon.
J'avale des baguettes. Ma dignité se vautre dans les dégobillements...

The scene changes to a contemporary image of the black man as entertainer and comic figure, an image propagated by films and theater shows in the years between the two world wars when black music began to come into vogue. The poet's primary preoccupation here is with the derogatory and condescending character of this image and its ideological implications. But the stanza also contains a severe moral addressed to the black people themselves for their acquiescence in the image thus projected and in the general decadence it subserves.

comme on nous aime!: antiphrasis, with ironical intent.

très doudous de jazz: the phrase combines a typical French West Indian word, **doudous** (meaning "dear one" and used as an adjective), frequently to be heard in the lyrics of music from the region, with the North American English term for black music.

sur leur excès d'ennui: an allusion to the role played by some white writers and artists in the promotion of the Harlem Renaissance: the poet implies that very often, these writers and artists were merely projecting their fantasies upon the black people they identified with, as a form of diversion from their inability to cope with their own neurosis.

le tracking, le Lindy-hop, les claquettes: forms of black American dancing associated with jazz in the inter-war years. "The Lindy-hop" is named after Carl Lindbergh, whose solo flight in 1927 across the Atlantic from St. Louis, Missouri, to Paris made aviation history; **claquettes** is tap dancing.

nos plaintes enrobées de oua-oua: a reference to the muted trumpet (**sourdine**) used to accompany the blues (alluded to here in **nos plaintes**); the poet's rejection of the black image connoted by the reference is indicated by the derisive onomatopoeia. Cf. Senghor's "A New York" for a more neutral reference .

Tout est dans l'ordre: the ironical tone carries a hint of menace.

Mon bon ange broute du néon: the apparent recognition of the black man's artistic gifts serves merely as a distraction from the reality of his oppression in white society; coming after the preceding phrase, this carries an even more ominous overtone.

J'avale des baguettes: the stereotype of the black man as performer of cheap stunts; the **baguettes** here are the drumsticks in the jazz ensemble, but the word also carries a secondary sense of French bread, with a suggestion of the popular image of the black man as an indolent element in Western industrial society, as a passive consumer.

Ma dignité...dégobillements: the demeaning effect of the black man's acceptance of a condescending image of himself; **se vautre** has the connotation of complacency, while the complement **dégobillements** ("vomit") carries with it a strong suggestion of sad resignation to a degraded situation.

86.

> **Soleil, Ange Soleil, Ange frisé du Soleil**
> **pour un bond par delà la nage verdâtre et douce des eaux**
> **de l'abjection!**

The poet's aspiration to intensity of life is expressed in this characteristic invocation to the sun, the central image of force.

Ange frisé: the sun personified in racial terms with curly hair (**frisé**).

pour un bond: the wish is for the muscular strength of a wild animal such as the tiger (see stanza 36); **bond** here gives added meaning to the previous occurrence of the word in stanza 60.

la nage verdâtre et douce: a compacted image, integrating the suggestion of muscular effort in **bond**; the idea is that the poet will swim clear, *beyond* the **eaux de l'abjection** to clean water, an agent of renewal anticipated in **douce**, which qualifies **la nage verdâtre**, an image with which it is thus directly associated; for the latter, cf. **hache verdâtre**, stanza 52.

87.

> **Mais je me suis adressé au mauvais sorcier. Sur cette terre exorcisée,**
> **larguée à la dérive de sa précieuse intention maléfique, cette voix qui crie,**
> **lentement enrouée, vainement, vainement enrouée,**

88.

> **et il n'y a que les fientes accumulées de nos mensonges — et qui ne répondent pas.**

A brief return in these two connected stanzas to the despondent mood of earlier passages, expressing the poet-prophet's profound dejection at the lack of response from his people to his vision; he has to reckon with the customary passivity of his people, recognizing at the same time that their unwillingness to respond to his exhortations and to make an effort towards their liberation is an immediate consequence of their conditioning by history.

mauvais sorcier: an African turn to the poet's expression; the context provides the meaning.

cette terre exorcisée: in keeping with the preceding phrase, Martinique seen as a land "exorcised" of the demon of revolt by the Christian church; the point is made again with **ceux qu'on domestiqua et christianisa** in stanza 108.

larguée à la dérive: disoriented; the adjective qualifies **terre**, taken here for the people cut adrift from any moral or spiritual moorings.

ses précieuses intentions maléfiques: of justified revolt, hence both **précieuses** and **maléfiques**.

cette voix qui crie: of the poet, in his enforced role of the prophet "crying in the wilderness."

les fientes accumulées: literally "compacted dung," a strong metaphor for the abject self-deception (**mensonges**) of the people.

89.

Quelle folie le merveilleux entrechat par moi rêvé au-dessus de la bassesse!
Parbleu les Blancs sont de grands guerriers
hosannah pour le maître et pour le châtre-nègre!
Victoire! Victoire, vous dis-je : les vaincus sont contents!
Joyeuses puanteurs et chants de boue!

The mocking tone of this inverted homage to the white conqueror combines a sardonic accent of irreverence with a deep feeling of resentment and indignation.

le merveilleux entrechat: a variation on **bond**, this time with the definite sense of a graceful step in a dance (**entrechat** is a technical term for a particular movement in Western ballet); the contrast between the poet's high aspiration and the reality he is confronted with is emphasized by the two opposed movements in the line.

les Blancs sont de grands guerriers: the whites represented in "native" terms; note the capitalization employed for ironic emphasis.

le châtre-nègre: agent of emasculation in the broadest sense.

les vaincus sont contents: the ultimate self-negation of the alienated black; observe, however, the note of irony which persists.

chants de boue: a deliberate use of bathos setting off the sarcasm of the entire passage.

90.

Par une inattendue et bienfaisante révolution intérieure, j'honore maintenant mes laideurs repoussantes.

This stanza announces the transformation of consciousness within the black poet, a process that constitutes the essential movement of the poem, and whose full development we are shortly to witness.

mes laideurs repoussantes: cf. **laideurs pahouines** of stanza 60.

91.

A la Saint-Jean-Baptiste, dès que tombent les premières ombres sur le bourg du Gros-Morne, des centaines de maquignons se réunissent dans la rue "De Profundis",

92.

dont le nom a du moins la franchise d'avertir d'une ruée des bas-fonds de la Mort. Et c'est de la Mort véritablement, de ses mille mesquines formes locales

(fringales inassouvies d'herbe de Para et rond asservissement des distilleries)
que surgit vers la grand'vie déclose l'étonnante cavalerie des rosses
impétueuses. Et quels galops! quel hennissements! quelles sincères urines!
quelles fientes mirobolantes! "un beau cheval difficile au montoir!" — "Une
altière jument sensible à la molette!" — "Un intrépide poulain vaillamment
jointé!"

Et le malin compère dont le gilet se barre d'une fière chaîne de montre,
refile au lieu de pleines mamelles, d'ardeurs juvéniles, de rotondités authentiques, ou les boursouflures régulières de guêpes complaisantes, ou les obscènes
morsures du gingembre, ou la bienfaisante circulation d'un décalitre d'eau
sucrée.

These two stanzas form an interlude consisting of a descriptive passage in which the
poet presents a typical scene at the horse fair in his native island and then, in the
stanza that follows, draws the moral as it applies directly to himself and to the collective situation which he represents. Stanza 91 gives us the setting, followed in stanza
92 by a description of the horse fair, with a close-up of one of the dealers and an
account of their fraudulent practices. Note the picturesque tone of the description,
despite its negative implications which the poet clearly insinuates in the parallel,
implied throughout the passage, between the miserable condition of the horses being
traded and that of the people.

la Saint-Jean-Baptiste: June 24, St. John the Baptist's Day in the Catholic calendar,
in which each day of the year is devoted to a saint.

Gros Morne: north of Fort-de-France, the capital of Martinique (see map).

maquignons: "horse dealers"; the word has a pejorative connotation in French, much
like "horse-trading" in English.

"De Profundis": the opening words of a Latin chant in the Catholic liturgy for the
dead.

des bas-fonds de la Mort: the name of the street "De Profundis" ("out of the
depths") is not only appropriate to the gloomy setting of the scene about to be
described; it also recalls to the poet his previous evocations of the material and moral
misery of the island.

fringales inassouvies d'herbe de Para: this refers to the horses which are being traded; as they are fed only on coarse elephant grass (**herbe de Para**), their constant need
for food cannot be satisfied (**fringales inassouvies**).

rond asservissement des distilleries: refers to the men and carries the obvious sense
of their addiction to alcohol (with a play on the familiar expression *être rond*, "to be
tipsy").

rosses impétueuses: the famished horses (**rosses**) suddenly acquire a semblance of
life as they are led out into the open ground; their excitement is described in the
exclamatory passages that follow.

"un beau cheval difficile au montoir!": this and the other expressions in quotation
marks are the cries of the dealers proclaiming the quality of their horses; there is the
suggestion that this is just how a slave dealer might advertise the humans he is sell-
ing.

altière: "proud": attributing to the horse a human quality.

molette: "spurs."

vaillamment jointé: "nobly built."

une fière chaîne de montre: fière is a transferred epithet; the horse dealer proudly sports on his waistcoat (**gilet**) a chain attached to a watch in its pocket.

refile: from the slang term *refiler*, "to fob someone off with something," to pass off something fake as genuine.

au lieu de: this adverbial phrase marks a parenthesis in the construction of the passage; the three epithets that follow fall within the parenthesis, so that the verb **refile** has as its complements the list of terms beginning with **ou les boursouflures régulières**, terms which describe the various ways in which the horses are specially doctored before their sale.

pleines mamelles...rotondités authentiques: these are the authentic qualities which the horses are supposed to have, in contrast to the false ones induced by the practices of the dealers as described in the next section.

boursouflures régulières: the horses are artificially bloated by being deliberately stung with wasps; *boursouflé* is an adjective used for a puffed-up face.

gingembre: they are also fed on ginger to produce the same effect.

décalitre d'eau sucrée: another method of treating the horses so as to give them a false air of well-being; **décalitre** is ten liters.

93.

> Je refuse de me donner mes boursouflures comme d'authentiques gloires.
> Et je ris de mes anciennes imaginations puériles.
> Non, nous n'avons jamais été amazones du roi du Dahomey, ni princes de Ghana avec huit cents chameaux, ni docteurs à Tombouctou Askia le Grand étant roi, ni architectes de Djenné, ni Madhis, ni guerriers. Nous ne nous sentons pas sous l'aisselle la démangeaison de ceux qui tinrent jadis la lance. Et puisque j'ai juré de ne rien celer de notre histoire (moi qui n'admire rien tant que le mouton broutant son ombre d'après-midi), je veux avouer que nous fûmes de tout temps d'assez piètres laveurs de vaisselle, des cireurs de chaussures sans envergure, mettons les choses au mieux, d'assez consciencieux sorciers et le seul indiscutable record que nous ayons battu est celui d'endurance à la chicotte...

The scene he has just described is now employed by the poet to characterize the inauthenticity of life in the colonial situation, one that makes for false values which distort the personality of the colonized (the theme is elaborated upon in stanza 173). The complement to his refusal of this state is his quest, stated in ironic terms here, for roots in an authentic African past. The poet's interrogation of that past implies not so much a simple identification with a legacy, imagined as heroic and illustrious, as an embittered reflection on the historic fall of the black race and its disastrous consequences, a reading confirmed by the four stanzas that follow. The sense of achievement in the past which the stanza initially evokes comes, therefore, to be dramatically and poignantly set against a sober recognition of the harsh reality of the present with which the poet has to contend. The stanza thus gives expression to a historical consciousness that is both complex and ambiguous.

Et je ris: a recourse once again to the device of antiphrasis; both the language and the context establish the ironic tone here.

amazones du roi du Dahomey: female warriors in the ancient African empire of Dahomey, with its capital at Abomey, now part of the Benin Republic; their historical role forms the background to the action in Paul Hazoumé's epic novel, *Doguicimi*.

princes de Ghana: of the ancient West African empire of Ghana, which was established in the early Middle Ages and flourished for some four centuries, and after which the modern state, formerly called The Gold Coast, is named.

docteurs à Tombouctou: Timbuktu, on the River Niger, was an outstanding intellectual center in the Middle Ages; the city is still in existence.

Askia le Grand: King of the African kingdom of Songhai from the late fifteenth to the early years of the sixteenth century; he is reputed to have made a pilgrimage to Mecca, accompanied by an impressive retinue of courtiers and servants.

architectes à Djenné: this city, situated in present-day Mali, was the seat of a famous university in the Middle Ages.

Mahdis: Islamic religious leaders in a holy war.

qui tinrent jadis la lance: the warriors (**guerriers** in the previous sentence).

le mouton broutant son ombre: an image of the limited mental horizon attributed to the black race in the colonial ideology.

d'assez consciencieux sorciers: another element of the stereotype of the African.

chicotte: "whip."

94.

> Et ce pays cria pendant des siècles que nous sommes des bêtes brutes; que les pulsations de l'humanité s'arrêtent aux portes de la négrerie; que nous sommes un fumier ambulant hideusement prometteur de cannes tendres et de coton soyeux et l'on nous marquait au fer rouge et nous dormions dans nos excréments et l'on nous vendait sur les places et l'aune de drap anglais et la viande salée d'Irlande coûtaient moins cher que nous, et ce pays était calme, tranquille, disant que l'esprit de Dieu était dans ses actes.

The stanza details, in a tone of bitter recrimination, the objective dehumanization and ideological devaluation of the black race during slavery, and its enduring effects of demoralization, restated in accents that express their firm hold upon the poet's consciousness.

ce pays: i.e., Europe, whose writers developed the racist ideology which denied a human quality to members of the black race, considered as worth no more than animals (**bêtes brutes**); it was in this way that slavery and colonial exploitation were rationalized.

négrerie: a variation on the pejorative term **négraille** employed earlier (stanza 10); the word, first used by Césaire in the title of his article in *L'Etudiant Noir*, has animal associations (on the pattern of *écurie*, horse stable).

fumier ambulant: literally, in the sense referred to in stanza 97 (**ça fait pousser la canne**), and metaphorically, as in the familiar expression.

et l'on nous marquait au fer rouge: a reference to the practice of branding slaves with hot iron, like cattle and horses.

l'aune de drap anglais: the slaves were considered a commodity to be bought and sold, comparable to such items on the market as a piece of English cotton material; **aune** is a unit of measure formerly used in France, equivalent to 1.2 meters, or just over a yard.

l'esprit de Dieu: the calm conscience with which the inhumanity of slavery was generally accepted in Europe despite Christian teaching of the brotherhood of mankind; the specific reference here is to theological arguments, based on the biblical story of Ham, that were frequently invoked as justification for slavery.

95.

Nous vomissure de négrier
Nous vénerie des Calebars
quoi? Se boucher les oreilles?
Nous, soûlés à crever de roulis, de risées, de brume humée
Pardon tourbillon partenaire!

96.

J'entends de la cale monter les malédictions enchaînées, les hoquettements des mourants, le bruit d'un qu'on jette à la mer...les abois d'une femme en gésine...des raclements d'ongle cherchant des gorges...des ricanements de fouet...des farfouillis de vermine parmi des lassitudes...

The references to the African past now prompt a recall in these stanzas of the immediate historical conditions of slavery and a reenactment of the agony endured by the slaves during the Middle Passage. The stanzas provide a further indication that the memory of slavery remains with the poet as a profound psychological experience; the recall of the Middle Passage develops here into an evocation of the nightmarish atmosphere of the slave ship as it takes the slaves across the sea into captivity; the dramatic quality of the evocation brings out the pathos and full horror of the voyage. It is of considerable interest to observe that, in the second chapter of his memoirs entitled *The Interesting Narrative of Olaudah Equiano* published in London in 1789, the eighteenth-century African writer, otherwise known as Gustavus Vassa, provides an account of his personal experience of the Middle Passage in terms that are almost identical with Césaire's poetic rememoration in these stanzas.

vomissure de négrier: a graphic image of the slaves, dirty and ragged, spilling out from the fetid hold of the slave ships like vomit (cf. **les descentes d'épaves** in stanza 66).

vénerie des Calebars: the victims of slavery were often hunted like animals for capture; **vénerie** is the art of hunting ("venery"); **Calebars** evokes the hold of the ship (cale) in which the slaves were confined like wild animals (bêtes brutes in the previous stanza), as well as Calabar, the coastal town in Southeastern Nigeria which was a major slave depot.

soûlés à crever de roulis: the violent roll (roulis) of the slave ship makes the slaves, who are packed like cargo in its hold, constantly dizzy; this distant experience is recreated by the poet as an immediate sensation.

risées: in the two senses of light wind and mockery of the slavers.

brume humée: the sickening effect of the stagnant air which the slaves are forced to breathe in the packed holds of the ships.

J'entends: the poet's imagination continually haunted by the tragic events of the past he recalls.

les malédictions enchaînées: of the slaves held in chains; another instance of transferred epithet.

hoquettements: "death gasps"; the same word used earlier to describe Toussaint L'Ouverture's death.

le bruit d'un qu'on jette à la mer: dead or sick slaves were thrown into the sea during the voyage.

les abois: in the sense both of animal-like baying from distress and of being trapped (être aux abois).

ricanements: links with risée above. In this and similar passages evoking slavery (e.g., stanza 75), Césaire attributes to the slave masters a sadistic disposition both as a matter of historical fact and as a polemical device which lends dramatic interest to his presentation.

farfouillis: a state of extreme commotion; the word is coined by Césaire from the slang verb farfouiller, "to create confusion."

parmi des lassitudes: the plural emphasizes the general character and extensiveness of the state of weariness of the slaves.

97.

Rien ne put nous insurger jamais vers quelque noble aventure désespérée.
Ainsi soit-il. Ainsi soit-il.
Je ne suis d'aucune nationalité prévue par les chancelleries
Je défie le craniomètre. Homo sum etc.
Et qu'ils servent et trahissent et meurent
Ainsi soit-il. Ainsi soit-il.
C'était écrit dans la forme de leur bassin.

A parody of racist ideas concerning the black race, in the same tone of antiphrasis as in previous passages.

Ainsi soit-il: i.e., "Amen," which echoes l'esprit de Dieu in stanza 94 above.

d'aucune nationalité: colonial subjects were denied political rights and were there-fore not recognized as full members of the community of nations; the phrase has a further resonance as an expression of the poet's sentiment of exile in the world.

Je défie le craniomètre: the reference is to the instrument designed by Dr. Gall, a German scientist, for measuring the size of skulls in animal and human fossils in the comparative study of the development of the brain, further developed in Europe by another German, Blumenbach, and by the Frenchman Broca, and in the United States by Morton. From these studies, it was concluded that features such as the shape of the skull, "facial angle," and size of the brain were significant factors in the development of intelligence in humans; the implication was further drawn that the supposed racial and cultural inferiority of Africans and other non-Western peoples was inborn, genetic.

Homo sum etc.: Latin for "I am a man"; the phrase is a quotation of the first part of a celebrated sentence spoken by a character in the play *The Self-Tormentor* by the comic playwright Terence. The rest of the original sentence (marked here by **etc.**) runs: *humani nihil a me alienum puto* ("and I consider nothing that is human foreign to me"). The fact that Terence was an African writing in the context of Roman colo-nialism must be considered to give a special meaning to Césaire's echo of his words here.

la forme de leur bassin: bassin is the pelvis. The phrase takes up the actual words of Arthur Gobineau, a nineteenth-century French writer who, in his *Essai sur l'inégalité des races*, argued the inequality of the races on the basis of a supposed correlation between physical characteristics and mental traits; drawing extensively on the writ-ings of the scientists whose activity is designated by **craniomètre** above, Gobineau employed biological arguments to sustain the theory of a congenital inferiority of the black race in particular. The original sentence runs: "Le caractère de l'animalité empreint dans son bassin lui impose sa destinée." The preceding line, **Et qu'ils ser-vent...meurent**, expressive of the attitude of the white supremacists to the black race, offers an ironic comment on the social and moral implications of Gobineau's words.

98.

Et moi, et moi,
moi qui chantais le poing dur
Il faut savoir jusqu'où je poussai la lâcheté.
Un soir dans un tramway en face de moi, un nègre.

This stanza dramatizes the poet's confrontation with the negative image of his race in colonial ideology, an image that comes to life, as it were, in the person of a fellow black and brings home to him the extent to which he has internalized this image. The stanza thus signals a moment of self-recognition, in the widest sense of the term.

le poing dur: suggesting the mere striking of an attitude; the vehemence of the poet's previous protestation on behalf of his race contrasted to his actual response in a real situation, whose details he is about to recount.

99.

C'était un nègre grand comme un pongo qui essayait de se faire tout petit sur un banc de tramway. Il essayait d'abandonner sur ce banc crasseux de tramway ses jambes gigantesques et ses mains tremblantes de boxeur affamé. Et tout l'avait laissé, le laissait. Son nez qui semblait une péninsule en dérade et sa négritude même qui se décolorait sous l'action d'une inlassable mégie. Et le mégissier était la Misère. Un gros oreillard subit dont les coups de griffes sur ce visage s'étaient cicatrisés en îlots scabieux. Ou plutôt, c'était un ouvrier infatigable, la Misère, travaillant à quelque cartouche hideux. On voyait très bien comment le pouce industrieux et malveillant avait modelé le front en bosse, percé le nez de deux tunnels parallèles et inquiétants, allongé la démesure de la lippe, et par un chef-d'oeuvre caricatural, raboté, poli, verni la plus minuscule mignonne petite oreille de la création.

C'était un nègre dégingandé sans rythme ni mesure.

Un nègre dont les yeux roulaient une lassitude sanguinolente.

Un nègre sans pudeur et ses orteils ricanaient de façon assez puante au fond de la tanière entrebâillée de ses souliers.

La misère, on ne pouvait pas dire, s'était donné un mal fou pour l'achever.

Elle avait creusé l'orbite, l'avait fardée d'un fard de poussière et de chassie mêlées.

Elle avait tendu l'espace vide entre l'accrochement solide des mâchoires et les pommettes d'une vieille joue décatie. Elle avait planté dessus les petits pieux luisants d'une barbe de plusieurs jours. Elle avait affolé le coeur, voûté le dos.

Et l'ensemble faisait parfaitement un nègre hideux, un nègre grognon, un nègre mélancolique, un nègre affalé, ses mains réunies en prière sur un bâton noueux. Un nègre enseveli dans une vieille veste élimée. Un nègre comique et laid et des femmes derrière moi ricanaient en le regardant.

Il était COMIQUE ET LAID,
COMIQUE ET LAID pour sûr.
J'arborai un grand sourire complice...
Ma lâcheté retrouvée!
Je salue les trois siècles qui soutiennent mes droits
civiques et mon sang minimisé.
Mon héroïsme, quelle farce!
Cette ville est à ma taille.
Et mon âme est couchée. Comme cette ville dans la crasse et dans la boue couchée.
Cette ville, ma face de boue.
Je réclame pour ma face la louange éclatante du crachat!...
Alors, nous étant tels, à nous l'élan viril, le genou vainqueur, les plaines à grosses mottes de l'avenir?
Tiens, je préfère avouer que j'ai généreusement déliré, mon coeur dans ma cervelle ainsi qu'un genou ivre.

This stanza enacts, in one of the most vivid passages in the poem, the drama of self-denial that is a troubling component of the alienated consciousness. The incident in the tram—which seems from the precision of the narration to have been taken from Césaire's real-life experience—thus takes us to the very heart of the psychological tension from which the poem proceeds. In its confessional tone, the passage provides another instance of the poet's mood of introspection; his dwelling on the incident he reports thus gives it significance as an acid test of his moral disposition and as the catalyst that impels him toward the expression of an affirmative consciousness.

un nègre grand comme un pongo: the detailed and realistic description that opens with this notation is intended to underline not only the miserable condition of the individual whom the poet finds before him but also his utter lack of self-confidence, despite his impressive bulk, as a result of his demoralization in a hostile environment. His physical appearance and his whole demeanor are deliberately exaggerated, presented in terms of a caricature which conforms to the standard portrait of the black man in the eyes of the white. The word **pongo** which sums up the description is the name of an ethnic group in the Congo, but has often been employed in French to mean "gorilla," in an association between Africans and primates.

Son nez...en dérade: as is well known, Africans usually have broader noses than those of other races; in this case, the man's nose seems to loom so large on his face as to have an existence of its own apart from the rest of his body, hence **en dérade**, "adrift."

et sa négritude: here, simply the fact of his blackness.

mégie: "tanning," the working of leather; an appropriate term for the effect inscribed upon the man's skin and general countenance by his miserable condition, emphasized in the next sentence by the personalisation.

Un gros oreillard subit: in apposition to **Misère** in the previous sentence; the agent responsible for the man's condition presented as a kind of malicious bat (**oreillard**) which has suddenly attacked him (**subit**, used here primarily as an adjective, also functions as an adverb) and left the traces of its claws on his face, as indicated by **cicatrisés**, which also suggests tribal marks.

îlots scabieux: the picture is of random patches of scab-covered lines on the man's face.

cartouche: the word in the singular means a cartoon or sketch, such as is used for pictures; here it conveys the sense of the man's miserable portrait which has been carefully and relentlessly fashioned by a cruel artist; this idea is developed in the rest of the paragraph.

le front en bosse: a reference to prognathism, considered a distinctive physical feature of the black race and indicative of a low level of mental development; the man's protruding forehead is so prominent as to become a deformity; **bosse** is used normally of the hunchback (*bossu*).

la lippe: thick, lower lip, also protruding; a calculated use here of a word which was often employed in French in a pejorative sense, in place of *lèvres*, when speaking of Africans.

raboté: "polished," as of a piece of furniture.

verni: "varnished"; the term belongs more to art than to the craftsman's trade and is thus in line with the presiding idea of portraiture in the passage.

petite oreille: totally out of proportion to the rest of the man's body, making him look ungainly, hence **sans rythme ni mesure** in the next sentence; the comic tone of this passage is indicated by the preceding ironic **mignonne**.

dégingandé: "ungainly."

sanguinolente: refers primarily to the bloodshot eyes of the man; the transferred epithet emphasizes the cause.

ses orteils ricanaient: the man's toes showing through his tattered shoes add to the comic effect of the portraiture; the verb employed here anticipates the snigger of the other passengers in which the poet later joins.

pour l'achever: in the double sense of poverty as an artist (**mégissier**), completing the man's whole portrait and "doing him in."

orbite: "socket of the eye"; the deep sunken eyes of the man add a sinister touch to his bloodshot eyes.

fardée, fard: related to make-up for actors.

chassie: "rheum," liquid from the eye.

entre l'accrochement solide de machoires...joue décatie: there is another suggestion of prognathism in this notation; the picture is one of an absurd discrepancy between the solid jaws and the cheeks shrunken by hunger and misery (**décatie** means "dull, without luster").

pieux: here,"stubbles"; the character is unshaven and therefore presents a somewhat sinister aspect.

affolé le coeur, vouté le dos: the cowed mien of the man; the psychological state linked to the physical.

un nègre hideux: the whole point of the portraiture; the rest of the passage provides variations on this theme through the repetitions.

grognon: with a disagreeable face, as in the expression *figure grogneuse*.

affalé: the man seems to have collapsed into himself.

sur un bâton noueux: a detail that brings out the tense and nervous condition of the poor black man lost in a sea of white faces.

élimée: "threadbare"; the coat the man is wearing is presumably second-hand.

Il était COMIQUE ET LAID: like the Albatross in Baudelaire's famous poem but without the spiritual significance of the mythical bird's exile on earth implied by the French poet; **pour sûr** at the repetition emphasizes the literary reference.

J'arborai un grand sourire complice: thus giving proof of his own complex of self-hatred; the use of the verb *arborer* here is ironic since the word is normally employed for the raising of a flag in a noble cause, while the poet's smile is rather a sign of abject betrayal, of moral defeat.

Ma lacheté retrouvée: the reprise of the moral term indicates the depth of the poet's remorse.

mes droits civiques et mon sang minimisé: **sang minimisé** contrasts with **la splendeur de ce sang** in the "coda" to the evocation of Toussaint L'Ouverture.

Et mon âme est couchée: in the double sense of his having been humbled by the experience he has just narrated, and as a sign of his repentance. (See **Je réclame pour ma face la louange éclatante du crachat** further in the stanza.)

Cette ville, ma face de boue: the phrase needs to be reversed for its concrete meaning: the poet recognizes that he is himself merely a part of the general abjection of his people, in this town in particular.

Alors, nous étant tels: the poet's new identification extends his self-doubt to his own people in these interrogations indicative of a moment of discouragement.

les plaines à grosses mottes de l'avenir?: the future seen as a vast landscape, waiting to be ploughed and sown, therefore rich with promise; the question mark underlines the hypothetical nature, in the circumstances, of the enterprise.

j'ai généreusement deliré: a self-accusation which acknowledges the inordinate measure of his messianic posture but nonetheless stresses the impulse to generosity it involves; the two senses are contained in the adverb.

mon coeur dans ma cervelle: the poet's emotions have overcome his power of reason, preventing him from a realistic appraisal of his situation; in view of the further development of the poem, this is merely a provisional statement of his position, with a slightly ironic tone to it.

genou ivre: complements **deliré** above.

100.

Mon étoile maintenant, le menfenil funèbre.

This single-line stanza announces a new upward movement in the poem, though its development is deferred until stanza 107, where its full meaning becomes clear.

Mon étoile: in the sense of a guiding star giving direction to his new resolve.

le menfenil: a Caribbean variety of the sparrow-hawk, with black plumage, hence **funèbre**; its sinister associations are in accord with the poet's malevolent design.

101.

Et sur ce rêve ancien mes cruautés cannibales:

A forthright statement of the poet's dream of violence as a means to liberation. The repetition of this line in stanza 103, with a slight variation to form another complete stanza, gives it the character of an incantation.

102.

(Les balles dans la bouche salive épaisse
notre coeur de quotidienne bassesse éclate
les continents rompent la frêle attache des isthmes
des terres sautent suivant la division fatale des fleuves
et le morne qui depuis des siècles retient son cri au dedans de lui-même, c'est
lui qui à son tour écartèle
le silence
et ce peuple vaillance rebondissante

et nos membres vainement disjoints par les plus raffinés supplices
et la vie plus impétueuse jaillissant de ce fumier — comme le corossolier
imprévu parmi la décomposition des fruits du jacquier!)

The whole stanza, standing in parenthesis between passages of the poet's reflection on his personal disposition in relation to his mission, develops for a while the import of the preceding stanza in a dream sequence filled with images of destruction which are nonetheless balanced by other images of renewal.

Les balles dans la bouche: the poet's words become weapons of struggle; this is the presiding idea of the title of Césaire's volume *Les Armes miraculeuses*.

les continents rompent...sautent: a reordering of the world at the poet's bidding; the geographical references seem to be specific to the American continent.

et le morne...au dedans de lui-même: cf. **l'incendie contenu du morne** in stanza 13.

qui à son tour écartèle le silence: that is, Martinique, imagined as breaking out of its passivity into articulate revolt.

vaillance rebondissante: in apposition to **ce peuple**; the resilience of the black people in America in the context of a difficult history. Césaire's perspective on this point has been given admirable expression in the following lines from the poem "Mémorial de Louis Delgrès" in the volume *Ferrements*: *Je veux au haut des vagues soudoyant le tonnerre de midi / la négrillone tête désenlisant d'écumes / la souple multitude du corps impérissable.*

nos membres vainement disjoints: a development of the idea of the collective survival of the race in the preceding line, but the immediate reference of the phrase is to the torture (**les plus raffinés supplices**) often inflicted on the slaves as punishment, whose gruesome details are provided further in the poem (see stanza 133).

et la vie...jacquier: a positive reprise of the idea of **fumier ambulant** in stanza 94. The terms of this evocation are based on the vegetation of the West Indies: **corossolier** is a tropical tree common in the West Indies and also found in parts of Africa; its fruit is called "soursop" in Jamaica and by a variety of other names in the English-speaking West Indies, and "sharp-sharp" in West African pidgin (it has no standard English equivalent); **jacquier** is the breadfruit tree, whose fruit was an important source of nourishment for the slaves and is still an item of West Indian diet.

103.

Sur ce rêve vieux en moi mes cruautés cannibales :

The variation to this refrain recalls **dans mes profondeurs** in stanza 1.

104.

Je me cachais derrière une vanité stupide le destin m'appelait j'étais caché derrière et voici l'homme par terre, sa très fragile défense dispersée,
ses maximes sacrées foulées aux pieds, ses déclamations pédantesques rendant du vent par chaque blessure.
voici l'homme par terre
et son âme est comme nue

et le destin triomphe qui contemple se muer
en l'ancestral bourbier cette âme qui le défiait.

Once again, and still in the critical light of the incident in the tram, the poet returns to his self-examination; a mood of disillusionment seems to pervade the passage, though this is soon to be dissipated.

le destin: here, the historic necessity of the poet's personal mission, in opposition to the apparent negative destiny of the black race alluded to in the repetition of **destin** further on in the stanza.

voici l'homme par terre: both the poet and humanity at large.

ses maximes sacrées: confirms the personal and general significance of **homme** above; the poet's personal ideal which he has failed to live up to is extended to the general sense of the humanistic ideal of Western civilization trampled upon by its representatives in the course of slavery and the colonial domination of black people.

ses déclamations pédantesques: the specific reference now is to the humanistic philosophy of the West whose denial in the concrete suffering inflicted upon the black race by the white renders its abstract principles meaningless, making them appear as so much "hot air," as one would say familiarly (**rendant du vent**).

cette âme: that of the poet, who seems unable to rise by an act of moral courage and noble defiance of fate above the general degradation of his people, expressed here as **bourbier**, "quagmire" or general mess.

105.

Je dis que cela est bien ainsi.
Mon dos exploitera victorieusement la chalasie des fibres.
Je pavoiserai de reconnaissance mon obséquiosité naturelle
Et rendra des points à mon enthousiasme le boniment galonné d'argent du pos-
tillon de la Havane, lyrique babouin entremetteur des splendeurs de la servi-
tude.

The apparent attitude of resignation to the general servile lot of his people expressed by the poet here is undercut once again by irony; nonetheless, there remains an ambiguous character to his expression. There is also a sense in which the stanza insists on the disabling effect of such resignation.

la chalasie des fibres: another instance of transferred epithet; it is the whip whose suppleness (**chalasie**), due to the fibers from which it is assembled, will "explore" the slave-poet's back.

Je pavoiserai de reconnaissance: the idea of the slave-poet putting out flags to celebrate his condition confirms the ironic tone of this passage; **obséquiosité naturelle** is of course an ironic echo of a standard prejudice.

Et rendra des points...servitude: Note the inversion in this complex sentence, whose subject is the nominal phrase **le boniment du postillon de la Havane**. This subject is itself qualified in another remarkable instance of transferred epithet by the phrase **galonné d'argent**. The reference is to the practice in Cuba during the slave period of employing a valet (**postillon**) dressed in silver embroidered boots (hence, **galonné d'argent**) whose duty it was to welcome newly arrived slaves with a flowery speech (**boniment**) extolling the attractions of life under slavery (**les splendeurs de la servitude**). The meaning of the line is that the poet's newly found enthusiasm for the servile condition will score points even against the lyrical efforts of this character.

lyrique babouin: the sarcastic intent of the stanza emerges clearly here where the valet is described as a monkey (**babouin**); the epithet **lyrique** applies, of course, to his **boniment**.

entremetteur: hired agent, with a hint here of "pimp."

106.

Je dis que cela est bien ainsi.
Je vis pour le plus plat de mon âme
Pour le plus terne de ma chair!

Note the stucture of this stanza, with its first line, a repetition of that of the previous stanza, serving as a refrain complemented by the parallelism of the two lines that follow; the phrases **le plus plat de mon âme, le plus terne de ma chair** stand in marked contrast to the dramatic development of the poem that begins in the next stanza.

107.

Tiède petit matin de chaleur et de peur ancestrales
je tremble maintenant du commun tremblement que notre sang docile chante
dans le madrépore.

The governing refrain of the poem is now recalled to sum up all the drama of consciousness that has gone before and to register the awakening of mind announced in this stanza. The poet's long exploration of the situation of his people and the process of self-scrutiny which has accompanied it have led to a clarity of vision which enables him to speak out of a new determination of will, in a swell of images that will carry the poem to its central theme of racial exaltation.

je tremble maintenant: the identification of the poet with his native land and his people is now complete; he participates as much in their collective trauma as in the warmth of feeling which animates them.

madrépore: coral reef, symbolizing Martinique and, by extension, the whole of the Caribbean area.

108.

Et ces têtards en moi éclos de mon ascendance prodigieuse!
Ceux qui n'ont inventé ni la poudre ni la boussole
ceux qui n'ont jamais su dompter la vapeur ni l'électricité
ceux qui n'ont exploré ni les mers ni le ciel
mais ils savent en ses moindres recoins le pays de souffrance
ceux qui n'ont connu de voyages que de déracinements
ceux qui se sont assouplis aux agenouillements

ceux qu'on domestiqua et christianisa
ceux qu'on inocula d'abâtardissement
tam-tams de mains vides
tam-tams inanes de plaies sonores
tam-tams burlesques de trahison tabide

The celebration of the black race which begins in this stanza rests on a paradox, that of a people whose apparent lack of accomplishment in Western terms is their very title to consideration in human and poetic terms. There is a deliberate emphasis in this celebration on the technological disadvantage of African civilizations in relation to the European; as pointed out in the Introduction (see pp. li), this forms part of Césaire's romantic valuation of peasant societies and cultures. Moreover, in the specific context of the poem, it is intended to set off the innocence of the black race as the historical victim of the white race in a sharp dichotomy whose polemical thrust is unmistakable: for the poet, the distinctive achievement of the white race, by comparison with the black, has been its use of technology for purposes of conquest and domination. The comparison thus implies a moral superiority of the black race whose collective spiritual endowments the poet proceeds to delineate in this section of the poem.

ces têtards en moi: the germs of his new resolution (**têtards**, "larvae"), ascribed by the poet to his distant African inheritance, his **ascendance prodigieuse**, in which the adjective has a strong sense conveyed by the root noun *prodiges*.

la poudre: gunpowder, whose invention has been attributed to the Chinese; its further development and use in war by Europeans was an important factor in their subjugation of other races.

la boussole: the invention of the compass in the sixteenth century was a decisive technological advance which greatly facilitated European voyages of exploration and was thus an important factor in the expansion of Western imperialism.

ni les mers ni le ciel: an indirect allusion to the invention of the telescope about the same time as the compass; while the latter made possible long voyages across the seas, the former became instrumental in the scientific observation of the heavenly bodies.

le pays de souffrance: in both a physical and spiritual sense; the comprehensive nature of the black experience is given in the phrase **en ses moindres recoins**.

déracinements: a thematic obsession in Césaire's poetry.

agenouillements: in the sense both of submission to a master and going down on one's knees in prayer; the phrase thus establishes a direct link between slavery and the Christian religion, made clear in the line **ceux qu'on domestiqua et christianisa** that follows, which further establishes an association between Christian influence and black docility.

ceux qu'on inocula d'abâtardissement: cf. **échouage hétéroclite**, stanza 17.

tam-tams de mains vides: powerless, without resources; the image is based on the action of drumming with open palms.

tams-tams inanes de plaies sonores: an inversion, in a complex association of images, of **l'affreuse inanité de notre raison d'être** in stanza 3. There is an underly-

ing appropriation here of Mallarmé's phrase "l'inanité sonore" to describe poetry—
apparently futile, but charged with significance—to represent the depressed historical situation of the black race; the transformation of this situation by a revolt provoked by suffering (**plaies**) is announced by the resonant accents of a poetry that
both documents the situation and is a signal of combat.

trahison tabide: another expression for **révoltes inopérantes; tabide** is derived from
the Latin *tabidus,* "wasting away."

109.

> Tiède petit matin de chaleurs et de peurs ancestrales
> **par-dessus bord mes richesses pérégrines**
> **par-dessus bord mes faussetés authentiques**

This short stanza is a restatement of the poet's attitude of refusal already declared in
stanza 109.

richesses pérégrines: acquired from his wanderings, in his exile, and therefore
against the grain of his native endowments, of his true self; the oxymoron **faussetés
authentiques** carries the same idea.

110.

> **Mais quel étrange orgueil tout soudain m'illumine?**

The poet now enters fully into his prophetic role with this announcement of a new
spirit and insight; the dominant image of light suggests a visionary import which is
developed in the stanza that follows. The line is a classical alexandrine, with a dis-
tinctly Racinian ring: it is as if Césaire is replicating the turning point of a classic
drama.

111.

> vienne le colibri
> vienne l'épervier
> vienne le bris de l'horizon
> vienne le cynocéphale
> vienne le lotus porteur du monde
> vienne de dauphins une insurrection perlière
> brisant la coquille de la mer
> vienne un plongeon d'îles
> vienne la disparition des jours de chair morte dans la chaux vive des rapaces
> viennent les ovaires de l'eau où le futur agite ses petites têtes
> viennent les loups qui pâturent dans les orifices sauvages du corps à l'heure où
> à l'auberge écliptique se rencontrent ma lune et ton soleil

In the series of predications that make up this stanza, the poet deploys a structure of
images expressing a personal scheme of values and an apprehension of the essential
life of the universe. His imagination moves from the immediate historical reference
of his theme to embrace different realms of experience to which it relates human
consciousness, in a statement of their profound unity. Furthermore, the progression
towards sexual symbolism, governed by the image of water, suggests his personal inti-

mation of the promise of rebirth as much in a historical sense, associated with the ideological intent of the poem, as in a more general poetic sense of a fundamental process of nature in which the whole of humanity itself is intimately involved.

vienne le colibri: the verb is in the subjunctive, used as an imperative to express an invocation; for the significance of **colibri**, see note to stanza 55.

l'épervier: this stresses the normal association of the eagle with a natural majesty, as opposed to the predatory connotation it receives in the earlier allusion to the imperial banner of Napoleon Bonaparte in stanza 45.

le bris de l'horizon: the poet's aspiration to a wider horizon of experience than that afforded by his immediate situation; **bris** (from *briser*) signifies the act of breaking through an obstacle, of making a breach through an opposing force.

le cynocéphale: a kind of African monkey, with a head resembling that of a dog (see Rudyard Kipling's drawing and explanation in his *Just So Stories*); the animal, which features in ancient Egyptian mythology, is noted for its great strength.

le lotus porteur du monde: the lotus flower has several associations in the various mythologies of the world; the reference here seems to be to the white lotus in ancient Egyptian mythology, symbol of Isis, goddess of the rising sun (hence **porteur du monde**), and is thus also a symbol of dawn (**petit matin**).

vienne de dauphins une insurrection perlière: note the inversion. The initial image in this extended metaphor derives from the characteristic action of dolphins, which, when plunging in water, send up sprays that catch the rays of the sun, making them appear like strings of pearls; the poet presents this gambolling action as an expression of a natural vitality (the dolphin is also a symbol of immortality) and of an irrepressible urge breaking through artificial restraints, hence **brisant la coquille de la mer** in the next line, which also echoes **bris de l'horizon** earlier in the stanza.

un plongeon d'îles: the islands activated, like the dolphins, by a natural energy.

chair morte: the collective body, earlier evoked by the poet in images suggestive of a spiritual death.

la chaux vive des rapaces: in this extremely compressed image, the poet identifies his movement of revolt both with the action of birds of prey (**rapaces**), who pick carcasses of dead bodies clean, and (at the same time) with quicklime (**chaux vives**), used to disinfect corpses on battlefields; **rapaces** suggests a determined aggressiveness and goes with **épervier** above and **sangliers** further in the passage.

ovaires de l'eau: in the same category of images as **têtards**; water is an essential element in the emergence of life, represented here in its elementary manifestation in new creations (**petites têtes**) which also presage the future; the image is further associated with the process of procreation developed in the remaining lines of the stanza.

viennent les loups: symbolic of unbridled instincts and therefore of the free play of natural impulses. This latter connotation links the notation with the Surrealist call for total freedom, especially in the sphere of the erotic; this explains the immediate transition to an erotic meaning in the next line which serves as complement to the notation.

les orifices sauvages du corps: the idea of savage freedom signified by **loups** is given a concrete and positive meaning in an oblique evocation of sexual encounter between male and female; that this encounter is a healthy one is suggested by the word **pâturent**, evocative of pastures and the bearing of fruit in the continuity of the life cycle in nature.

à l'auberge écliptique: the poet proceeds further to give sexual union a cosmic significance (cf. stanza 35); the two partners are the cosmic pair who have met as if in a tryst (**auberge**) and fuse into one another as in an eclipse of the sun and the moon.

ton soleil: the reference is to Suzanne Césaire, whose radiance this notation celebrates; the conventional character of the image is avoided by its function in the extended metaphor of which it forms a part; moreover, it anticipates a second extended metaphor in the following stanza, built around **tes yeux** and reinforced by **ta lumière**.

112.

il y a sous la réserve de ma luette une bauge de sangliers
il y a tes yeux qui sont sous la pierre grise du jour un conglomérat frémissant de coccinelles
il y a dans le regard du désordre cette hirondelle de menthe et de genêt qui fond pour toujours renaître dans le raz-de-marée de ta lumière
(Calme et berce ô ma parole l'enfant qui ne sait pas que la carte du printemps est toujours à refaire)

This stanza reflects with special clarity the Surrealist strain in Césaire's poetry, as much in its style as in the underlying thought on which the imagery is built. The association of the feminine figure with spiritual values was a standard feature of Surrealist poetry, for example in André Breton's L'Amour fou or Louis Aragon's Les Yeux d'Elsa; Césaire extends this feature into a spiritualized eroticism through a celebration of the feminine principle, as in this stanza.

ma luette: the uvula, the bit of tissue at the back of the tongue opening into the throat; the mobilization of the poet's physical resources for a revolt which involves his whole being; cf. the title of the volume Corps perdu.

une bauge: an animal lair; the **sanglier** to which the word refers represents yet another instance of animal force with which the poet identifies.

Il y a tes yeux: the radiance of the poet's female companion, expressed in the image of the sun employed earlier to describe her, is further elaborated in this metaphor, in which the brightness of her eyes is compared to the shimmer of a swarm of beetles (**conglomérat frémissant de coccinelles**); Césaire probably has in mind the particular variety of the beetle dotted with bright spots and sometimes called "ladybird" due to its birdlike wings and fragile aspect.

la pierre grise du jour: i.e., the harshness of day and of experience in general, which the poet's wife helps to alleviate. Note the slight transfer of the epithet **gris** which applies to **jour** as well as to **pierre**, which it directly qualifies.

le regard du désordre: the revolutionary vision, projected beyond the momentary need of revolt towards a better future.

cette hirondelle de menthe et de genêt: the swallow is the harbinger of spring which brings renewal of vegetal life represented here by the varieties of mint plants (**men-**

the) noted for the freshness of their leaves, and broom plant (**genêt**); the plants mentioned have medicinal properties and therefore a wholesome significance.

le raz-de-marée de ta lumière: this variation on a previous notation emphasizes the compelling impact and inspirational role of the poet's wife.

l'enfant: a reference to the child which Césaire's wife was expecting at the time of the composition of the poem; the wider significance of the reference is developed in the next stanza.

la carte du printemps: anticipated in the reference to **hirondelle** above; this sums up the import of the whole stanza: the poet's revolutionary will is directed towards the constant renewal of life and consciousness.

113.

Les herbes balanceront pour le bétail vaisseau doux de l'espoir
le long geste d'alcool de la houle
les étoiles du chaton de leur bague jamais vue
couperont les tuyaux de l'orgue de verre du soir puis
répandront sur l'extrémité riche de ma fatigue
des zinnias
des coryanthes
et toi veuille astre de ton lumineux fondement tirer
lémurien du sperme insondable de l'homme la forme non osée
que le ventre tremblant de la femme porte tel un minerai!

The poet now projects an intense vision of the universal order which is at the same time an affirmation of the primacy of life. The stanza breaks into two parts: the first, governed by verbs in the future tense, is a presentation of this vision in general terms; the second is an invocation, with a more personal implication, in which the profound association of human existence with the natural processes is given a triumphant expression. The movement of the stanza is determined by a rapid succession of images linking the terrestrial and the cosmic and coming to rest on an intimate note to establish the active interaction of various elements that compose the whole realm of being.

Les herbes...houle: there is a conflation of two images in these lines. The first image is that of a broad expanse of land which serves as pasture for cattle (cf. Leconte de Lisle's poem "Midi"); the sinuous movement of the wind sweeping through tall grass in an open field suggests the abrupt transition of this image into that of the open sea and of a ship laden with goods representing the promise of the future (**vaisseau doux de l'espoir**)—and thus presaging a new era of celebration (**le long geste d'alcool**)— riding over the sea's heaving waves (**houle**). A sensuous note runs through the passage, explicitly given in the epithet **doux** and associated with the pastoral tenor of the opening line, and the erotic suggestion of **le long geste** which links the movement of the waves with the idea of fecundity (cf. **le ventre tremblant de la femme** further in the passage.)

les étoiles...verre du soir: the passage brings together images of light and music in a complex association with human experience. Despite its Surrealist cast, the imagery here is built on a simple, almost conventional, comparison of the stars illuminating the heavens to rare gems (cf. **pierres precieuses** in stanza 36): the stars are seen as embossed (**chatons**) in the dome of the sky, forming a circle in a mystic ring (**leur bague jamais vue**); the image thus established then proceeds in a kind of synesthesia from one area of experience to another: the brilliance of the stars cuts through the fading light of the evening, producing the resonance of celestial music, of a truly cosmic Aeolian harp.

repandront sur l'extrémité riche de ma fatigue des zinnias et des coryanthes: a transitional passage; the subject is still **étoiles**; the profusion of the stars in the sky is likened to a flowering of the land which will bring a conclusive end to the poet's ordeal; **extrémité** is a Latinate expression signifying "final phase"; **zinnias** and **coryanthes** are tropical flowers.

et toi: the invocation that follows is addressed to the sun (**astre**), the source of the light and warmth that conditions all life (**lumineux fondement**).

lémurien: the lemur is a species of monkey, small in size and found generally in Africa and parts of Asia. The word as used here by Césaire to refer to the fetus in the mother's womb stresses the relationship in the evolutionary line betwen primates and homo sapiens; it is also an indirect allusion to the Latin *lemures*, in Roman belief spirits thought to inhabit the shades; both the reference and the allusion have possibly been suggested by the peculiar situation of the fetus as a human being still in formation and secluded in the darkness of the womb.

sperme insondable de l'homme: cf. **tétards** and **ovaires** in previous stanzas, to which the present notation adds a new dimension in its emphasis on the miracle of reproduction. The parallelism of the two lines that close the stanza enacts the vital collaboration between man and woman in the renewal of life.

tel un minerai: Césaire's telluric vision expressed here as a direct association of woman with the earth.

114.

ô lumière amicale
ô fraîche source de la lumière
ceux qui n'ont inventé ni la poudre ni la boussole
ceux qui n'ont jamais su dompter la vapeur ni l'électricité
ceux qui n'ont exploré ni les mers ni le ciel
mais ceux sans qui la terre ne serait pas la terre
gibbosité d'autant plus bienfaisante que la terre déserte
davantage la terre
silo où se préserve et mûrit ce que la terre a de plus terre

115.

Ma négritude n'est pas une pierre, sa surdité ruée
contre la clameur du jour
ma négritude n'est pas une taie d'eau morte sur l'oeil
mort de la terre

ma négritude n'est ni une tour ni une cathédrale
elle plonge dans la chair rouge du sol
elle plonge dans la chair ardente du ciel
elle troue l'accablement opaque de sa droite patience.

In this celebrated passage, one of the high points of the poem, we are offered a
vibrant affirmation of racial pride which is all the more telling for coming after a
long process of personal and collective introspection in the preceding parts of the
poem. The attitude to which the passage gives expression derives quite evidently
from a partisan rejection of the scientific and technological culture of the West. It
needs to be pointed out, however, that beyond its polemical intent, the passage is
also a poetic statement of an alternative path to knowledge—that of an intuitive
grasp of the reality of a living universe in intimate relation to human consciousness
and sensibilty.

ô fraîche source de la lumière: this continues the invocation to the sun (cf. astre
and lumineux fondement in the previous stanza), with the added sense of light as
spiritual illumination; the epithet fraîche suggests primal origin.

mais ceux sans qui la terre ne serait pas la terre: the qualification here not only
confirms the irony of the poet's previous negative catalogue of the black man's non-
technical attributes, but also establishes an absolute claim as to the essential value of
his race to the life of the world, a theme that is developed in the ensuing sections of
the poem.

gibbosité d'autant plus bienfaisante: the point of the previous line is emphasized in
this deliberate paradox; gibbosité is an ugly excrescence, and the epithet bienfaisante contributes to the effect of the oxymoron.

silo où se préserve...de plus terre: in a similar expression, the nineteenth-century
black ideological leader Edward Wilmot Blyden called Africa "the spiritual granary
of the world."

Ma négritude: the poet now ascribes a new meaning to this word, to denote a collective personality of the race, based upon an essential racial endowment, itself defined
and sustained by specific spiritual values.

sa surdité: the word refers of course to pierre, which symbolizes the insensitive character of Western civilization as depicted by the poet, characterized further in
clameur du jour, which suggests a confused din of machines; the same lack of
responsiveness to life is suggested by the words tour and cathédrale further in the
passage; cf. also pétition de la pierre in stanza 48.

une taie d'eau morte: a dramatic reversal by the poet of earlier associations of his
people with the spiritual death implied by a lackluster condition of the collective
life.

elle plonge dans la chair rouge du sol / elle plonge dans la chair ardente du ciel:
the image on which these two lines are built is derived from the characteristic motif
of Dogon and Bambara statuettes representing a man with his hands raised to the sky
while his feet are firmly planted on the ground, symbolic of mankind uniting the two
realms in itself and therefore in harmony with the entire universe. The symbol has
been adopted in a modified form as a logo by the Présence Africaine organization.

elle troue l'accablement opaque de sa droite patience: the collective body of the race is likened to a mole patiently burrowing beneath the earth until it comes up into the light of day; the word **accablement** refers to the burden of history which the black race had to bear, while **droite patience** (in which the noun has the same etymological meaning as in stanza 65) is a compaction of the two ideas: the long-suffering nature of the race throughout its experience, and its justified revolt which will lead to an inevitable triumph.

116.

> Eia pour le Kaïlcédrat royal!
> Eia pour ceux qui n'ont jamais rien inventé
> pour ceux qui n'ont jamais rien exploré
> pour ceux qui n'ont jamais rien dompté
> mais ils s'abandonnent, saisis, à l'essence de toute chose
> ignorants des surfaces mais saisis par le mouvement
> de toute chose
> insoucieux de dompter, mais jouant le jeu du monde

After the summary definition, the poet proceeds in this and the next two stanzas to a celebration of négritude in ecstatic lines which reverse both the terms of his perceptions of the race in the earlier parts of the poem and its negative representation in Western ideology.

Kaïlcédrat: a tree typical of the West African Savanah, with royal significance. Cf. Senghor's "Lettre à un poète" (in *Chants d'ombre*), a poem addressed to Césaire in which the word occurs with this meaning.

mais ils s'abandonnent etc: it is of interest to observe that Senghor has pressed these lines into service in his elaboration of the theory of négritude, which posits an intensely emotive disposition of the black race.

ignorants des surfaces: the phenomenal and therefore superficial aspects of the world as grasped and described by Western science, as opposed to its elusive and deep (numinous) reality (**l'essence de toutes choses**); this opposition is a central one in all Césaire's poetry.

le jeu du monde: the inner movement of the universe.

117.

> véritablement les fils aînés du monde
> poreux à tous les souffles du monde
> aire fraternelle de tous les souffles du monde
> lit sans drain de toutes les eaux du monde
> étincelle du feu sacré du monde
> chair de la chair du monde palpitant du mouvement
> même du monde!
>   Tiède petit matin de vertus ancestrales

This stanza contains perhaps the extreme point of the glorification of the black race in the poem. The unabashed celebration of négritude which it continues from the previous stanza is intensified here in the forceful interplay of expressive sonorities combined with effect of anaphora within the structure of parallel lines.

les fils aînés du monde: an echo of Césaire's description of the common people in his *L'Etudiant Noir* article, extended here to the black race. It might be noted that the conception of the black race as the earth's first children anticipates in a curious way the findings of archaeologists who have discovered the earliest human remains in Africa. Césaire was later to make use of this fact in a speech given to the character Lumumba in his play *Une Saison au Congo.*

vertus ancestrales: reverses **peurs ancestrales** in stanza 107; the governing refrain of the poem is now employed to mark the poet's access to a firm consciouness of his ancestral heritage; the epithet **tiède** suggests an intimate warmth of feeling that goes with this stage of his adventure; it also leads directly to another evocation of the sun in the stanza that follows.

118.

> Sang! Sang! tout notre sang ému par le coeur mâle du soleil
> ceux qui savent la féminité de la lune au corps d'huile
> l'exaltation réconciliée de l'antilope et de l'étoile
> ceux dont la survie chemine en la germination de l'herbe!
> Eia parfait cercle du monde et close concordance!

Although this stanza begins as an exaltation of the race in terms that appear to be biological and thus have a racist tone, it progresses in fact to an elaboration of values that are essentially imaginative, expressed in vegetal imagery that creates the sense of a poetic vitalism which comes to stand as an ideal in itself.

tout notre sang...soleil: this postulation of a vital reciprocity between the black race and the universal energy should be understood in its context: it is more the expression of a polemical stance than a reflection of consciously-held ideas. Moreover, as pointed out in the Introduction, blood functions as a cardinal reference in the structure of primordial images that underlies and animates the poem and it constitutes a fundamental element of the poet's imaginative apprehension.

féminité de la lune: this image is suggested by the association between the menstrual cycle and the periodic appearances of the moon and forms part of a whole scheme of agro-lunary and vegetal references in the poem.

corps d'huile: the sexual reference in the preceding notation is further extended in this image which, in its evocation of the female body, connects with the theme of rebirth. Cf. "Femme noire" of Senghor.

antilope, étoile: the idea of an intimate connection between the black race and the sun leads to this image of a more extended *correspondance* in the universe; Césaire may be thinking here of the antelope-horn motif in African sculpture, which would give the **reconciliation** a visual dimension.

germination de l'herbe: the vegetal imagery that runs through the stanza is given direct expression here; note the active quality given to the noun **survie** by the verb **chemine** leading to the notation here.

parfait cercle; close concordance: complementary terms in a triumphant affirmation; the poet proclaims the total coincidence of his race with the imaginative universe he has just evoked; once again, the partisan reference need not exclude a consideration of this as the expression of a universal ideal of spiritual perfection, stressed by the poet further in the poem (see stanza 125).

119.

Ecoutez le monde blanc
horriblement las de son effort immense
ses articulations rebelles craquer sous les étoiles dures
ses raideurs d'acier bleu transperçant la chair mystique
écoute ses victoires proditoires trompeter ses défaites
écoute aux alibis grandioses son piètre trébuchement
Pitié pour nos vainqueurs omniscients et naïfs!

After the excitement of the preceding stanzas, there is a lowering of the key in this stanza in which the poet returns to an indictment of the Western world. The entire stanza relies on antithesis and paradox for effect.

horriblement las: spiritual weariness as an effect of overexertion in the realm of the material. Cf. Cheikh Hamidou Kane's *L'Aventure ambigüe* for a similar idea of the deadening effect of Western technological civilization.

ses raideurs d'acier bleu: consider earlier evocations of Europe (stanzas 1 and 68 in particular) and compare Senghor's "A New York," which paints a similar picture of a bleak and even sinister universe dominated by machines.

victoires proditoires: "Pyrrhic victories"; the dehumanizing effects of science and technology make its vaunted triumphs ultimately hollow, conveyed by **proditoires**, which has the primary meaning of "deceptive."

omniscients et naïfs: the paradox in this reference to the disposition of the white race complements the earlier description of the black race as **ignorants des surfaces**.

120.

Eia pour ceux qui n'ont jamais rien inventé
pour ceux qui n'ont jamais rien exploré
pour ceux qui n'ont jamais rien dompté

121.

Eia pour la joie
Eia pour l'amour
Eia pour la douleur aux pis de larmes réincarnées.

The return of this exultant cry first heard in stanza 116 heralds a new insight: the close association of Joy, Love, and Sorrow, in a trinity which carries obvious religious overtones, gives to the black experience a millenial dimension.

la douleur aux pis des larmes réincarnées: the poet is now able to celebrate the tragic experience of the race whose historical passion has elected it to a special place in the world; **larmes réincarnées** is a metonymic representation of the black race, which has been weaned on a long history of sorrows, like a child that has suckled milk from its mother's breast (**pis**); the phrase thus announces a second coming that will see the race, fortified by this experience and transfigured by it, re-emerge into universal history.

122.

et voici au bout de ce petit matin ma prière virile
que je n'entende ni les rires ni les cris, les yeux fixés
sur cette ville que je prophétise, belle,
donnez-moi la foi sauvage du sorcier
donnez à mes mains puissance de modeler
donnez à mon âme la trempe de l'épée
je ne me dérobe point. Faites de ma tête une tête de proue
et de moi-même, mon coeur, ne faites ni un père, ni un frère,
ni un fils, mais le père, mais le frère, mais le fils,
ni un mari, mais l'amant de cet unique peuple.

After the exultant mood of the preceding passages, the poem now proceeds in a devotional tone in this and the next four stanzas, a tone that is in keeping with the deeply introspective character of the poem momentarily obscured in the preceding passages. The prayer which begins here is addressed to the poet's heart as the seat of his being and defines for him a quasi-messianic role already implicit in the stances he has adopted in the earlier part of the poem.

les yeux fixés sur cette ville: this makes clear the visionary import of **le regard du désordre** in stanza 112; the transformation of **ville** into a positive image indicates the change that has now occurred in the poet's vision of his people and of their destiny.

la foi sauvage du sorcier: a firmness both of faith and of will; a deliberate transformation of the earlier connotation of **sorcier** in stanza 93.

la trempe de l'epée: the poet's soul refined by combat as the steel blade of the sword is tempered by fire; this confirms the import of **larmes réincarnées** above, the same import as in the opening lines of "Soleil Serpent" from *Les Armes miraculeuses*: *Soleil serpent oeil fascinant mon oeil / et la mer pouilleuse d'îles craquant aux doigts de rose / lance-flamme et mon corps intact de foudroyé.*

je ne me dérobe point: contrary to his early gesture of flight.

une tête de proue: figurehead of a ship; the poet at the forefront of his people's combat, whose symbolic enactment in terms precisely of a slave revolt on the high seas, will bring the poem to its conclusion. (See stanzas 162 ff.)

123.

Faites-moi rebelle à toute vanité, mais docile à son génie
comme le poing à l'allongée du bras!
Faites-moi commissaire de son sang
Faites-moi dépositaire de son ressentiment
faites de moi un homme de terminaison
faites de moi un homme d'initiation
faites de moi un homme de recueillement
mais faites aussi de moi un homme d'ensemencement

124.

Faites de moi l'exécuteur de ces oeuvres hautes
voici le temps de se ceindre les reins comme un vaillant homme —

This litany, running over two stanzas, of the poet's aspiration for service on behalf of his people is sustained by the device of parallelism and the play of expressive sonorities lending a tone of determination to the stanza. The two lines of stanza 124 summarize the preceding one and define its meaning for the poet himself.

le poing à l'allongée du bras: the idea here is the same as that conveyed by **tête de proue**; the poet envisions himself as forceful extension of his people's will and energy.

commissaire de son sang: as one charged with a *vital* mission.

un homme de terminaison: persevering, so as to see his mission through and thus bring to an end his people's historical distress.

un homme d'initiation: both as one who is initiated, in the religious sense of the word, and as pathfinder.

un homme de recueillement: in both a devotional and moral sense.

un homme d'ensemencement: this expresses a cardinal idea related to the theme of growth and renewal that runs through the poem, as indeed all Césaire's expression.

l'exécuteur de ces oeuvres hautes: there is a reference here to the formal designation *maître des hautes oeuvres* for the executioner (*bourreau*); the expression now acquires a new and positive meaning for the poet, who aspires to function as agent of future accomplishments of his race, notably in the realm of the spiritual, which will stand as monuments to its genius.

voici le temps de se ceindre les reins: an echo of God's injunction to Job, "Gird up thy loins like a man" (Job 38.3). The phrase also occurs in Césaire's presentation of *Tropiques*, a fact that attests to the urgency he attaches to its import.

125.

Mais les faisant, mon coeur, préservez-moi de toute haine
ne faites point de moi cet homme de haine pour qui
je n'ai que haine
car pour me cantonner en cette unique race
vous savez pourtant mon amour tyrannique
vous savez que ce n'est point par haine des autres races
que je m'exige bêcheur de cette unique race
que ce que je veux
c'est pour la faim universelle
pour la soif universelle
la sommer libre enfin
de produire de son intimité close
la succulence des fruits.

This stanza, one of the most admirable in the poem, is a restatement of the essential relationship between the poet's racial passion and the universal humanism that informs his poetic vision. The liberation that the poet proposes is not only a condition for fulfilment for the poet's race but corresponds as well to a universal ideal.

cet homme de haine: the need for moral purity which alone can break the cycle of hatred against which the poet takes an unambiguous stand here.

pour me cantonner: a formal construction, used in place of the more customary *bien que* followed by the subjunctive: despite the poet's immediate preoccupation with his race, his vision is not an exclusive one; *se cantonner* means to confine oneself to something, with the additional sense here of billeting, as during a military campaign.

bêcheur: from the verb *bêcher*, to cultivate intensively (cf. **ensemencement** above); another sense of the verb, meaning "to run someone down," is also suggested: the poet's uncompromising exposure of the moral lapses of his people in the opening sections of the poem is now revealed as a sign of strong attachment—his **amour tyrannique** earlier in the stanza.

la faim universelle, la soif universelle: the parallel lines give emphasis to the idea. This passage was used in the poster for the First Congress of Black Writers organized in 1956 in Paris by Présence Africaine, as the text of an illustration by Picasso depicting a *tête de nègre*.

sommer: complements the preceding sentence; in its primary legal meaning of "to summon," "to give someone an imperative order" (a meaning somewhat attenuated here by the qualifying word **libre**), the word confers a solemn and urgent note to the universal message proclaimed by the stanza.

la succulence des fruits: not only as an expression of inner genius (**intimité close**) but also as the manifestation of a collective vitality, an idea that is developed in the image of the tree in the next stanza.

126.

> Et voyez l'arbre de nos mains!
> il tourne, pour tous, les blessures incises
> en son tronc
> pour tous le sol travaille
> et griserie vers les branches de précipitation parfumée!

This expands on the last line of the previous stanza. The poet must be imagined addressing the world in this representation of the collective self of his race in typically organic terms, with which he associates the rest of mankind. The stanza gathers up in one single comprehensive symbol the idea of total harmony with the cosmic order which presides in the poem.

l'arbre de nos mains: recalls the imagery in the poet's affirmation of his négritude in stanza 115; **nos mains** suggests a spreading out of the hands in a gesture of reconciliation, a reading suggested by the meditative tone of the whole stanza.

les blessures: a reformulation of the idea in **larmes réincarnées:** just as some plants, like the rubber tree, thrive on incisions made to their trunk to produce sap, so the black race is seen as having derived spiritual benefit from its painful historical experience.

le sol travaille: the subject here, inverted for emphasis, is anticipated by the pronoun two lines above; the whole line evokes the silent revolution of the earth and its vigorous life as grasped by the poet's intuition. Compare the following lines from the poem "Tam Tam II" in *Les Armes miraculeuses: à petits pas de secousse sismique / les ignames dans le sol marchent à grands pas de trouées d'étoiles.*

griserie: "exhilaration"; refers here to the rushing action of sap mounting in the tree.

précipitation parfumée: this completes the sense of **succulence des fruits** in the previous stanza: the end result of the organic relationship between tree and soil is the blooming of flowers and their ripening into fruit.

127.

Mais avant d'aborder aux futurs vergers
donnez-moi de les mériter sur leurs ceintures de mer
donnez-moi mon coeur en attendant le sol
donnez-moi sur l'océan stérile
mais où caresse la main la promesse le l'amure,
donnez-moi sur cet océan divers
l'obstination de la fière pirogue
et sa vigueur marine.

128.

La voici avancer par escalades et retombées sur le flot
pulvérisé
la voici danser la danse sacrée devant la grisaille du bourg
la voici barir d'un lambi vertigineux
voici galoper le lambi jusqu'à l'indécision des mornes

129.

et voici par vingt fois d'un labour vigoureux la pagaie
forcer l'eau
la pirogue se cabre sous l'assaut de la lame, dévie un instant
tente de fuir, mais la caresse rude de la pagaie la vire,
alors elle fonce, un frémissement parcourt l'échine de la vague,
la mer bave et gronde
la pirogue comme un traîneau file sur le sable.

The invocation begun in stanza 122 now leads to an extended metaphor developed as a narrative sequence over these three stanzas. The concrete basis of the metaphor is the familiar activity of local fishermen in Martinique (as indeed in many coastal areas of Africa and the underdeveloped world) who, in plying their trade, have to go far out to sea in their dug-out canoes. The image of the canoe (**pirogue**) confronting the sea and riding defiantly over its swell on the return journey to land becomes figurative of the poet's aspiration to a moral ideal. The passage also foreshadows the triumphant reversal of the Middle Passage enacted towards the end of the poem. (See stanzas 162-67.)

futurs vergers: this image is typical of visions of utopia: as island (**sur leur ceinture de mer**) and as garden.

la promesse de l'amure: the idea here is the same as that expressed by **vaisseau doux de l'espoir** in stanza 113; **amure** is part of a sail.

cet océan divers: refers to the numerous islands of varying sizes forming the Caribbean archipelago.

l'obstination de la fière pirogue: this serves as the object of the imperative **donnez-moi**; the complement **vigueur marine** in the closing line expands on the sense of stubborn attachment to an ideal which the phrase suggests.

escalades et retombées: the very movement of the lines suggests the rise and fall of the canoe on the waves and the widening scope of the imagery which comes to associate sea and land in a comprehensive perspective.

le flot pulvérisé: describes the spray of the sea water as the canoe cuts a path through the sea; **pulvérisé** carries the additional suggestion of a rout, as of an enemy.

la danse sacrée: the canoe and its occupants are involved in a drama of elemental proportions.

la grisaille du bourg: the village as it appears from the sea in the misty distance, presumably in the evening; cf. **la houle grise** in stanza 30.

lambi: the shell of the conch used as a musical instrument; it makes a trumpeting sound, like that of an elephant tusk, hence **barir**; for the significance of **lambi**, see note, stanza 131 below.

l'indécision des mornes: as scene painting, this complements **grisaille du bourg** above to refer to the vague outline of the hills on land, but with an additional moral connotation.

par vingt fois: presumably twenty pairs of hands working the paddle (**pagaie**) in total unison.

se cabre: rears up on the waves, like an unruly horse.

tente de fuir: the application of this notation to the people is clear.

la caresse rude: just as the poet-prophet, in his **amour tyrannique**, has tried to guide his people with his harsh but well-meant admonitions to action.

la vire: in order to set the canoe in the right direction.

la mer bave et gronde: in keeping with **la mer démontée** below; the foaming and roaring breakers on the shoreline represent the final obstacle to be confronted.

comme un traîneau: a detail from observation: the fishing canoes are built to ensure in landing the kind of smooth movement on the soft sand described here; **traîneau** is a sledge.

130.

 Au bout de ce petit matin, ma prière virile :

131.

donnez-moi les muscles de cette pirogue sur la mer démontée
et l'allégresse convaincante du lambi de la bonne nouvelle!

The reprise of the major refrain of the poem now brings to a conclusion the invocation begun in stanza 122.

les muscles: the physiological turn to the imagery is characteristic.

l'allégresse convaincante: as opposed to **l'allégresse mauvaise** of stanza 68.

du lambi de la bonne nouvelle: the conch was often used by runaway slaves to send messages to one another, and so became associated with liberation; it denotes here a prophetic signal heralding a new dispensation.

132.

Tenez je ne suis plus qu'un homme, aucune dégradation, aucun crachat ne le conturbe,
je ne suis plus qu'un homme qui accepte n'ayant plus de colère
(il n'a plus dans le coeur que de l'amour immense et qui brûle)

The calmer tone of this stanza, coming after the animation of the preceding lines, bespeaks a lessening of tension in the poet as he endeavors to overcome his feeling of bitterness in a gesture of reconciliation, but as the succeeding stanzas indicate, the effort remains inconclusive, testifying to the intensity of his emotions.

conturbe: a verb taken direct from the Spanish *conturbar*, meaning "to disturb," "to harass"; the original derivation is from the Latin *conturbare*, "to confound."

133.

J'accepte... j'accepte... entièrement, sans réserve...
ma race qu'aucune ablution d'hysope et de lys mêlés
ne pourrait purifier
ma race rongée de macules
ma race raisin mûr pour pieds ivres
ma reine de crachats et de lèpres
ma reine de fouets et de scrofules
ma reine de squasmes et de chloasmes
(oh ces reines que j'aimais jadis aux jardins printaniers et lointains avec derrière l'illumination de toutes les bougies de marronniers!)
J'accepte. J'accepte.
et le nègre fustigé qui dit : "Pardon mon maître"
et les vingt-neuf coups de fouet légal
et le cachot de quatre pieds de haut
et le carcan à branches
et le jarret coupé à mon audace marronne
et la fleur de lys qui flue du fer rouge sur le gras de
mon épaule
et la niche de Monsieur Vaultier Mayencourt, où j'aboyai six mois de caniche
et Monsieur Brafin
et Monsieur de Fourniol
et Monsieur de la Mahaudière
et le pian
le molosse
le suicide
la promiscuité
le brodequin
le cep
le chevalet
la cippe
le frontal

Despite its calm beginning, a carry-over from the somewhat meditative tone of the previous passage, this stanza initiates a new catalogue of grievances, with specific reference to the infamous *Code noir* enacted in 1685, setting out forms of punishment for slaves in the French West Indian colonies. Although its provisions were really an extension of contemporary European practice, with its heavy reliance on instruments of torture, the harsh application of the code led to widespread abuses, provoking both disaffection among the slaves and an ever stronger movement of protest by European humanists, who came to employ the barbaric treatment of black slaves as an argument in favor of abolition. This was in particular the case with Victor Schoelcher, alluded to earlier in stanza 9, on whose writings Césaire has drawn here for some of the details of slave experience.

qu'aucune ablution d'hysope et de lys mêlés ne saurait purifier: a pointed denunciation of the historic collusion of the Catholic Church with slavery, which explains the poet's anticlerical attitude declared at the very outset of the poem. Two references are explicitly combined in the phrase here: hyssop is an aromatic plant mentioned in the Latin chant (beginning with the words *Asperges me*) that accompanies the ritual sprinkling of the congregation with holy water before High Mass in the Catholic Church; the chant, whose text is taken from the Psalms (51.7), is a prayer for the devotee to be cleansed whiter than snow (*super nivem*); this suggests in turn the whiteness of the lily, the emblem of the Bourbon monarchy in France. An intimate connection is thus established between the general system of references within Western culture and the symbolism of the Church which, as its principal component, this symbolism helps to sustain.

macules: spots on the skin ("macula" in medical terminology).

raisin mûr: in the traditional process of making wine, the grapes are crushed by stamping vigorously on them with the feet, hence **pieds ivres**.

scrofules: abscess from tuberculosis ("scrofula").

ma reine de squasmes et de chloasmes: a contrived collocation, reinforced by onomatopoeia, suggestive of an insistence upon the negative history of the black race; **squasmes**, habitually written *squames*, denotes scales on the skin; **chloasmes**, possibly derived from the Greek word *chloasma* meaning "paleness," carries a connotation of sickness, as a culmination of the pathological direction of the imagery in the passage. Note the way in which the word **race** converts to **reine**, leading to the visionary evocation contained in the parenthesis in the next three lines, and preparing the imaginative ennobling of the race in a line of stanza 170 (see note infra).

(oh ces reines...marronniers!): two complementary perspectives of vision are brought together in this dream sequence which intervenes as an interlude set against the somber evocations of the passage: the exclamation is to be understood in the immediate sense of a nostalgic recall of the original state of the race in the idyllic setting of the ancestral homeland, denoted by **jardins printaniers et lointains** and associated with the image of chestnuts in bloom (**bougies des marronniers**); the word **marronniers**, in its other meaning of runaway slaves (see stanza 51 and **audace marronne** below) in turn suggests the secondary sense—founded on the events of the Haitian revolution—of heroic liberation, marked by the celebratory assembly of the race in triumph.

fustigé: "flogged."

vingt-neuf coups de fouet légal: the limit prescribed by the *Code noir*, though this was regularly exceeded by the slave owners.

cachot: underground prison cell; the detail **quatre pieds de haut** is mentioned in Schoelcher's description of one such cell.

le carcan: an iron collar (or yoke) fixed around the neck.

le jarret coupé: Article 38 of the code specifically stipulated that a captured slave should have his leg cut off at the knee after more than three escape attempts; despite the severity of the punishment, many slaves attempted to flee, hence **mon audace marronne**, at the same time a salute to their indomitable spirit and a mode of identification with them.

et la fleur de lys qui flue du fer rouge: under the provisions of the Code, recaptured slaves were to be branded with the royal emblem; cf. **et l'on nous marquait au fer rouge** (stanza 94) and **fleurs de sang** (stanza 3).

et la niche...six mois de caniche: a reference to an incident recounted by Schoelcher in which a slave died after having been caged for six months in a dog's kennel by his master (named here). Although brought to trial for the atrocity, the master was acquitted.

et Monsieur Brafin: in another incident recounted by Schoelcher, this slave owner caused the suicide of two of his slaves on account of an unjust accusation and punishment; he too was tried and acquitted. M. de Fourniol was the judge at the trial.

le pian: "yaws," a skin disease with which the slaves were habitually afflicted.

le molosse: bloodhound; it was common practice to hunt down runaway slaves with the help of ferocious dogs.

le suicide: both a direct reference to the tragic outcome of the incident involving M. Brafin and a general observation on the desperation of the slaves; cf. stanza 15.

la promiscuité: combines the two senses of the word in French, to refer to the cramped living conditions of the slaves and the impossibility of leading any kind of moral life under these conditions.

le brodequin: designates the stocks in which the victim's legs were locked and held immobile for hours.

le cep: also called *barre*, the iron rings (or shackles) placed around the slave's ankles.

le chevalet: "rack" in English, originally the frame on which the victim's body was placed and the limbs pulled in opposite directions ("drawn") till they came apart from the body; a modified form was later used to attach the body of an offender so as to keep him immobile during flogging.

la cippe: an elevated construction where slaves were publicly flogged; the word originally refered to a kind of low tombstone.

le frontal: a form of punishment in which a cord was wound tightly round the head of the slave.

134.

> Tenez, suis-je assez humble? Ai-je assez de cals aux genoux? Des muscles
> aux reins?
> Ramper dans le boues. S'arc-bouter dans le gras de la boue. Porter.
> Sol de boue. Horizon de boue. Ciel de boue. Morts de boue, ô noms à
> réchauffer dans la paume d'un souffle fiévreux!

The detailed recall of slavery in the previous stanza leads to this summing up of the
bleak perspectives of being and existence implied by the West Indian's historical
experience. The two stanzas provide further evidence of the poet's profound internal-
ization of the historical passion of his race - registered earlier by the refrain **J'accepte**
- and serve to articulate his sense of Caribbean identity, given increasing prominence
in the rest of the poem.

cals aux genoux: "calluses on the kneecap"; got both from praying and submission to
the master; this echoes **ceux qui se sont assouplis aux agenouillements** in stanza
108.

muscles aux reins: therefore well-suited for strenuous work; slaves, especially the
males, were valued for their physique.

Porter: the slave as beast of burden. Césaire was later to center his sense of the
epochal nature of the black condition upon this word in the following passage from
the poem "Depuis Akkad, depuis Elam, depuis Sumer" in *Cadastre*: *Maître de trois
chemins, tu as en face de toi un homme qui a beaucoup porté / Depuis Elam. Depuis
Akkad. Depuis Sumer. / J'ai porté le corps du commandant. J'ai porté le chemin de fer du
commandant. Jai porté la locomotive du commandant, le coton du commandant. J'ai porté
sur ma tête laineuse qui se passe bien du coussinet de Dieu, la machine, la route—le Dieu
du commandant. / Maître de trois chemins j'ai porté sous le soleil, j'ai porté dans le brouil-
lard j'ai porté sur les tessons de braise de fournis manians / j'ai porté le parasol j'ai porté
l'explosif j'ai porté le carcan. / Depuis Akkad. Depuis Elam. Depuis Sumer.*

Sol de boue...Ciel de boue: note the progression in this statement of the comprehensive degradation of the slaves, which assumes the character of an interminable
collective destiny.

Morts de boue: the poet's slave ancestors, whose painful memory and whose spirit
the poet wishes to revere and keep alive through his anguished expression (**souffle
fiévreux**).

135.

> Siméon Piquine, qui ne s'était jamais connu ni père ni mère; qu'aucune
> mairie n'avait jamais connu et qui toute une vie s'en était allé—cherchant son
> nom

136.

> Grandvorka — celui-là je sais seulement qu'il est mort, broyé par un soir de
> récolte, c'était paraît-il son travail de jeter du sable sous les roues de la locomo-
> tive en marche, pour lui permettre, aux mauvais endroits, d'avancer.

137.

Michel qui m'écrivait signant d'un nom étrange. Michel Deveine adresse
Quartier Abandonné et vous leurs frères vivants
Exélie Vêté Congolo Lemké Boussolongo quel guérisseur de ses lèvres
épaisses
sucerait tout au fond de la plaie béante le tenace secret du venin?

These three stanzas present close-up portraits of ordinary individuals who, each in
his own way, becomes representative of the tragic experience of the people. These
stanzas, added to the original version of the poem in the definitive edition published
in 1956, seem to reflect Césaire's activity as mayor of Fort-de- France and deputy for
Martinique in the years after the Second World War. They have their place in the
poem as evidence of the poet's direct acquaintance with the lot of the people.
Moreover, they confer a concrete and as it were documentary value, underlined by
an intense note of pathos, to the poem's testimony of life in the Caribbean in the
colonial period.

qu'aucune mairie n'avait jamais connu: in the French system of local government,
the mayor's office has the responsibility for recording births and deaths (*l'état civil*) of
all the inhabitants in its area of jurisdiction; this links up with **je ne suis d'aucune
nationalité prévue par les chancelleries** in stanza 97.

cherchant son nom: in quest of his original identity, a preoccupation with blacks in
the New World; consider the title of James Baldwin's novel *Nobody knows my name*
and the extraordinary success of Alex Haley's *Roots*.

Grandvorka: from the context, a casual laborer. There is a note of real commiseration in this account, possibly factual, of a typical work accident in the sugar-cane
fields.

d'un nom étrange: "Deveine" means "out of luck" (*veine*, "luck" in colloquial
French); it is, however, a regular surname.

Quartier Abandonné: indicative of the man's mood of total despair.

Exélie etc.: the poet now addresses his compatriots by their African names in a symbolic reversal of Siméon Piquine's situation, in order to affirm their original identity
before slavery; the point is emphasized by the play on the word *exil* in the first name.

lèvres épaisses: another deliberate emphasis on the physical feature of the black race
despised by whites, but now seen as an attribute of innate force; the poison (**venin**)
which is to be sucked out is primarily that in the mind, the insidious effect of humiliation.

138.

quel précautionneux sorcier déferait à vos chevilles la tiédeur visqueuse des
mortels anneaux?

139.

Présences je ne ferai pas avec le monde ma paix sur votre dos.

The interrogation in the first of these two stanzas is rhetorical, as is borne out by the
affirmative tone of the second.

précautionneux sorcier: defines the poet's conception of his mission as healer of minds, the **guérisseur** of the previous stanza; cf. **la foi sauvage du sorcier** in stanza 122.

anneaux: literally, chains or shackles binding the ankles of slaves (see **chevalet** in stanza 133 above), used here as a metaphor for the mental alienation of the people.

sur votre dos: "at your expense," a colloquial expression; the line provides a strong indication of the moral dilemma presented by the colonial situation to the assimilated intellectual in his relation to the rest of the black population.

140.

Iles cicatrices des eaux
Iles évidences de blessures
Iles miettes
Iles informes

141.

Iles mauvais papier déchiré sur les eaux
Iles tronçons côte à côte fichés sur l'épée flambée du
Soleil
Raison rétive tu ne m'empêcheras pas de lancer absurde sur les eaux au gré des
courants de ma soif
votre forme, îles difformes
votre fin, mon défi.

These two stanzas begin a continuous evocation of the islands in terms that counterpose a new and dominant feeling of attachment to the strongly articulated sense of disgust in earlier evocations.

cicatrices des eaux: as a result of the **blessures** in the next line, historical wounds which are not fully healed. Cf. **vieilles plaies** in stanza 145.

miettes: scattered all over the Caribbean Sea, as is clear from the map.

informes: without a well-defined collective personality.

mauvais papier: same idea as **miettes** above; the idea of waste papers, which can be collected on a pointed stick, generates the next image.

tronçons côte à côte: the islands are represented as pieces on a spit, grilled by the sun (**sur l'epée flambée du Soleil**) in a kind of cosmic barbecue; the main idea is that of the incompleteness of the islands, their need for a larger connection: compare in this regard these lines from "Dit d'errance" in *Cadastre*: *île maljointe île disjointe / toute île est veuve / toute île appelle.*

Raison rétive: the poet's project of reconstruction defies logic, which does not admit of the possibility of other forms of knowledge and experience outside the framework of its rigid categories. The poet's mission is intended, however, to give definition to the islands through the improbable means of poetry, his *armes miraculeuses*, whose powers transcend the narrow bounds of conventional reason. The epithet **rétive** ("stubborn") applies as much to **Raison** which it qualifies as to the poet himself, by transfer. Note the structure of the passage which is composed of one long, highly alliterative sentence: the main clause is **Raison rétive, tu ne m'empêcheras pas de lancer...mon défi**; the confidential address to **îles** serves as parenthesis within this structure.

mon défi: in apposition to **votre fin** and qualified by **absurde**.

142.

Iles annelées, unique carêne belle

143.

Et je te caresse de mes mains d'océan. Et je te vire de mes paroles alizées. Et je te lèche de mes langues d'algues.
Et je te cingle hors-flibuste

These lines, though they apply to the Caribbean in general, are addressed specifically to Martinique. They complete the sequence of evocations to express, in terms of the local landscape, the poet's sense of a sacred mission deriving from a profound devotion to his native island.

anneleés: the islands strung out in the Caribbean Sea suggest a ceremonial procession.

unique carêne: Martinique, compared to the hull of a mythical ship rising out of the sea.

mains d'océan: in the sense both of a common familiarity with the sea and the scope and quality of his feelings, wide and deep as the ocean itself.

paroles alizées: the word **alizées**, used here as an adjective, is normally a substantive designating the trade winds which blow from the Caribbean across the Atlantic to the west coast of Africa.

mes langues d'algues: the phrase denotes the specific grounding of Césaire's poetry in the West Indian landscape, with the suggestion of a steadfast attachment, as of seaweed (**algues**.)

hors-flibuste: beyond the reach of the pirate, to which the slave ships are assimilated, and in a new and positive direction; **cingler** is to steer a ship in a chosen direction. The line anticipates the final section of the poem.

144.

O mort ton palud pâteux!
Naufrage ton enfer de débris! j'accepte!

In the appropriate metaphor of a shipwreck at sea, these lines give voice to Césaire's conception of slavery as an original catastrophe from which all Caribbean history flows, as a kind of epochal disaster which overwhelmed his people in their African homeland and forced them into the hell of slavery in exile.

palud pâteux: the collective existence depicted as taking place in a kind of moral and spiritual swamp; the epithet **pâteux** adds the combined effects of alliteration and onomatopoeia to the notation.

145.

Au bout du petit matin, flaques perdues, parfums errants, ouragans échoués, coques démâtées, vieilles plaies, os pourris, buées, volcans enchaînées, morts mal racinés, crier amer. J'accepte!

This stanza, which takes us back with the refrain to the beginning of the poem, prolongs the meaning of the previous one in an enumeration, and as a random catalogue, of some of the consequences of slavery as they have not only affected the poet's people but imprinted themselves on his mind; the writing is expressive of the rush of bitter emotions. The return of the refrain gives to the poet's catalogue of grievances in this part of the poem a finality which comes to have an ominous ring.

flaques perdues, parfums errants: intimations of an earlier spirituality, no longer immediately available.

coques démâtées: as in a shipwreck; **coque** is the hull of a ship; the completeness of the disaster is emphasized by **démâtées** which refers to the masts, to give the sense of a total undoing.

buées: literally, "condensation"; refers here to the blurring of the collective vision.

crier amer: crier is used as substantive.

146.

Et mon originale géographie aussi; la carte du monde faite à mon usage, non pas teinte aux arbitraires couleurs des savants, mais à la géométrie de mon sang répandu, j'accepte

This stanza serves as a succinct summary of and complement to the presentation of the historical adversity of the black race in stanza 42.

la carte du monde: the major colonial powers used to indicate their territories painted in distinctive colors on the map; the poet adopts here a different and personal perspective on history, in order to insist on its real and tragic implications for his race; **mon sang répandu** places in their wider context the terms of his earlier evocation of the islands in stanza 14.

147.

et la détermination de ma biologie, non prisonnière d'un angle facial, d'une forme de cheveux, d'un nez suffisamment aplati, d'un teint suffisamment mélanien, et la négritude, non plus un indice céphalique, ou un plasma, ou un soma, mais mesurée au compas de la souffrance

This stanza is a reformulation of stanza 97, whose ironic tone has given way to a more openly bitter indictment. Taken together with the preceding stanza, it provides the clearest statement in the poem of négritude as designating, in the first place, a community of suffering.

angle facial: in physical anthropology, this was taken to be an indication of brain power.

mélanien: "dark skinned."

indice céphalique: a formula used to determine the average bulk of the head in the different races.

plasma: the clear fluid which carries the components of blood.

soma: the Greek word for body; here, the physical aspect as differentiated in the various races.

compas: the extensive scope, in terms both of geography and of historical import, of black people's suffering.

148.

et le nègre chaque jour plus bas, plus lâche, plus stérile, moins profond, plus répandu au dehors, plus séparé de soi-même, plus rusé avec soi-même, moins immédiat avec soi-même,

149.

j'accepte, j'accepte tout cela

The focus here is on the subjective aspects of the black experience, the psychological and moral implications arising from the objective historical and sociological situation of the race.

150.

et loin de la mer de palais qui déferle sous la syzygie suppurante des ampoules, merveilleusement couché le corps de mon pays dans le désespoir de mes bras, ses os ébranlés et, dans ses veines, le sang qui hésite comme la goutte de lait végétal à la pointe blessée du bulbe...

The effect of this stanza resides in the dramatic contrast between the agony of the land, represented as a wounded body, filling the foreground in a painting, and the vigor and majesty of the encircling sea in the background.

la syzygie suppurante des ampoules: syzygie is the alignment of the sun and the moon; the whole phrase presents a perspective in which the hillocks, the *mornes*, referred to here as **ampoules**, are seen as markers of the relationship between the island and the sea which laps with its waves around it (**syzygie** also means tides); the epithet **suppurante** recalls the pathological imagery of earlier stanzas.

le corps de mon pays: the qualification **merveilleusement couché** suggests a formal tableau, typical of the various versions of the *Pietà* in Italian Renaissance art.

le sang qui hésite: the immediate reference is to the blood slowly dripping from the wounded body like sap from a plant which has been cut; however, the verb **hésite**, with its suggestion of pondering, prepares for the dramatic turn of events in the next stanza, which marks a major development in the poem.

151.

Et voici soudain que force et vie m'assaillent comme un taureau et l'onde de vie circonvient la papille du morne, et voilà toutes les veines et veinules qui s'affairent au sang neuf et l'énorme poumon des cyclones qui respire et le feu thésaurisé des volcans et le gigantesque pouls sismique qui bat maintenant la mesure d'un corps vivant en mon ferme embrasement.

The abrupt transition here, though characteristic, has been anticipated in previous notations which come to a head in this stanza initiating the final movement of the poem. The images as they are deployed function as a determined reversal of previous evocations of the island's lifelessness and of the passive disposition of the people, to enact a general awakening; the new and positive affirmation that emerges here is centered on the poet's awareness of the elemental potential of his island and the spiritual resources of his people. Henceforth, the dominant note in the poem will be one of confident assurance, which even the brief return to a previous mood of despondency in some of the passages to come only serves to emphasize.

comme un taureau: embodying a monumental strength combined with an aggressive instinct; despite the qualifying verb, the poet *absorbs* these qualities of the bull.

l'onde de vie: the vitalist strain of the evocations in the stanza is conveyed principally through this metaphor which represents the inner principle of all manifest life as a wave surging with energy through the entire being; the verb **circonvient** suggests a movement that is both circular and engulfing.

la papille du morne: a notation in keeping with the poet's habitual depiction of the Martinican landscape as a female body, and the **morne** as a breast: the new flood of life rises over the land right up to each nipple (**papille**; cf. **gras téton des mornes** in stanza 22).

qui s'affairent au sang neuf: a quickening and a renewal of vital processes in the collective body, described further on as **corps vivant**, as opposed to its posture of limp prostration depicted in the preceding stanza.

le feu thésaurisé des volcans: the energies that had previously been represented as dammed up (**l'incendie contenu du morne** in stanza 13) are now seen as having only been stored up as in a treasury (**thésaurisé**), ready to be turned to positive account.

le gigantesque pouls sismique: this connects with and enlarges the reference to volcanic action; the earthquake, a formidable manifestation of elemental life, provokes a violent reordering in nature and is thus a regular image of revolution in Césaire's poetry.

qui bat...la mesure: the collective body now attuned to the regulatory principle of the earth itself.

en mon ferme embrasement: recalls **le blanc embrasement des sables abyssaux** in stanza 66; the poet's role as agent in the transformations he has just evoked proceeds from his fierce identification with the land.

152.

Et nous sommes debout maintenant, mon pays et moi, les cheveux dans le vent, ma main petite maintenant dans son poing énorme et la force n'est pas en nous, mais au-dessus de nous, dans une voix qui vrille la nuit et l'audience comme la pénétrance d'une guêpe apocalyptique. Et la voix prononce que l'Europe nous a pendant des siècles gavés de mensonges et gonflés de pestilences,
car il n'est point vrai que l'oeuvre de l'homme est finie
que nous n'avons rien à faire au monde
que nous parasitons le monde
qu'il suffit que nous nous mettions au pas du monde

The note of identification which is struck in the preceding stanza modulates, as it were, into the sustained tone of an annunciation: that of the prophetic role of the poet. The rhetorical ring of the last four lines brings out the character of a consciously directed exhortation which this stanza assumes.

les cheveux dans le vent: the natural vigor of the Martinican landscape, previously evoked in stanza 80, now directly associated with the people; the mystical significance of **vent** is made clearer in the final stanzas of the poem.

dans une voix qui vrille la nuit: the poet is obviously the agent of this prophetic voice which breaches the silence of night to awaken the people from their spiritual slumber. Note the focused meaning of the verb *vriller*, previously employed in stanza 26 in a more indeterminate sense.

et l'audience: the noun refers to the faculty of hearing (Latin *audire*), the immediate target of the voice; its effect extends to the totality of the senses so that it becomes an imperious summons impossible to ignore.

la pénétrance d'une guêpe apocalyptique: possibly an allusion to the affliction of the Egyptians by the pests as a prelude to the liberation of the Israelites in Exodus; **pénétrance** continues the sense of **vrille**: the sound and the sting are both penetrating.

gavés de mensonge: the reprise of the phrase **pendant des siècles** indicates that this is a formal negation of the defamation of the black race enumerated in stanza 94.

au pas du monde: that is, of the Western world.

153.

> mais l'oeuvre de l'homme vient seulement de commencer
> et il reste à l'homme à conquérir toute interdiction immobilisée aux coins de sa ferveur
> et aucune race ne possède le monopole de la beauté, de l'intelligence, de la force
> et il est place pour tous au rendez-vous de la conquête et nous savons maintenant que le soleil tourne autour de notre terre éclairant la parcelle qu'a fixée notre volonté seule et que toute étoile chute de ciel en terre à notre commandement sans limite.

The note of exhortation in the previous stanza is sustained here in lines that integrate the poet's expression of his ideological preoccupations into a truly poetic statement of an imaginative consciousness and vision.

aux coins de sa ferveur: the phrase denotes the full scope of human possibility; the underlying concept, expanded in the imagery in the latter part of the stanza, is that of the cardinal points marking a comprehensive delimitation of space.

et aucune race...de la force: this continues the tenor of **gavés de mensonges** in a pointed reference to Gobineau's *Essai sur l'inégalité des races*, in which (in Chapters XII and XIII) he argues the superiority of the white race in terms of the precise qualities restated here; as against the ironic echo of Gobineau's text in stanza 97, the reference here is an explicit refutation of his extravagant racial claims. Note also that the black poet gives a new meaning to the idea of force, which acquires here a primarily moral and spiritual connotation.

le soleil tourne autour de notre terre: this wilful assertion contradicts the heliocentric conception of the universe introduced by Copernicus and accepted by Western science, in order to affirm the privileged status of the poet's race in the universal realm, a status that endows it with spiritual authority (see also stanza 61 and **notre commandement sans limite** further in this passage); in a wider sense, it also implies the unbounded nature of human possibility.

toute étoile...sans limite: an insistence on the significance of the preceding statement and on the potency of the poetic word as both an anticipation of the collective will and operative force.

154.

> Je tiens maintenant le sens de l'ordalie : mon pays est la "lance de nuit" de mes ancêtres Bambaras. Elle se ratatine et sa pointe fuit désespérément vers le manche si c'est de sang de poulet qu'on l'arrose et elle dit que c'est du sang d'homme qu'il faut à son tempérament, de la graisse, du foie, du coeur d'homme, non du sang de poulet.

This stanza functions as an interlude, as a moment of reflection on the part of the poet upon the severe disposition required of his race in order to assume its heroic destiny. The stanza makes direct use of African references both to establish the poet's racial and spiritual link with the ancestral continent and to enforce in a very striking way the message he wishes to convey.

l'ordalie: a form of trial in many traditional societies in which an accused person was exposed to danger—usually the drinking of poison—in order to prove his or her guilt or innocence; the English word "ordeal" was originally derived from the French in this sense.

la "lance de nuit": a reference to the ritual by which Bambara warriors consecrated their spears with human blood in order to ensure their efficacy; the quotation marks indicate Césaire's avowal of the derivation of this detail from anthropological literature and its character here as the basis of a metaphor, which extends from this stanza into the next. The image also confirms the heroic connotation of **qui tinrent jadis la lance** in stanza 93, with the further suggestion of *fer de lance*, a highly venomous snake, as an image of aggression.

mes ancêtres Bambara: the Bambara are an ethnic group concentrated in the present-day Republic of Mali; their language serves as a lingua franca over a wide area of West Africa. Césaire's claim here to a specific Bambara ancestry is of course purely literary; it can be accounted for by the historical importance of the group and their prominence in anthropological literature. From historical records and other less formal indications, it is in fact almost certain that the population of Martinique is made up largely of descendants of the Ibo and related ethnic groups in Southeastern Nigeria.

Elle se ratatine...vers le manche: this elaboration on the Bambara myth is simply an illustration of the need for self-sacrifice in the heroic undertaking to which the poet invites his people.

du sang d'homme: the literal sense of the Bambara ritual now receives a clear metaphorical application in this notation, dwelt upon in **du coeur d'homme** and **coeur viril** in the next stanza, to stress the point that it is resolute and brave men—valiant hearts—that the country stands in need of for its salvation; the final phrase **sang de poulet** can be taken as equivalent to the English expression "chicken-hearted," which gives by contrast a sense of the meaning intended by the passage.

155.

Et je cherche pour mon pays non des coeurs de dattes, mais des coeurs d'homme qui c'est pour entrer aux villes d'argent par la grand'porte trapézoïdale, qu'ils battent le sang viril, et mes yeux balayent mes kilomètres carrés de terre paternelle et je dénombre les plaies avec une sorte d'allégresse et je les entasse l'une sur l'autre comme rares espèces, et mon compte s'allonge toujours d'imprévus monnayages de la bassesse.

The reflection begun in the previous stanza is continued here in a further statement of the heroic ideal which the poet proposes to his people. This ideal is contrasted with the immediate reality of their lives in a long digression which is to extend over several stanzas and provides another occasion for moral analysis. As the development in later stanzas shows, the discrepancy which the poet once again discovers between his ideal and the depressing spectacle offered by reality no longer has the same disheartening effect on him as on previous occasions.

aux villes d'argent: a metaphor for a visionary future.

la grand'porte trapézoïdale: the trapezoid is a geometrical figure with four sides of unequal length, a primordial motif that occurs frequently in the architecture of ancient civilizations; the image here evokes the triumphant march of a victorious army through a monumental archway serving as a gate into a city.

et mes yeux etc.: the sweep of the poet's eyes over the land reveals further areas of moral failings which he explores with a peculiar enthusiasm.

comme rares espèces: like precious coins or pieces of jewelry.

d'imprévus monnayages de la bassesse: that is, new instances of moral decrepitude constantly brought to the poet's attention; the image is derived from the minting-of coins, but also carries the sense of a sordid exchange, as shown in the denunciation in the next stanza.

156.

Et voici ceux qui ne se consolent point de n'être pas faits à la ressemblance de Dieu mais du diable, ceux qui considèrent que l'on est nègre comme commis de seconde classe : en attendant mieux et avec possibilité de monter plus haut; ceux qui battent la chamade devant soi-même, ceux qui vivent dans un cul de basse fosse de soi-même; ceux qui se drapent de pseudomorphose fière; ceux qui disent à l'Europe : "Voyez, je sais comme vous faire des courbettes, comme vous présenter mes hommages, en somme, je ne suis pas différent de vous; ne faites pas attention à ma peau noire : c'est le soleil qui m'a brûlé."
Et il y a le maquereau nègre, l'askari nègre, et tous les zèbres se secouent à leur manière pour faire tomber leurs zébrures en une rosée de lait frais.
Et au milieu de tout cela je dis hurrah! mon grand-père meurt, je dis hurrah! la vieille négritude progressivement se cadavérise.
Il n'y a pas à dire : c'était un bon nègre.

Les Blancs disent que c'était un bon nègre, un vrai bon nègre, le bon nègre à son bon maître.
Je dis hurrah!
C'était un très bon nègre,
la misère lui avait blessé poitrine et dos et on avait fourré dans sa pauvre cervelle qu'une fatalité pesait sur lui qu'on ne prend pas au collet; qu'il n'avait pas puissance sur son propre destin; qu'un Seigneur méchant avait de toute éternité écrit des lois d'interdiction en sa nature pelvienne; et d'être le bon nègre; de croire honnêtement à son indignité, sans curiosité perverse de vérifier jamais les hiéroglyphes fatidiques.

The satirical note on which this stanza begins deepens into one of frank invective directed primarily at the middle class, whose attitude of self-negation is a major cause of demoralization for the common people; the first part of this stanza thus parallels the poet's indictment of this class in stanza 17. The connection between cause and effect in this social perspective is made clear in the portrait of the grandfather in the latter part of the stanza.

Et voici...du diable: Christian iconography and general symbolism as promoting factors in the self-hatred of the black subject.

avec possibilité de monter plus haut: see note to **poussis surnuméraires** in stanza 17.

ceux qui battent la chamade devant soi même: refers to the attitude of resignation to racial humiliation. The expression *battre la chamade* derives from the practice in former times of beating a special drum as a signal for capitulation and is now used colloquially to designate a state of panic; the original sense survives here.

pseudomorphose: "taking on a false personality"; the word is coined by Césaire on the model of *métamorphose*, and recalls the oxymoron **faussetés authentiques** in stanza 109; the context makes clear its reference to the inauthentic life of the black bourgeoisie.

c'est le soleil qui m'a brûlé: the phrase is a literal quotation from the First Song of the "Woman" (now generally identified with the Queen of Sheba) in The Song of Songs (or The Song of Solomon) 1.6; the same song contains her celebrated declaration: *Nigra sum sed formosa* ("I am black but beautiful").

le maquereau nègre: maquereau is slang for "pimp," so that the phrase here recalls **entremetteur des splendeurs de la servitude** in stanza 105, with practically the same meaning.

askari nègre: a uniformed black in the service of a white master, like the **askari**, colonial soldiers in East Africa; the word is Swahili.

tous les zèbres...rosée de lait frais: a variation on the biblical text on the impossibility of the leopard changing its spots or the black man his color (Jeremiah 13: 23); there is also a suggestion here of a parallel with the crow who is decked out in borrowed feathers in one of Aesop's fables. The passage amplifies on an even more caustic note the previous commentary on the desperate lengths to which the black élite often went in order to conform to white standards (**rosée de lait frais**, an image which also recalls the Queen of Sheba's description of Solomon's eyes as "washed in milk"—The Song of Songs 5.12).

mon grand père meurt: a poetic restatement of Césaire's conclusion to his article in *L'Etudiant Noir*. Again, this is less a personal than a collective reference to the passing away of the older generation of blacks (**la vieille négritude se cadavérise**) whose Uncle Tom-like submissiveness to injustice and humiliation (detailed later in 156-61) is now to be replaced by the more determined attitude of the younger generation represented by the poet; hence the exultant cry, **Je dis hurrah!**

c'était un bon nègre: the portrait of the grandfather presented here draws succinctly on the same elements as those employed to describe the anonymous black man encountered by the poet in the tram, thus establishing a parallel between the two figures.

une fatalité...qu'on ne prend pas au collet: the challenge to fate represented in characteristic physical terms, as an aggressive posture.

en sa nature pelvienne: cf. **la forme de leur bassin** in stanza 97.

les hiéroglyphes fatidiques: hieroglyphics were the characters in ancient Egyptian writing; their mysterious associations have to do with the fact that they were for a long time undeciphered (this was eventually accomplished by the French archaeologist Champollion) and are associated with ritual. The idea here is that the **lois d'interdiction**, inscribed in incomprehensible letters, had been pronounced by an evil god to seal the individual's fate (**fatalité** and **fatidiques** derive from the Latin *fatum*, the latter formed from a combination with *dicere*, "to say"); an association is also suggested with the Bible story of the Ten Commandments handed by God to Moses on tablets of stone.

157.

C'était un très bon nègre

158.

et il ne lui venait pas à l'idée qu'il pourrait houer, fouir, couper tout, tout autre chose vraiment que la canne insipide

159.

C'était un très bon nègre.

160.

Et on lui jetait des pierres, des bouts de ferraille, des tessons de bouteille, mais ni ces pierres, ni cette ferraille, ni ces bouteilles...
O quiètes années de Dieu sur cette motte terraquée!

161.

et le fouet disputa au bombillement des mouches la rosée sucrée de nos plaies.

The portrait of the grandfather merges in these lines into a composite picture of the black rural labor force and of the hardships it had to endure in the colonial regime that replaced slavery; the evocation moves through a progression from the individual to the collective that culminates in another bitter expression of historical grievance.

houer: "to hoe."

fouir: "to dig."

couper tout: with the further suggestion of *couper court à tout*.

canne insipide: describes the drab life of the sugar cane field worker in ironic contrast, as in stanza 4, to the sweetness of the crop he has to cut; the epithet **insipide** is thus transferred for emphasis on this idea.

quiètes années de Dieu: calm resignation sanctioned by religion; cf. **l'esprit de Dieu** in stanza 94.

cette motte terraquée: recalls **palud pâteux** in stanza 144.

Et le fouet...nos plaies: the passage here from the individual to the collective plane seems natural and inevitable; **fouet** is the standard symbol of servitude and humiliation in Césaire's poetry; the picture of flies buzzing over **la rosée sucrée de nos plaies** contains both an implied contrast to **rosée de lait frais** above and an insistence on the discrepancy between the bitterness of the lives of the black population and the benefits derived by the colonial master from the fruits of their labor.

162.

Je dis hurrah! La vieille négritude
progressivement se cadavérise
l'horizon se défait, recule et s'élargit
et voici parmi des déchirements de nuages la fulgurance d'un signe
le négrier craque de toute part... Son ventre se convulse et résonne... L'affreux
ténia de sa cargaison ronge les boyaux fétides de l'étrange nourrisson des mers!
Et ni l'allégresse des voiles gonflées comme une poche de doublons rebondie, ni
les tours joués à la sottise dangereuse des frégates policières ne l'empêchent
d'entendre la menace de ses grondements intestins

163.

En vain pour s'en distraire le capitaine pend à sa grand'vergue le nègre le plus
braillard ou le jette à la mer, ou le livre à l'appétit de ses molosses

The enactment of black revolt broken off by the poet's reflections now enters an active phase in this stanza. It is as if the poet's cry of triumph produces a change of scene, to a dramatic presentation of an insurrection on board a slave ship during the Middle Passage. The details of the description and the imagery represent an extension, leading to a direct reversal, of the poet's rememoration of the Middle Passage in stanza 96. The scene itself, as presented here, is an imaginative reconstruction of historical data concerning the numerous uprisings of slaves during the Middle Passage and in this respect can be compared to similar accounts in literature, such as Prosper Merimée's short story *Tamango*, or Herman Melville's *Benito Cereno*, more familiar to English-speaking readers. Césaire's poetic re-enactment has, however, a much more immediate ideological and symbolic significance.

la fulgurance d'un signe: an allusion to the clap of thunder rending the sky in the Old Testament story of Moses on Mount Sinai; the religious connotation is already anticipated by **dans une voix qui vrille la nuit** in stanza 152, which this notation amplifies.

Son ventre se convulse: the pathological imagery establishes the continuity between the earlier evocation of the slave ship (cf. **farfouillis de vermines** in stanza 96) and the present one.

ténia: tapeworm, a tropical parasite which lives in the intestines of its victims.

l'étrange nourisson des mers: the slave ship in its fully monstrous aspect.

Et ni l'allégresse...poche de doublons: another example of Césaire's habitual compaction of images and rapid shift of ideas: the bulge of the slave ship's sails, well filled out by favorable winds, not only indicates its speed and steady course towards its destination but also the prospects of ample payment for the crew for their human cargo; this induces a sense of satisfaction in the crew, so that **allégresse** becomes displaced as a description of the sails to that of the mental state of the crew (with a meaning akin to the colloquial expression *avoir le vent en poupe*) as they look forward to filling their pockets with the gold with which they expect to be paid (**doublon** is an old Spanish coin; in English "doubloons"); the whole picture is shot through with dramatic irony.

les tours joués...frégates policières: this notation draws on historical fact: the slave ship is represented as running a gauntlet of patrol ships (**frégates policières**) which used to be sent out from England to police the West African coast in the period after its official abolition by Britain; they were often outwitted by the clever maneuvers of the slavers (conveyed here by **les tours joués**) which rendered their mission ineffective.

grand'vergue: "yard-arm," wooden beam laid across the main mast in a sailing ship as a support, habitually used to hang mutineers.

braillard: brawler, troublemaker; there exists an alternative form - *brailleur*.

164.

La négraille aux senteurs d'oignon frit retrouve dans son sang répandu le goût amer de la liberté

This stanza rings out like a proclamation, conveying in simple but strong imagery the new historical determination of the blacks in revolt projected by the poet.

aux senteurs d'oignon frit: suggestive of a pungent, trenchant nature; the positive connotation now assumed by the word **négraille**, previously encountered as a term of contempt in stanza 90, is emphasized by this qualification.

165.

Et elle est debout la négraille

166.

la négraille assise
inattendument debout
debout dans la cale
debout dans les cabines
debout sur le pont
debout dans le vent
debout sous le soleil

debout dans le sang
  debout
    et
      libre
debout et non point pauvre folle dans sa liberté et son dénuement maritimes
girant en la dérive parfaite
et la voici :
plus inattendument debout
debout dans les cordages
debout à la barre
debout à la boussole
debout à la carte
debout sous les étoiles
  debout
    et
      libre
167.
et le navire lustral s'avancer impavide sur les eaux écroulées.
Et maintenant pourrissent nos flocs d'ignominie!

These stanzas compose a narrative sequence that moves the poem's theme toward its culmination. Stanza 166 builds on the enumerations which produce the effect of a scene of generalized combat as the slaves storm every part of the ship; the device not only has an obvious dramatic value but also serves to propel the narrative through the two series of progressions that determine the movement of the stanza, the first ending with **soleil** and the second with **étoiles**. The poet thereafter proceeds to invest the drama he has presented with a heroic and spiritual significance: the slaves are regenerated by their action and the slave ship itself, now a mythical figure, becomes symbolic of the invigorating properties of the elements in whose essence the freed slaves participate.

dans le sang: this notation has two senses: the first is immediate to the context and relates to the shedding of blood for a justified cause, in this case freedom from a dehumanizing bondage; it is relevant to note here the overt formulation of the restorative value of violence for the slave and the oppressed by "le Rebelle," the principal character of Césaire's dramatic poem *Et Les Chiens se taisaient*, who concludes his account of a slave revolt with these words: *je frappai, le sang gicla: c'est le seul baptême dont je me souvienne aujourd'hui*. (The influence of this aspect of Césaire's work on Frantz Fanon for the latter's formulation of his psychology and ethics of violence is undeniable.) The second sense restates the affirmation of stanza 164: the blacks in revolt are now at last acting true to their profound nature, proclaimed earlier in the dynamic link between **sang** and **Soleil**, and emphasized by the parallelism which connects this line to the previous one.

et non point pauvre folle...dérive parfaite: these lines compose a picture of the slave ship in momentary disarray and adrift at sea after its take-over by the slaves. The poet, however, stresses the lucid disposition of the slaves (**non point folle**, referring to **la négraille**) in their precarious freedom (**dans sa liberté et son dénuement maritimes**) and the positive nature of this drifting (**dérive parfaite**) both in the sense of the moral victory it represents and that of its spiritual significance, made clear in the next stanza.

et le navire lustral: the ship taken in itself and as a comprehensive image of its occupants; the metonymic device, anchored in the epithet **lustral** which relates to rites of purification, draws attention to the transformation of the slaves now cleansed by their act of revolt.

s'avancer: the infinitive is employed here in place of the past tense, as in certain Latin constructions, for narrative effect.

impavide: boldly, without fear (Latin *impavidus*).

les eaux écroulées: cf. **flot pulvérisé**, and similar context in stanza 128.

Et maintenant...flocs d'ignominie: this line can be read as a solemn and jubilant proclamation of a definitive end to the deplorable historical situation of the black race; **flocs** is an interjection representing the sound of a falling object, with a slight effect of bathos setting off the solemnity of the proclamation which is marked by the inversion.

168.

par la mer cliquetante de midi
par le soleil bourgeonnant de minuit
écoute épervier qui tiens les clefs de l'orient
par le jour désarmé
par le jet de pierre de la pluie

169.

écoute squale qui veille sur l'occident

These stanzas link up in an apostrophe that brings together the essential elements of Césaire's polemical stance in the poem: its character as a diatribe is overlaid by the menacing tone in which the prospect of a universal social and cosmic revolution is predicated. The parallelism reinforces the effect of the sound values to suggest the particular urgency of the poet's dissident mood.

la mer cliquetante de midi: this notation combines visual and auditory effects: the brilliance of the sun on the shimmering sea at the height of the day and in a tropical environment is perceived in terms of sharp sound (*cliqueter* is the regular verb for the clanging of metal) which is further associated with the roar of the waves, the whole expressive of an elemental vigor.

le soleil bourgeonnant de minuit: this image involves a complex scheme of associations central to the structure of images and symbols in Césaire's poetry. The primary reference here is to the rising sun, slowly spreading light and warmth over the earth, with the connotation of the budding of life registered in the epithet **bourgeonnant**; this is extended by the complement **de minuit** to a projection of the black race emerging from the night of a negative historical situation to a new day, one of forceful manifestation of its collective being. In its further allusion to the phenomenon of the midnight sun at the poles, the image connects with **la mer...de midi** in the previous line as a parallel reference, to designate the conjunction of opposites within the seamless totality of the cosmological order; in this sense, it incorporates a Surrealist conceit of the reconciliation of contrary principles which analytical thought isolates, but which are brought into harmony at a higher, poetic level of apprehension, a conceit that Césaire employs directly in the following lines from *Les Armes miraculeuses*:

Jour nocturne / nuit diurne / qu'exsude / la Plénitude. A further underlying meaning is suggested by the weaving of subtle echoes of Nerval into the poem, echoes which become more distinct in the next stanza. (See notes below.)

épervier: this is a generalization of the earlier indirect reference to Napoleon Bonaparte.

le jet de pierre de la pluie: the basis for this image is the phenomenon of hailstones, made symbolic of revolution in both its aggressive, violent aspect and its regenerative potential.

squale: "shark"; the white master characterized as a predator.

170.

écoutez chien blanc du nord, serpent noir du midi
qui achevez le ceinturon du ciel
Il y a encore une mer à traverser
oh encore une mer à traverser
pour que j'invente mes poumons
pour que le prince se taise
pour que la reine me baise
encore un vieillard à assassiner
un fou à délivrer
pour que mon âme luise aboie luise
aboie aboie aboie
et que hulule la chouette mon bel ange curieux.
Le maître des rires?
Le maître du silence formidable?
Le maître de l'espoir et du désespoir?
Le maître de la paresse? Le maître des danses?
C'est moi!

The stanza opens with a striking presentation of the antagonists in a struggle which divides the universe into two areas of life; the apostrophe is then resumed in a series of incantations which carry forward the vein of the previous stanza into an expression of messianic fervor.

chien blanc du nord: carries forward the association of **molosse** already encountered in stanza 133.

serpent noir du midi: refers to the poet himself; **midi**, in the sense both of South and midday, designates his universe, marked by an intensity of being. The phrase functions as a parenthesis intended to sharpen the sense of confrontation implied in the apostrophe. The totemic identification with the snake - which features as a sacred symbol in many African rituals and is associated with the tutelary spirit of rivers ("Damballa Wedo") in Haitian Vodun, a religion derived from African sources - is a pervasive feature of Césaire's poetry and a central element of his poetic mythology. The image is also associated with Nerval's "le soleil noir" in "El Desdichado," more directly echoed in other references in the stanza.

encore une mer à traverser: in a reversal of the Middle Passage, and as a return to the poet's African antecedents; more broadly still, the phrase implies a future still to conquer.

pour que j'invente mes poumons: in order to give cosmic resonance to his voice; cf. **l'énorme poumons des cyclones** in stanza 151.

pour que le prince se taise: another reference to Nerval's sonnet, in which the prince is symbol of dereliction ("le Prince d'Aquitaine à la tour abolie," a line incorporatèd into T. S. Eliot's *The Waste Land*); there is a shift here from its "decadent" associations to a determined call for the abolition of all systems of social hierarchy.

pour que la reine me baise: the Nerval reference in the previous line is pursued in this one with which it forms a neat rhymed couplet: it recalls Nerval's "Mon front est rouge encore du baiser de la reine" which functions as a transformation image within his sonnet; it is employed here to give resonance to the black poet's aspiration for total union with his land and with his race, previously ennobled as **ma reine** in the series of evocations in stanza 133.

un vieillard à assassiner: to ensure the final demise of **la vieille négritude**.

un fou à délivrer: a variation on the valorization of madness in stanzas 48 and 49.

pour que mon âme luise: spiritual illumination as the poet's fundamental aspiration.

aboie: in justified anger.

la chouette: the owl as a totem animal which serves as the poet's guardian angel, expressed in **bel ange curieux** in which the adjective has the etymological sense deriving from the Latin *cura* ("care"), as well as the conventional association of the owl with Minerva, the goddess of wisdom in classical Greek mythology.

Le maître du silence formidable: the black man's apparent resignation to fate now becomes an ominous portent.

Le maître des danses: the symbolic implications of this notation, which derives from the black stereotype, provide the theme of the poem's penultimate stanza.

171.

et pour ce Seigneur
les hommes au cou frêle
reçois et perçois fatal calme triangulaire

This is a travesty of the rite of sacrifice and dedication; the poet abandons the undeserving among his race to the Christian God, before he proceeds to detail his own forceful prerogatives in the next stanza.

les hommes au cou frêle: the weak-hearted; the phrase functions as the complement of **reçois et perçois**.

fatal calme triangulaire: qualifies **Seigneur** in an irreverent allusion to the representation of the Trinity in Christian iconography by the triangle; because of the association of this geometric figure with the slave trade (made clear in the next stanza), it has a sinister connotation for the poet, hence the epithet **fatal**.

172.

Et à moi mes danses
mes danses de mauvais nègre
à moi mes danses
la danse brise-carcan
la danse saute-prison
la danse il-est-beau-et-bon-et-légitime-d'être-nègre
A moi mes danses et saute le soleil sur la raquette de mes mains
mais non l'inégal soleil ne me suffit plus
enroule-toi, vent, autour de ma nouvelle croissance
pose-toi sur mes doigts mesurés
je te livre ma conscience et son rythme de chair
je te livre les feux où brasille ma faiblesse
je te livre le chain-gang
je te livre le marais
je te livre l'intourist du circuit triangulaire
dévore vent
je te livre mes paroles abruptes
dévore et enroule-toi
et t'enroulant embrasse-moi d'un plus vaste frisson
embrasse-moi jusqu'au nous furieux
embrasse, embrasse NOUS

173.

mais nous ayant également mordus
jusqu'au sang de notre sang mordus!
embrasse, ma pureté ne se lie qu'à ta pureté
mais alors embrasse
comme un champ de justes filaos
le soir
nos multicolores puretés
et lie, lie-moi sans remords
lie-moi de tes vastes bras à l'argile lumineuse
lie ma noire vibration au nombril même du monde
lie, lie-moi, fraternité âpre
puis, m'étranglant de ton lasso d'étoiles
monte, Colombe
monte
monte
monte
Je te suis, imprimée en mon ancestrale cornée blanche.

The poem moves toward a resolution in these two stanzas. In an impassioned invocation to the wind, felt as the current of life in the universe, the poet works off his burden of anguish, in a "sloughing off" of his historical personality in order to advance toward a new reality of the self and a new apprehension of the world. The dominant image is that of a rising sea-breeze, appropriate to the invocation and the context of the action in the poem: a blowing away of the old and blowing in of the new, as well as an elevation to a higher plane of being.

mes danses de mauvais nègre: of a dissident and therefore liberated consciousness; the next five lines develop the idea.

la raquette de mes mains: the poet's power to manipulate the forces of the universe, even to play with them, **jouant le jeu du monde**, as in stanza 116.

enroule-toi, vent: an imperative by which the poet forces a widening of his horizons in order to acquire an unbounded vista on the world; the mystic significance of **vent** is shortly to intervene.

ma nouvelle croissance: the poet becomes aware of an expansion of his being.

mes doigts mesurés: a variation on the idea of **la raquette de mes mains** above, highlighting the process of absorption of the poet's finite frame into the realm of the infinite.

je te livre ma conscience: the poet is now able to abandon his temporal preoccupations in his ascent to a higher consciousness.

son rythme de chair: as opposed to that of the spirit; see note to **jusqu'au nous** below.

les feux où brasille ma faiblesse: *brasiller* is to sparkle: the poet's human weaknesses (for example, the moral failure he narrates in stanza 99) are to be consumed in an experience from which he will emerge with a soul tempered and a being purified.

le marais: the difficulties and reverses of black history figured as a vast historical morass; cf. **palud pâteux**, stanza 144.

le chain-gang: black slaves were often chained together, like the desperate criminals with which this word, borrowed from English, is normally associated.

l'intourist du circuit triangulaire: a reference to the triangular route of the slave ships which went from Europe with goods in exchange for slaves taken in Africa to be sold in the Americas, from which the ships then returned to Europe with produce such as sugar and cotton.

mes paroles abruptes: the abrasive language the poet has so far been obliged to employ.

dévore et enroule-toi: the wind as it unwinds also infuses the poet with its propitious powers.

vaste frisson: the poet assimilated to the universe in a mystic trance; the notation anticipates **ma noire vibration** below and the final lines of the poem.

jusqu'au nous furieux: the inner self of the poet, seething with strong emotions; it is the Greek word *nous* (spirit or essence) that Césaire employs here.

embrasse, embrasse NOUS: the capitalization indicates both a reversion to French and a progression from the individual to the collective consciousness.

jusqu'au sang de notre sang: "right to the marrow"; a use of the Hebrew superlative, made familiar by the Bible, as in "Holy of Holies."

ma pureté…ta pureté: the context suggests an aside in which the poet addresses himself to a companion in a declaration of universal brotherhood, stated later as **nos multicolores puretés**; the phrase also implies the poet's humble submission to the cleansing power of the wind in an attitude of religious devotion.

champ de justes filaos: filao is the casuarina tree, a tropical variety of the pine; it usually grows tall and straight, hence the epithet **justes**, given here a moral and spiritual connotation.

nos multicolores puretés: extends to **ma pureté** above a universal significance (see **faim universelle** and **soif universelle** in stanza 125 and **il est place pour tous au rendez-vous de la conqête** in stanza 153); the imperative **embrasse** is doubly charged with the two meanings of the word, to characterize the all-encompassing and welcoming nature of the poet's ideal of universal reconciliation.

à l'argile lumineuse: two closely related levels of meaning are suggested by this image: the poet's aspiration to a perfection of being manifested in an organic bond with his native environment (cf. **ce pays dont le limon entre dans la composition de ma chair,** stanza 48) expands into a broader telluric vision of union with the earth and the forces of the universe.

au nombril même du monde: for the restoration of an original and fundamental attachment, a broadening of **cordon ombilical** in stanza 21.

ton lasso d'étoiles: with this image, we must imagine the poet drawn into the vast perspectives of the constellations.

monte, Colombe: the dove is the symbol of Pentecost in Christian iconology, from which it has acquired its conventional meaning of peace; in the present context, it assumes an almost totemic significance for the poet, parallel to that of **colibri.**

mon ancestrale cornée blanche: the reciprocity between poet and bird is here signified in the inscription of the dove's essence upon the poet's agent of vision, denoted here by **cornée** ("the cornea," the transparent tissue that protects the sensitive parts of the eye).

174.

monte lécheur de ciel
et le grand trou noir où je voulais me noyer l'autre lune
c'est là que je veux pêcher maintenant la langue maléfique
de la nuit en son immobile verrition!

The difficulty of interpretation posed by this final stanza of the poem is appreciably reduced if it is read as the expression of an aspiration to an ecstatic experience which the poet envisions as a form of the fulfilment of the imaginative adventure enacted by the whole poem.

lécheur de ciel: the dove riding on the wind becomes an inseparable part of its motion and cleansing action.

le grand trou noir: there are two possible readings of this: it may be considered to have an equivalence, on an even more intense register, to **cul de basse fosse de soi-même** in stanza 156 and thus to refer to the anguish and despair fostered by the black experience which is now to be dissipated in the poet's ultimate transfiguration. There may also be a suggestion of a whirlwind or tornado, at the center (or "eye") of which is the fixed point around which the elements turn; in this sense, it locates **ma noire vibration** in the universal motion and looks forward to the significance of **immobile verrition** below.

l'autre lune: again, two readings are possible here. The immediate context suggests an indication, in something of an Africanism ("a moon ago"), that the poet's somber thoughts are now in the past. Taken, however, with other notations in Césaire's poetry, the image forms part of an aspiration to a total experience, concretized by a full vision of the moon embracing its other half, which is never turned towards the earth: this meaning is clarified by these lines from *Cadastre*: *le fruit coupé de la lune toujours en allée / vers le contour à inventer de l'autre moitié.*

la langue maléfique: cf. **mes paroles abruptes** above; the poet's symbolism of aggression, inspired by a negative historical experience, now to be translated into a different key of expression.

son immobile verrition: this image, which has been the subject of much speculation as to its reference and its significance within the poem's symbolic scheme, is built on the seeming paradox of the co-existence in the same object of rapid movement (**verrition**, a word coined by Césaire from the Latin *vertere*, "to spin") and absolute stasis, to convey a sense of the profound unity of experience intimated by the cosmic order itself, a truth which ordinary experience is unable to perceive or verify, but which is directly accessible to the profound intuition of the poet. English-speaking readers will be familiar with this idea expressed in the image of the gyre in Yeats's "The Second Coming" and which finds memorable expression in the final lines of his poem "Among Schoolchildren." It also provides the essential thought in the development of Eliot's *Four Quartets*, in particular Part II of "Burnt Norton" ("At the still point of the turning world"). The import of Césaire's image comes to this: the universal pulse becomes incarnated in the poet, whose turbulent progress through history leads to an encounter with the cosmic realm; his agitated existence, which has been the subject of the poem, thus comes to hold the promise of fulfilment in a higher mode of experience, of an integration into the Absolute.

SELECTED BIBLIOGRAPHY

[Place of publication Paris unless otherwise indicated]

I. WORKS BY AIME CESAIRE.

For a complete listing of Césaire's writings, published speeches, and interviews up to 1978, with commentary on each item, see Thomas Hale, *Les Ecrits d'Aimé Césaire* (special publication of *Etudes Françaises*, Vol. 14, Nos. 3-4). Montreal: Les Presses de l'Université de Montréal, 1978); see also Frederick Ivor Case, *Aimé Césaire: Bibliographie* (Toronto: Manna, 1973), which lists the works of Césaire as well as the secondary literature up to the year of its publication.

A. *Cahier d'un retour au pays natal.*

The following are the various editions that contain the French text:

1. Bilingual edition, French and English (with poem's title rendered as *Memorandum on my Martinique*); Preface by André Breton, "Un Grand Poète Noir"; translation of poem and preface by Yvan Goll and Lionel Abel. New York: Brentano's, 1947. André Breton's preface is reprinted in *Martinique, charmeuse de serpents*. Editions Jean-Jacques Pauvert, 1972.

2. French text of above, with minor revisions, Bordas, 1947.

3. Revised and expanded edition, French text only, with Preface by Petar Guberina. Présence Africaine, 1956.

4. *Zurück ins Land der Geburt*, bilingual edition, French text of 1956 edition and German translation by Janheinz Jahn. Frankfurt am Main: Insel-Verlag, 1962.

5. *Cuaderno de un Retorno al Pais Natal*, bilingual edition, French text of 1956 edition and Spanish translation, with introduction, by Agusti Bartra. Mexico City: Ediciones Era, 1969.

6. *Return to my Native Land*, bilingual edition, French text of 1956 and English translation by Emile Snyder. Présence Africaine, 1968.

7. *Oeuvres Complètes,* Volume I (Poésie), pp. 41-78. French text of 1956 edition. Fort-de-France: Editions Désormeaux, 1976.

8. *Aimé Césaire: The Collected Poetry,* bilingual edition, French text of 1956 edition and English translation, pp. 34-85 (title in English as *Notebook of a Return to the Native Land*); translation by Clayton Eshelman and Annette Smith. Berkeley and Los Angeles: University of California Press, 1983.

9. Reprint of 1956 edition with corrections to the text and Appendices, including Breton's 1947 preface. Présence Africaine, 1983.

B. **Other Poetic and Dramatic Works.**

Les Armes miraculeuses, poems. Gallimard, 1946; reissued in revised edition with Postface, 1970 (Collection "Poésie").

Soleil cou coupé, poems. Editions K, 1948.

Corps perdu, poems, with illustrations by Picasso. Editions Fragrance, 1949.

Et Les Chiens se taisaient, stage version of dramatic poem previously published as part of *Les Armes miraculeuses.* Présence Africaine, 1956.

Ferrements, poems. Editions du Seuil, 1960.

Cadastre, containing *Soleil cou coupé* and *Corps perdu* in revised versions of both volumes. Editions du Seuil, 1961.

La Tragédie du Roi Christophe, play. Présence Africaine, 1963.

Une Saison au Congo, play. Editions du Seuil, 1966.

Une Tempête, play. Editions du Seuil, 1969.

moi, laminaire, poems. Editions du Seuil, 1982.

Extracts in the the following historic anthologies:

Léon Damas: *Poètes d'expression française.* Editions du Seuil, 1947.

Léopold Sédar Senghor: *Anthologie de la nouvelle poésie nègre et malgache,* Presses Universitaires de France, 1948; second edition, 1970. Contains Jean-Paul Sartre's preface, "Orphée noir"; this is reprinted in *Situations II,* Gallimard, 1949; English translation by Samuel Allen under the title *Black Orpheus,* Présence Africaine, 1963.

English Translations.

In addition to *Collected Poetry* above:

State of the Union. Trans. Clayton Eshelman and Denis Kelly. Bloomington: Caterpillar Press, 1966.

Return to my Native Land. Trans. John Berger and Anna Bostock, with Introduction by Mazisi Kunene. Harmondsworth: Penguin Books 1968.

Cadastre, bilingual edition. Trans. by Emile Snyder and Sanford Upson. Introduction by Emile Snyder. New York: Third Press, 1973.

Non-Vicious Circle: Twenty Poems of Aimé Césaire, Selection, French texts and English translations, with introduction and notes, by Gregson Davis, Stanford: Stanford University Press, 1984.

Lyric and Dramatic Poetry: 1946-82, containing French texts with English translations of stage version of *Et Les Chiens se taisaient* and complete text of the volume *moi,laminaire*. Trans. Clayton Eshelman and Annette Smith. Charlottesville: University of Virginia Press, 1990 (CARAF Books). The volume also contains an Introduction by A. James Arnold and his English translation of "Poésie et Connaissance" under the title "Poetry and Knowledge."

See also Ellen Conroy Kennedy (ed.), *The Negritude Poets*, New York: Thunder's Mouth Press, 2nd ed. 1989, for selections in English translations.

C. Selected Cultural, Historical and Political Writings.

Early articles in *Tropiques*, Tome I, 1941-42, Tome II, 1943-45, Editions Jean-Michel Place, 1978. (The first volume contains an interview with Jacqeline Leiner, "Entretien avec Aimé Césaire," pp. v-xxiv, and an introduction, "Pour une lecture critique de *Tropiques*" by René Ménil, pp. xxv-xxxv.)

Introduction, *Esclavage et colonisation* (Selected writings of Victor Schoelcher). Presses Universitaires de France, 1948.

Discours sur le colonialisme. Editions Réclame, 1950; Présence Africaine, 1955. Trans Joan Pinkham, *Discourse on Colonialism*. New York: Monthly Review Press, 1972.

"Sur la poésie nationale," *Présence Africaine*, Oct.-Nov., 1955, pp. 39-41.

"Culture et colonisation" in *Présence Africaine*, juin-novembre, 1956, pp. 190-205.

Lettre à Maurice Thorez. Présence Africaine, 1956.

"L'Homme de culture noir et ses responsabilités," in *Deuxième Congrès des écrivains et artistes noirs*, Présence Africaine, Feb.-March, 1959, pp. 116-122.

"La Martinique telle qu'elle est," *French Review*, Vol. 53, No.2, December, 1979, pp. 183-89.

Toussaint Louverture: La Révolution française et le problème colonial, Présence Africaine, 1962.

"Société et littérature dans les Antilles," *Etudes Littéraires*, Québec, Vol 6, No 1, April 1973, pp. 9-20.

II. SECONDARY LITERATURE.

A. **Studies devoted to** *Cahier*.

Maryse Condé: *Cahier d'un retour au pays natal* (Collection "Profil d'une oeuvre"). Hatier, 1976.

Séminaire de l'ILENA: *Cahier d'un retour au pays natal d'Aimé Césaire*, Abidjan: Les Nouvelles Editions Africaines, 1985.

Lilyan Kesteloot: *Comprendre le* Cahier d'un retour au pays natal *d'Aimé Césaire* (Collection "Comprendre"). Issy-les-Moulineaux: Editions Saint Paul, 1982.

B. **Studies devoted wholly or in part to the work of Aimé Césaire.**

Régis Antoine: *La Littérature franco-antillaise*. Editions Karthala, 1992.

A. James Arnold: *Modernism and Negritude: The Poetry and Poetics of Aimé Césaire*. Cambridge, Mass.: Harvard University Press, 1981.

Marianne Wichmann Bailey: *The Ritual Theater of Aimé Césaire*. Tübingen: Gunter Narr Verlag, 1992.

Jean-Claude Bajeux: *Antilia retrouvée*, Editions Caribbéennes, 1993.

Simon Battestini: *Aimé Césaire, poète martiniquais* (Série "Littérature africaine"). Fernand Nathan, 1967.

Bernadette Cailler: *Proposition poétique: une lecture d'Aimé Césaire*. Sherbrooke: Editions Naaman, 1976.

Jacques Corzani: *La Littérature des Antilles-Guyane françaises*. Fort-de-France: Désormeaux, 1978, 6 vols.

Selwyn R. Cudjoe: *Resistance and Caribbean Literature*. Athens, Ohio: Ohio University Press, 1980.

Gregson Davis: *Aimé Césaire*. Cambridge: Cambridge University Press (forthcoming in the series "Cambridge Studies in African and Caribbean Literature").

Daniel Delas: *Aimé Césaire*. Hachette, 1991.

Susan Frutkin: *Aimé Césaire, Black Between Worlds*. University of Miami, Centre for Advanced International Studies, 1973.

Edouard Glissant: *L'Intention poétique*. Editions du Seuil, 1978.

——*Le Discours antillais*. Editions du Seuil, 1981.

——*Poétique de la Relation*, Gallimard, 1990.

Rodney Harris: *L'Humanisme dans le théâtre d'Aimé Césaire*. Ottawa: Editions Naaman, 1973.

Michel Hausser: *Pour une poétique de la Négritude*. Vol.I, Editions Silex, 1988; Vol. II, Editions Nouvelles du Sud, 1991.

Abiola Irele: *The African Experience in Literature and Ideology*. London, 1981; rpt. Bloomington: Indiana University Press, 1990.

Janheinz Jahn: *Muntu*. London: Faber and Faber, 1961.

——*A History of Neo-African Literature*. London: Faber and Faber, 1968.

Hubert Juin: *Aimé Césaire, poète noir*. Présence Africaine, 1956.

Lilyan Kesteloot: *Aimé Césaire* (Collection "Poètes d'aujourd'hui"). Editions Seghers, 1962.

——*Les Ecrivains noirs de langue française*. Bruxelles: Institut Solvay, 1965. Trans. by Ellen Conroy Kennedy, *Black Writers in French*. Washington D.C.: Howard University Press, 1991.

——*Négritude et situation coloniale*. Yaoundé: Editions CLE (Collection "Point de vue"), 1970.

——with Barthélémy Kotchy: *Aimé Césaire: l'homme et l'oeuvre* (Collection "Approche"), Présence Africaine, 1973; contains preface by Michel Leiris, "Qui est Aimé Césaire?" and first complete published text of Césaire's "Poésie et Connaissance."

Josaphat Kubayanda: *The Poet's Africa*. Westport, CT: Greenwood Press, 1990.

Jacqueline Leiner: *Imaginaire, langage, identité culturelle, Négritude* Tübingen: Gunter Narr Verlag/Editions Jean Michel Place, 1980.

——*Aimé Césaire: Le terreau primordial*. Tübingen: Gunter Narr Verlag, 1993.

Clément Mbom: *Le Théâtre d'Aimé Césaire*. Editions Fernand Nathan, 1979.

Jean-Claude Michel: *Les Ecrivains noirs et le Surréalisme*. Sherbrooke: Editions Naaman, 1982.

Bernard Mouralis: *Les Contre-littératures*. Presses Universitaires de France, 1975.

Georges [M. & M.] Ngal: *Aimé Césaire: un homme à la recherche d'une patrie*. Dakar: Nouvelles Editions Africaines, 1975.

Albert Owusu-Sarpong: *Le Temps historique dans l'oeuvre théâtrale d'Aimé Césaire*. Sherbrooke: Editions Naaman, 1986.

Janis L. Pallister: *Aimé Césaire*. New York: Twayne Publishers, 1991. (Twayne World Authors Series, No 821.)

Mireille Rosello: *Littérature et identité aux Antilles*. Editions Karthala, 1992.

Ronnie Leah Scharfman: *Engagement and the Language of the Subject in the Poetry of Aimé Césaire*. Gainesville: University of Florida Press, 1980.

Aliko Songolo: *Aimé Césaire: une poétique de la découverte*. Editions L'Harmattan, 1985.

Patrick J. Taylor: *The Narrative of Liberation*. Ithaca, N.Y.: Cornell University Press, 1989.

Roger Toumson: *La Transgression des couleurs: Littératures et langages des Antilles, XVIIIe, XIXe et XXe siècles*. Editions Caribbéennes, 1989, 2 vols.

Marcien Towa: *Poésie de la Négritude: Approche Structuraliste*. Sherbrooke: Editions Naaman, 1983.

Auguste Viatte: *Histoire littéraire de l'Amérique française des origines à 1950*. Presses Universitaires de France, 1954.

Keith Louis Walker: *La Cohésion poétique de l'oeuvre césairienne*. Tübingen: Gunter Narr Verlag, ("Etudes littéraires" series) and Editions Jean-Michel Place, 1979.

Claude Wauthier: *L'Afrique des Africains: Inventaire de la Négritude*. Editions du Seuil, 1964.

Bernard Zadi Zaourou: *Césaire entre deux cultures*. Dakar: Nouvelles Editions Africaines, 1978.

C. Collective volumes.

Aimé Césaire ou l'athanor d'un alchimiste. Editions Caribbéennes, 1987.

Etudes Littéraires, Vol. 6, No. 1, April 1973, Les Presses de l'Université Laval, Montreal.

Jacqueline Leiner (ed.): *Soleil éclaté*. Tübingen: Gunter Narr Verlag, 1984.

Négritude africaine, négritude caraïbe., Editions de la Francité, 1973.

Georges [M. & M.] Ngal and Martin Steins (eds.): *Césaire 70*. Editions Silex, 1984.

III. BACKGROUND AND GENERAL:

Jean Benoist: *L'Archipel inachevé*. Montréal: Presses Universitaires de Montréal, 1972.

Alain Ph. Blérald: *Négritude et Politique aux Antilles*. Editions Caribbéennes, 1981.

Frantz Fanon: *Peau noire, masques blancs*. Editions du Seuil, 1952.

Daniel Guérin: *Les Antilles décolonisées*, with Preface by Aimé Césaire. Présence Africaine, 1969.

Michel Leiris: *Contacts de civilisation en Martinique et en Guadeloupe*. UNESCO and Gallimard, 1969.

René Ménil: *Tracées*. Editions Robert Laffont, 1981.

L. V. Thomas: *Les Idéologies négro-africaines d'aujourd'hui*. Publications de la Faculté des Lettres, Université de Dakar, Dakar, 1965.

IV. PERIODICALS.

Présence Africaine, published in Paris since 1947, is the principal reference.

In addition to *Tropiques*, the following journals that are directly related to the development of Césaire's work have now been made available:

Légitime Défense, Editions Jean-Michel Place, 1979 (facsimile reprint of original number, with Introduction by René Ménil).

La Révue du monde noir: 1931-32, Editions Jean-Michel Place, 1992. (Facsimile reprint of the original six numbers, with a Preface by Louis-Thomas Achille.)

Abiola Irele was formerly Professor of French at the University of Ibadan, and is now Professor of African, French, and Comparative Literature at The Ohio State University.